Contents

Foreword by Dr Rowan Williams, Archbishop of Canterbury

With every year that passes, Tyndale's stature as an independent Christian thinker becomes more and more evident. It is no longer possible to see him as a rather prosaic adapter of Luther, or as a moralist whose main concern is practical exhortation. Dr Werrell in this excellent introduction to Tyndale's theology establishes beyond doubt that Tyndale is indeed a serious and creative intellect, following through a systematic and original vision, not Lutheran or Calvinist or Zwinglian, but distinctive, comprehensive, profoundly biblical.

The essence of this theology. as Dr Werrell demonstrates is a set of convictions about covenant; and Tyndale's originality lies in the place he gives to God's covenant with himself, the covenant between the three Persons of the Trinity whereby God the Father establishes eternally how he will be the father of his creatures, through the incarnation and sacrifice of the Son and the gift of the Spirit. Thus – although Tyndale might have been rather surprised to be told this – his theology is aligned with some of the profoundest themes of patristic and early mediaeval theology in insisting on the nature of salvation as incorporation into the trinitarian relations; but he is quite distinctive in grounding this so firmly in the biblical concept of covenant,

In this light, the whole of his theological vision unfolds with impressive coherence. We see how his doctrine of creation allows a positive valuation of social order and lawful community, insofar as it sets all human beings on the same level, as potential children of God; and we see also how his very radical convictions about our universal moral obligations, to unbelievers as well as believers, are a natural consequence of this. We can understand why he so rarely resorts to forensic metaphors in discussing salvation, because his central concern is with how God shows himself a father to his children. We are helped to grasp his sacramental theology as a further exploration of covenanted relationship, the visible signs renewing in us the awareness of the eternal disposition of the covenanting God towards us, the God who has determined that by the death of the Son our sins are removed and the Spirit set free to work in us. Mediaeval abuses are seen in the light of a breaking of the covenant, replacing the fatherly generosity of God to us with a self-interested scheme of power-broking for the clerical elite.

This study, in allowing Tyndale largely to speak for himself conveys vividly the richness and the warmth of Tyndale's thinking. 'I understand my father's words as they sound', wrote Tyndale. 'and after the most merciful manner'. The whole of this book helps us see why this is always Tyndale's method and goal. I hope it will stimulate more of the research that Tyndale so abundantly deserves, and meanwhile that it will introduce many people to a true theological master.

Rowan Williams
Archbishop of Canterbury

Prologue

There were certain considerations regarding methodology that were taken into account when I started writing about William Tyndale's theology. I could easily have written my own account of Tyndale's theology. However, many people had written various conflicting accounts of what they believed Tyndale had written. False statements about Tyndale's theological beliefs abound; one recent example will have to suffice. Diarmaid MacCulloch in his book, *Reformation,* wrote: "Luther openly affirmed soul sleep, . . . William Tyndale shared Luther's belief."[1] Yet what Tyndale wrote about it was: "he that determineth aught of the state of them that be departed, doth but teach the presumptuous imaginations of his own brain."[2] The question arises: who has understood and written something William Tyndale would have accepted as a statement of his theological position? My account of Tyndale's theology would just be yet another statement of Tyndale's thought. The fact that it contradicted what most scholars had written since Sir Thomas More wrote about Tyndale's theology meant it would have been considered as untrue.

Therefore I am letting William Tyndale speak for himself rather than putting his thought into my own words. There are many disadvantages in this approach, the smoothness of the work has, to a certain extent, been lost by the insertion of a large number of quotations in the English of four centuries ago. But this is counterbalanced by the accuracy in letting William Tyndale himself state what his theological position was. Some of the quotations might seem to be long, even unduly long, but, if we are to follow Tyndale's advice about not taking things out of context, in those places the context will be seen to be important.

The spelling in quotations used in the text has been modernised, but the original spelling is to be found in the footnotes where obsolete letters are in italics and conform to modern spelling where possible. In some Middle English quotations, where clarity of meaning is more important than strict modernising of spelling, I have felt free to express the meaning; the original text is in the footnote.

To assess Tyndale's doctrine I extracted every occurrence of passages relating to almost forty doctrines in Tyndale's writings and marginal notes (there were between a few hundred to nearly a thousand extracts for each doctrine). I then looked for any doctrinal changes that may have happened in each doctrine between 1525 and 1536. But Tyndale's doctrine proved to be consistent with only minor changes which did not alter his thought – for example the change of 'testament' and 'appointment' to 'covenant'. If I had found any significant changes they would have been noted in the final statement of Tyndale's theology. The next stage was to discover Tyndale's understanding of each doctrine, and, finally, to create a coherent theology which did justice to those doctrines and also the whole tenor of Tyndale's writings.

I am also grateful to those who have read the manuscript and made constructive comments which have improved it and made it more readable as a book: Dr. Alec Ryrie, and especially Dr. Anne O'Donnell S.N.D. and Mr. Brian Johnson who have spent much time editing the script and guiding me to those places where additional clarity was needed. Without their help this book would be struggling to see the light of day.

Notes

1. MacCulloch, Diarmaid, *Reformation: Europe's House Divided,* p. 580f.
2. Tyndale, William, *Exposition of 1 John, P.S-2* p. 185

Introduction

For a long time Tyndale's genius lay hidden, lost and ignored, with only his skill as a translator of the Bible and his importance in the formation of Modern English being recognised. I leave it to others to write of Tyndale's greatness as a translator,[1] and of his place in the development of the English language. I can only feel the vitality of Tyndale's translation nearly five hundred years after he was putting pen to paper and compare it with the mechanical lifeless work of so many modern translations and paraphrases. Even to criticise him for his "Tudor vulgarity"[2] sounds weak when we compare Tyndale's worst with passages from Sir Thomas More or Martin Luther – let alone with what passes as *fit for the family* on television today. Also some of Tyndale's *vulgarities* only arise because standard words of the sixteenth-century are now considered *not fit for polite society*.

As a theologian Tyndale is still unrecognised. He is assumed to have been merely a follower of Luther or of Wyclif. Whatever great name or movement we associate him with, we will find that we are in good company with others who have written about his theological position. Of course, scholars narrow down the field in different ways, but often they have to propose several changes in Tyndale's theology in the last ten to twelve years of his life to make their theory work. But in all this Tyndale is not allowed to speak: and selectivity from his writings can prove whatever theory one wants to prove.

Scholars who study the Reformation have made certain basic assumptions, and to suggest that those assumptions may not be true is as great a heresy as any found by the Inquisition in the sixteenth century. All too often the works of various scholars are mentioned in bibliographies, but their findings have been totally ignored simply because it disagrees with the thesis being propounded. In the next chapter I draw attention to some of these, especially regarding Tyndale's *Prologue to the Epistle to the Romans.* This is commonly regarded as a pure translation of Luther's *Preface* to the same epistle, in spite of Leonard Trinterud's analysis that one eighth of Tyndale is a translation of one half of Luther![3]

In the fourteenth century John Wyclif made many attacks on the papal Church, and most of his doctrines found their way, in a modified form, into the Churches of the Reformation. Wyclif's reforms would have brought the Church more than half way towards the position of the Reformed Churches of Europe. His writings were not confined to England but also spread to the Continent. Luther often refers to Wyclif in his writings. Yet, "No Luther, No Reformation!" is commonly accepted, as if Wyclif had never existed and a bolt out of the blue suddenly struck Luther and the Reformation was born. A study of the books Luther read and other possible influences on his thinking before his "conversion" may possibly throw some further light on what lay behind his disquiet with the papal Church; and led him to realise that "justification by faith" was a key to an understanding of Christianity. We must give credit where credit is due, but we do Luther an injustice if we try to force others into his mould. We must beware of having blinkered vision, as Gottfried Locher wrote:

> Luther is made the norm for every reformer. Whatever conforms to the phenomenon of Luther is valid, and whatever does not conform is alien. As if it were impossible for the Holy Spirit to lead each one of us, just as we are, in our own way![4]

We do an injustice to both Luther and Tyndale if we try to make Tyndale a Lutheran at any time. But we also do an injustice to them if we try to exaggerate or diminish Luther's work or the use Tyndale made of Luther's writings from the start of the European Reformation in 1517 into the 1530s.

The greatest injustice done to Tyndale has been the denigration of his intellect. Those who have written about his theology assume that Tyndale was influenced by and followed the lead given by Continental Reformers. Alister McGrath wrote of Tyndale "making extensive use of Luther", but unlike Luther he "tends to interpret justification as 'making righteous'. Tyndale's emphasis upon the renewing and transforming work of the Holy Spirit within man is quite distinct from Luther's emphasis upon faith."[5] Can we fairly say Tyndale depended on Luther for the doctrine of Justification by Faith when he understood justification in a different way to Luther, and his doctrine of faith was totally different to Luther's? When we examine the reasons for the different understanding of that doctrine we find that Tyndale differed from Luther's theology on *every* point.

My approach to Tyndale has been to examine his writings, from his first to his last, to see if there were any changes or alterations in his theological position. In drawing out from his writings the theology which undergirded them I was not, at first, concerned with seeing whether his thinking stemmed from patristic, medieval or reformation sources. I discovered that Tyndale had a consistent, logically developed theology that he backed by scripture – in fact he was prepared to modify or alter his theology if it could be proved that any part of it was not a faithful interpretation of the word of God. Only after I had established what Tyndale's theology was could I start to compare it with that of other theologies. Although Tyndale showed the independence of his thought and his unswerving reliance on the scriptures of the Old and New Testaments, his thinking had links with humanism, especially with Erasmus, and also with Lollardy. Augustine influenced Tyndale's theology, although this can probably be traced to Wycliffism. Linking Tyndale's thinking with these possible background influences is not easy because anything in them which relied on Aristotle, Plato or any other Greek philosopher – or anything which could not be proved from "authentic scripture" – was discarded by Tyndale. The certainties we can go on come from Tyndale's writings alone; the rest can only be probabilities or speculations.

Christian doctrinal systems are like dumb waiters,[6] where God is at one end and man the other. Different theologies of salvation vary in the importance they give to man in God's scheme to save him from his rebellion and sin. But the more important we make man's salvation and lift man higher we find that, at the same time, God's place becomes lowered. As far as I know, only Tyndale's theology puts God in the highest possible position and places man at the very bottom. As a result his doctrine of God is paramount and every other doctrine stems from it. Although he does not refer to it in his writings, the last verse in *Revelation* 4 could be considered as a key to Tyndale's theology: "Thou hast created all things, and for thy will's sake they are, and were created."[7]

Although my doctoral dissertation[8] contains much more about the background to Tyndale's theology than this book, I am doing further research into *The Roots of Tyndale's Theology.* This seems to be confirming Tyndale's Wycliffite background and the influence of Erasmus on his thinking, as well as his total reliance on Scripture and his rejection of any Greek philosophical influence. It is also showing that there is a greater division between his theology and that of Martin Luther than I had realised when I was working on *Tyndale's Theology.*

On the whole, the terminology used by Tyndale is easily understood. The one exception is the use of *spiritualty* and *temporalty.* Before the Reformation the clergy were the *spiritualty,* and the laity were the *temporalty,* but the two were separated from each other. Tyndale taught that the *temporal realm (temporalty)* included both the clergy and the laity, and that the *spiritual realm (spiritualty)* included all Christians, both lay and cleric, as Tyndale wrote: "The lay people be as well of the church as the priests."[9] Where possible I have used *clergy* to express the *spiritualty* when it refers only to the ordained members of the Church.

For most theological systems in the sixteenth century the *spiritual realm* was above the *temporal realm*. The Bull *Clericis Laicos* (1296) stated:

> That laymen have been very hostile to the clergy antiquity relates; and it is clearly proved by the experiences of the present time. For not content with what is their own the laity strive for what is forbidden and loose the reins for things unlawful. Nor do they prudently realize that power over clerks or ecclesiastical persons or goods is forbidden them.[10]

However, for Tyndale the temporal realm, or regiment, was a creation ordinance embracing the whole of mankind. The spiritual realm, or regiment, was secondary and consisted of those who had been baptized.

Tyndale's doctrine of the covenant differed from other covenant doctrines of the Reformation. Instead of being a covenant between God and man, Tyndale believed that the covenant was between the three Persons of the Trinity. The covenant was not primarily for the salvation of man but for the restoration of creation; man's salvation was necessary because it was man's sin that had caused the purity of creation to be broken.

God the Son covenanted to become man and shed his blood in order that God could "be just, and the justifier"[11] of those who would become God's children. God the Father covenanted to be a Father to those who, through Christ's blood, were born again as the children of God. God the Holy Spirit covenanted to apply the blood of Christ to those who had been chosen to be God's children. It is, therefore, through the work of the Holy Spirit that the Christian is brought into a covenant relationship with God.

Through the Fall man was "dead in trespasses and sin".[12] For Tyndale this meant that the only way man could be restored to fellowship with God was through being born again. The alternatives were all flawed because we are dead. The Church of Rome believed that our good works merited God's mercy for our salvation. Luther and the south German Reformers believed that our faith enabled us to be saved. Both of these ideas depend on the sinner having some life remaining in him, however weak and helpless this life might be. Tyndale quoted Ephesians 2 and wrote: "The text is plain: we were stone dead, and without life or power to do or consent to good."[13] Again, he wrote: "They that do good are first born of God, and receive of his nature and seed; and, by the reason of that nature and seed, are first good ere they do good, by the same rule."[14] In that way Tyndale had separated his theology not only from that of the Roman Church, but also from Luther and the other Continental Reformers.

Once we had been born again, and through faith had committed ourselves to the fulfilment of God's purpose for the restoration of his creation, we entered into a covenantal relationship with God. God's promises or covenants to us as his children were conditional. As Michael McGiffert expressed it: "The view of covenant as contract receives support from Tyndale's coupling of the gracious *if/then* with a lethal alternative, reserved for those who, having entered into covenant, later broke trust."[15] Tyndale believed that the pope, and his church, had broken the covenant between God and his people.

William Tyndale's theology is consistent throughout and relies solely on the scriptures. There are gaps in our knowledge; there are questions we would like answered. Tyndale faces up to these: he admits that there are places where we wished the Bible had given us the answers we looked for, but, we must not speculate if God had kept the answer from us. Tyndale wrote: "Moreover we by the light of faith see a thousand things which are impossible to an infidel to see: so likewise, no doubt, in the sight of the clear vision of God we shall see things which now God will not have known. For pride ever accompanieth high knowledge, but grace accompanieth meekness. Let us therefore give diligence rather to do the will of God, than to search his secrets, which are not profitable for us to know."[16] William Tyndale opened up the scriptures in a new way; he revealed the theological unity of the Old and New Testaments by linking the Old Testament sacraments of circumcision and the Passover with the New Testament sacraments of baptism and the Lord's Supper. Tyndale's stress on the blood of Christ also fulfilled the Mosaic Law and its emphasis on the blood in the Old Testament sacrifices.

Notes

1. Lawton, David, *Faith, Text and History*: see also others mentioned in Daniell, David. *The Bible in English*
2. Moynahan, Brian, *If God Spare My Life*, p. 53
3. Trinterud, L.J., "A Reappraisal of William Tyndale's Debt to Martin Luther." p. 26.
4. Locher, Gottfried W., *Zwingli's Thought: New Perspectives*, p. 3
5. McGrath, *Iustitia Dei*, vol 2. p. 99
6. A dumb waiter is a lift comprising two compartments joined by a rope passing over a pulley used to transfer food and dirty crockery between floors.
7. Tyndale, William, *The New Testament, 1534*, (Modern Spelling edn.) p. 374
8. Werrell, Ralph S., *The Theology of William Tyndale*
9. Tyndale, William, *Answer*, p. 3/158
10. Bettenson, Henry, *Documents of the Christian Church*, p. 157
11. Romans 3:26
12. Ephesians 2:1ff
13. Tyndale, William, *1st Epistle of St. John, PS2*, p. 199
14. ibid. p. 190
15. McGiffert, Michael, "William Tyndale's Conception of Covenant", p. 173.
16. Tyndale, William, *Mammon, PS-1*, p. 89.

2

The Background to Tyndale's Theology

Before we can start a serious study of Tyndale's theology we have to examine a common claim made by scholars: that Tyndale's theology changed between the years 1525 and 1536 (the years from the earliest of his writings to his death). Unless there was a consistency in all his writings there could be no single theological influence that related to William Tyndale. My research into his theology did not show any significant changes that had altered his basic theological position between 1525 and 1536. The research of Paul Lauchlin and Judith Mayotte confirm my own findings that there was no change in his theology.[1]

The authenticity of *The Supper of the Lord*, printed in the *Parker Society* edition of Tyndale's works, needs clarification. This is the only writing attributed to Tyndale whose theology differs from every authentic work that Tyndale wrote.[2] The most significant reason for dismissing it is that its eucharistic doctrine is based on *John* 6. In *The Sacraments.* Tyndale acknowledges that the papists and Lutherans believe Christ was referring to the sacrament in this chapter; he then expounds the meaning of *John* 6 and concludes: "And therefore must it be understood of faith only, and not of the sacrament."[3]

It is not until we have discovered what the theology of William Tyndale was that we can compare it with earlier theologies that may have influenced him. Scholars have approached Tyndale's writings with preconceived ideas. He must have been influenced by Luther or, to a lesser degree, by one of the other theological systems present in the first quarter of the sixteenth century. Therefore, whatever did not fit their theory had to be cut away and ignored. Whenever this process became too drastic it was assumed that Tyndale's theology must have changed. This mutilation of Tyndale's works is what I call the *Glass Slipper Syndrome*; only Cinderella's foot would fit the glass slipper, so there can only be one theology that applies to William Tyndale. Tyndale's writings have to conform, often by mutilation, or ignoring the context, but more usually by selectivity. However, Tyndale's writings must not be made to fit one's own theory, but used to inform us in the quest to discover his theology. If, between 1525 and 1536, Tyndale's theology changed it is his writings alone which must inform our thinking. If his theology was consistent during those years it is to Tyndale's writings only we must turn, and let them guide us in our quest for the truth.

Was Tyndale's theology consistent?

The person who has most influenced our thinking about Tyndale's theology is William A. Clebsch, who claimed that there had been two major shifts in Tyndale's thinking.[4]

Even scholars who do not follow Clebsch's position to the letter very often accept that in the beginning Tyndale was a Lutheran, and that his theology changed from Lutheran to a covenant theology in the early 1530s. One of the main reasons for taking this view is the word change Tyndale made between "testament" and "covenant". His early writings used "testament" and his later writings "covenant". There are some works, written between his early and late writings, which use both "testament" and "covenant" and Tyndale made it clear that the change of word did not mean a change of theology. "God . . . hath made a testament or a covenant, and hath bound himself, and hath sealed his obligation with Christ's blood." Again Tyndale wrote, "to testify and confirm the testament or covenant made in Christ's blood and body."[5]

The roots of Tyndale's theology

It is impossible to go into the possible background to Tyndale's theological thinking in any depth in a book dealing with his theology – the subject matter is too great. His belief that it is in the Scriptures alone that we can find the truth does not mean that he did not read widely and try what others had written against the Word of God. However, it is a help for us to have some idea of what lay behind his thinking and what led him to his understanding of the Christian faith.[6]

Luther

Because of the almost universal claim that Tyndale was at some time a Lutheran, this is obviously the place to start.

Although Tyndale made use of Luther's writings, his supposed "translations" are full of Tyndale's alterations and digressions from Luther's text. For example, Tyndale's *Prologue to the Epistle to the*

Romans has been claimed as proof of his Lutheranism, e.g. Tyndale's "pioneering work of Bible translation went hand in hand with translations of sections of Luther's biblical commentaries presented in discreet anonymity."[7] And Tyndale's translation of "Luther's celebrated *Preface to Romans*" could be read by Englishmen "without knowing it was by the arch-heretic. . . . Thomas More, in spite of his great erudition, never realised this."[8] Of course it was not surprising that Thomas More failed to spot that Tyndale's *Prologue* was a translation of Luther's *Preface* because, as we have already noted, "About one eighth of Tyndale's prologue consists of a good translation of roughly half of Luther's prologue."[9] More understood Tyndale's theology and rightly said he "hath also in many thynges farre passed" Luther, and he listed many ways Tyndale was a greater heretic than Luther.[10]

Tyndale differed from Luther in most doctrines.[11] Luther's hidden God becomes Tyndale's Father who we see "with a lovely and amiable countenance."[12] Luther's "Theology of the Cross" is not in Tyndale, who only mentions the cross six times in a theological sense; for Tyndale it is "the blood of Christ" which is important. For Tyndale the Holy Spirit has an importance in the Christian's life that is not found in Luther. Luther accepts the *Apocrypha* and almost rejects the *Epistle of James;* Tyndale ignores the *Apocrypha* and accepts all the books of the Old and New Testaments unreservedly. Tyndale rejects Luther's doctrine of consubstantiation and also some other aspects of Luther's sacramental theology. Whilst Luther believed Confession was important, Tyndale held that it was the work of Satan.

Although Tyndale's terminology often echoed that of Luther, his usage of the words differed. Although Tyndale wrote of "justification by faith alone," he understood it in a different way to Luther. For Luther justification was the "imputation of righteousness" but for Tyndale it was "making righteous."[13]

Laughlin found three phases in man's justification, and wrote: "These three phases corresponded roughly to the three persons of the Trinity and to the particular activity most closely associated with each of them: election by the Father, justification in the Son, and perfection through the Spirit."[14] We will see the importance of the Trinity in Tyndale's soteriology when we examine his covenant theology.

Thomas More's assessment that Tyndale's theology was much further from the medieval Catholic Church than Luther's was correct. Tyndale defended Luther (especially in his *Answer to Sir Thomas More's Dialogue*) because he wanted to present the Reformation as a united movement away from the errors of the papal Church towards a Church based on the word of God. *Sola scriptura* bound all the Reformers together, and they should support one another in spite of their differences.

Trevisa and Lollardy

John Trevisa, a contemporary of Wyclif at Oxford, had been Vicar of Berkeley and chaplain to Lord Berkeley about a hundred years before Tyndale was born. Berkeley is close to where Tyndale grew up, and not far from where he worked as tutor to the Walsh children.

Although Trevisa is considered to have been orthodox in his theology, I believe the influence on Tyndale of Trevisa and of Lollardy were similar and probably dated back to his childhood. That Trevisa's translations into the vernacular were known to Tyndale is beyond doubt. He wrote that when he was a boy he had read the *Polychronicon.* Possibly Tyndale had access to others whilst still a boy in the vale of Berkeley.[15]

In contemporary vernacular writings "Passover" was usually spelled "pasque" (or its variants). Trevisa, in his translation of Bartholomew's *On the Properties of Things,* wrote:

> And this Easter of the Jews was a figure and waiting for the Easter of Christian men, in the which Easter, by the blood of the clean lamb, without blemish, that took away the sins of the world. All that are chosen are freed and ransomed out of the devil's service. . . .[16]

In Tyndale's translation of the New Testament we find he translated "the Passover" as "Easter"; for instance, in *John* 6:4 we read: "And Easter, a feast of the Jews was nigh."

In *The Practice of Prelates* Tyndale mentions Higden's "English *Polycronicon*".[17] Tyndale may have been influenced by the *Dyalogue* in the *Polycronicon* and the seeds of his translation work were perhaps sown by Trevisa. The *Dyalogue* deals with the need for a translation of the Bible in English.

> And it may not be told in English what the Latin is to mean without translation out of Latin into English. Then it needs to have an English translation, and to keep it in mind, that it is not forgotten, it is better that a translation is made and written, than said and not written. . . . Also King Alfred . . . translated . . . a great deal of the Psalter out of Latin into English.[18]

Thomas More wrote, "that finally no man can please him, but Wyclif. the first founder here of that abominable heresy."[19] Although Tyndale's theology had moved much further from the medieval Church than had Wyclif or the Lollards, he was, in many ways, closer to the Wycliffite movement than he was to Luther.

St. Augustine was the favourite Church father of John Wyclif and the Lollards, and we find that William Tyndale's theology was strongly

Augustinian. Tyndale's comments that William Tracy "was a learned man, and better seen in the works of St Austin twenty years before he died, than ever I knew doctor in England."[20] This dates Tracy's knowledge of Augustine to 1510, and probably links Tracy, and possibly Tyndale, to Lollardy. Other Church fathers are also found in Wycliffite and Tyndale's writings: Chrysostom, Cyprian, Jerome, and Origen. Research is needed to see if Tyndale was linked to these Church fathers through the Lollards.

Tyndale was also involved in the publication of Lollard tracts. Recently a document has been found that "proved to be in the handwriting of William Tyndale". This contained pages of the Lollard tract *A Compendious Olde Treatyse,* so linking Tyndale with its publication at the time of the Reformation.[21] Tyndale also probably edited *The Praier and Complaynte of the ploweman vnto Christe* and *The Examination of Thorpe and Oldcastle.*[22] By editing and publishing these Lollard tracts, Tyndale shows that he had an interest in the Wycliffite movement in England.

Tyndale used words in a way that linked him to the Lollard movement, and that would have been recognised as such by both the Lollard and the Catholic Church. It has been pointed out that Henry Knighton (a monk of Leicester Abbey in the reign of Henry IV) in his *Chronicle* "makes several comments about the mode of speech and style of argument favoured by the heretics." Knighton also wrote about their use of "Trewe Prechoures, False Prechoures" and that the "*trewe prechoures* are those who propound Wycliffite doctrine, *false prechoures* those who controvert this, or who preach orthodox beliefs rejected by the Lollards."[23] Throughout all his writings Tyndale used "true" and "false" in a way which showed an affinity with Lollardy.

Tyndale also used "authentic" and "ground" in a way which was familiar to the Wycliffites. Tyndale challenged Thomas More and wrote: "We can confound your false doctrine with authentic and manifest scripture."[24] "Ground" means "not the bland *M.E.D.* sense 'justify', but the more precise 'establish as deriving from the Bible'."[25] It was in this sense that Tyndale used it, for "the scripture hath but one sense, which is the literal sense. And that literal sense is the root and ground of all."[26] There may also be other words, which had a specific Lollard meaning, that Tyndale used, linking him to Wycliffism.

"On matters of doctrine, church polity, and ethical standards, as well as criticism of clerical abuses, Lollardy largely anticipated the Protestant position."[27] But as many of those themes were common to all Reformers, and some are common to Erasmus and other humanists, care has to be taken before we can claim that it was Lollardy that influenced Tyndale.

Donald Smeeton claimed that there may have been a link between

Lollardy and Tyndale. The weakness of his argument lies in the selectivity of his texts. Unless they are firmly rooted in the context of both Lollardy and Tyndale to justify the argument, they are valueless; also quotations taken out of their context are unreliable as proof of a common tradition. He does warn of this danger: "It is the thesis of this book that Lollardy's impact on Tyndale has too frequently been ruled out, even though on the other hand, its influence 'must not be too lightly assumed.' The age of Tyndale presents an ebb and flow that denies simplifications."[28]

However, by looking more broadly at Wycliffite theology, found in Wyclif and other Lollard writings, we discover many Lollard doctrines are present in Tyndale and also many of the Continental Reformers. Even justification by faith (which is usually counted as a "re-discovery" of Luther) lies behind Lollard thinking. Walter Brute, in the early 1390s,[29] is credited with saying:

> Wherefore, in my judgement, it seemeth that the keys of the kingdom of heaven are faith and hope: for by faith in Jesus Christ, and hope in him for the remission of sins, we enter the kingdom of heaven.[30]

In *How Antichrist and his clerks travail to destroy holy writ* we read:

> but Christian men take their faith of God by his gracious gift, when he gives to them knowledge and understanding of the truths necessary to save men's souls; and grace to assent in their heart to such truths; and this men call faith.[31]

Nevertheless, there are places where there is a closeness between Tyndale's and Wycliffite writings that a direct link between them seems impossible to avoid. There are also lines of thought which are peculiar to the Lollards and to Tyndale, or where they both are more extreme in their statements than the unreformed Church or most other Reformers. In a world where the role of women was minimal both the Lollards and Tyndale were prepared to give them an increased place in the Church. Because women had the right to baptize in emergencies, the Lollards argued that they could perform other priestly functions.[32] It was from this power of women to baptize that Tyndale wrote that they could (in situations of great emergency) also celebrate the Lord's Supper or even ordain.

> Do not our women now christen and minister the sacrament of baptism in time of need? Might they not, by as good reason, preach also, if necessity required? . . . And why might she not, by the same reason, minister the sacrament of the body and blood of Christ? . . . O poor women, how despise ye them![33]

Also Tyndale's statements that the Christian's duty to help the Turk or unbeliever in their need[34] appears to be a development of the argument in Purvey's *Remonstrance Against Romish Corruptions in the Church.*[35]

Humanism

There are strong links between Tyndale and humanism, especially with Erasmus. Tyndale believed that we should return to the sources, and therefore he turned to the Hebrew and the Greek for his Bible translations. However, unlike both scholasticism and humanism he rejected any form of Greek philosophy. *Sola scriptura,* for Tyndale, meant that only the scriptures were able to guide us into an understanding of the truth, and that we did not need any help from pagan philosophers.

Tyndale translated the *Enchiridion Militis Christiani* of Erasmus into English. He also recommended Erasmus' *Annotations* as worth reading.[36] There are also signs in Tyndale's own writings that he had knowledge of what Erasmus had written for there are many instances where ideas for his wording had come from different works of Erasmus. For example, some of Tyndale's attacks on the monks and friars[37] bear a strong resemblance to passages from *In Praise of Folly.*[38] Some other passages relating to Scripture appear to owe something to the *Enchiridion.*[39] Although the context is different, did Tyndale read about "filthy Priapus" in Erasmus' *Colloquies,* so that he could use it in his own work?[40]

Erasmus was in favour of translating the scriptures, and he wrote in his *Paraclesis:* "I am totally against those who do not want the Holy Scripture to be read by the laity in their vernacular, . . . Thus I would like the farmer to sing Scripture as he plows." Did that influence on Tyndale when he said to one cleric, "If God spared him life, ere many years he would cause a boy that driveth the plough, to know more of the Scripture than he did".[41] (However, in making this suggestion we must not forget that there was a large body of *Ploughman* literature in England – some of which was heterodox in its theology.) In his translation of the New Testament Tyndale had translated *ecclesia* as *congregation*, and Tyndale asked Thomas More why he had not criticised Erasmus, as he had criticised Tyndale, for making the same translation.[42]

Although some scholars have suggested that Dean Colet[43] might have had some influence on Tyndale,[44] I have not been able to find any evidence of this. There are some similarities in certain places, but when these are examined within the context in which they were written any thought of dependence ends.

Many of the attacks on scholastic doctrines in Tyndale's writings could be paralleled in humanist writings;[45] these can also be found in Wycliffite writings, but "The divergencies from the Scriptural interpretation of Erasmus in the exegetical method of Tyndale pose some problems for a study of his Christian humanism."[46]

Tyndale had links with humanism, and in many ways he had a respect for Erasmus. However, as Anne Richardson wrote: "We are so accustomed to assume all great Renaissance figures were humanists, that Tyndale's independence from that powerful movement – even as he joins it in repudiating scholastic theology – comes as a shock."[47]

Notes

1. Paul Laughlin. In his doctoral dissertation, "The Brightness of Moses' Face", he examined four important doctrines in Tyndale's writings according to the date they had been published. Laughlin started his research following Clebsch, who he thought was the most thorough interpreter of Tyndale. However, his research led him to the discovery that Tyndale's thought had not changed: "Tyndale's thought was internally consistent throughout his career. For though he used two different theological schemata that together suggested the discrepant and inimical frameworks of two very divergent theological traditions. . . . It is not surprising, then, that Tyndale's free use of disparate schemata and terminology has beguiled some interpreters into positing either a basic inconsistency or a momentous shift in his thought. But it is now clear that he by no means employed two different theological frameworks, either simultaneously or successively, but rather maintained consistently throughout his writings an essentially covenantal framework for theological reflection and discourse." (p. 267f). Judith Mayotte also came to the same conclusion in her doctoral dissertation, "William Tyndale's Contribution to the Reformation in England". She wrote, "Clebsch either did not see, or else did not consider the fact that Tyndale worked throughout his life from the primary foundation of a 'testament betwene' God and man, freely given by God with the attendant response from man of love of God and neighbor." (p. 77).
2. See Appendix 1.
3. Tyndale, William, *Sacraments,* p. 1/368f
4. Clebsch, William A., *England's Earliest Protestants,* in the three Chapters of that work, "Tyndale as Luther's Protégé, 1524-1529"; "Tyndale's Rediscovery of the Law, 1530-1532"; "Tyndale's Theology of Contract 1532/3-1536".
5. Tyndale, William, *Obedience,* p. 1/292: Tyndale, *Sacraments,* p. 1/381: et al.
6. My present research at The University of Birmingham is "The Roots of Tyndale's Theology" which I hope to complete by 2008.
7. MacCulloch, Diarmaid, "England", p. 171
8. Lindberg, Carter, *The European Reformations,* p. 314f
9. Trinterud, L.J., "A Reappraisal of William Tyndale's Debt to Martin Luther," p. 26
10. More, Thomas, *A Dialogue Concerning Heresies, CWM 6,* pp. 424-426
11. My paper given at the Society for Reformation Studies Conference, Cambridge,

April 2002. "Tyndale's Disagreement with Luther in his Prologue to the Romans."

12. Tyndale, William, *Exposition Matthew,* p. 2/26
13. McGrath, Alister, *Iustitia Dei,* vol 2. pp. 14, 99. "Believers are righteous on account of the alien righteousness of Christ which is imputed to them – that is, treated as if it were theirs through faith." McGrath, Alister, *Reformation Thought,* p. 106
14. Laughlin, Paul, "The Brightness of Moses' Face," p. 69
15. See my article "John Trevisa and William Tyndale" in *The Tyndale Society Journal* No 24, April 2003; pp. 22-26
16. Trevisa, John, "And *th*is estir of Iewis was figure and bodynge of *th*e estir of cristene men in *th*e whiche estir, by *th*e blood of *th*e clene lambe wi*th*outen wemme *th*at took away synnes of *th*e worlde, al *th*at be*th* ichose be*th* iquyt and iraunsoned out of *th*e seruyse of fendis, . . ." *Of the Properties of Things,* p. 546
17. Tyndale, William, *Prelates,* p. 2/294. This refers to Trevisa's translation of Higden's work.
18. Trevisa, John, *Polycronicon,* (Lambeth Palace Library. 1495.5) "And it may not be tolde in englysshe what the latyn is to mene without translacion out of latyn in to englysshe. Thenne it nedeth to haue an englysshe translacion / and for to kepe it in mynde that it be not foryete*n* it is better that suche a translacion be made & wryten than sayd & not wryten / . . . Also kynge Alurede . . . translated . . . a grete dele of the Psalter out of latyn in to Englysshe. . . ."
19. More, Thomas, "yt fynally no man can please hym, but wyclyffe the fyrst founder here of that abominable heresye." *The Confutation of Tyndale's Answer, CWM-8,* p. 587
20. Tyndale, William, *Exposition of Tracy's Testament,* PS-3, p. 279
21. Cooper, William, "A Newly Identified Fragment in the Handwriting of William Tyndale," *Reformation* vol 3 1998. pp 323-347
22. Parker, Douglas H., *The praier and complaynte of the Plowemen vnto Christe,* p 42f.
23. Hudson, Anne, *Lollards and their Books,* p 165f Quote from *Chronicon Henrici Knighton,* vol 2. p. 179
24. Tyndale, William, *Answer,* p. 3/128
25. Hudson, Anne, *Lollards and their Books,* p. 172
26. Tyndale, William, *Obedience,* p. 1/304
27. Cooper, Kenneth Schaaf, "The Revival of Lollardy," p. 246f
28. Smeeton, Donald Dean, *Lollard Themes in the Reformation Theology of William Tyndale,* p. 36
29. Walter Brute – "From October 1390 to October 1393 bishop Trefnant of Hereford found himself dealing with a Lollard from his diocese, one Walter Brut." Hudson, A., "'Laicus literatus'; the paradox of Lollardy." p. 222. Brute described himself as a "sinner, layman, farmer, christian, having my origin from among the Britons from each parent." John Foxe, *Acts and Monuments* vol 3, pp 131-186 gives an account of his trial before Bishop Trefnant, including a long translation from *Registrum Johannis Trefnant* of the trial.
30. Foxe, John, *Acts and Monuments,* vol 3, pp. 168, 173
31. Matthew, F.D., "but cristene men taken here fei*th* of god bi his gracious *g*ifte, wha*n*ne he *g*eue*th* to he*m* knowynge & vnd*er*stondynge of treu*th*es nedful for

to saue menn*us* soulis bi, & grace to assente in here herte to suche treu*th*es; & *th*is men clepen fei*th*." *The English Works of Wyclif hitherto Unprinted,* p. 260f

32. Aston, Margaret, *Lollards and Reformers,* pp. 52f, 68f. "The Lollards, who produced some famous women preachers in their time and promoted the religious and educational equality of the sexes, had at least raised the theoretical possibility of having women priests."
33. Tyndale, William, *Answer,* p. 3/18
34. Tyndale, William, *Mammon,* p. 1/99; *Pathway,* p. 1/26
35. Purvey, John, *Remonstrance,* pp 62-65. Although Purvey does not go as far as Tyndale and refer to the Turks.
36. Tyndale, William, *Obedience,* p. 1/316
37. We must not rule out similar attacks both orthodox (e.g. FitzRalph), Wycliffite, or other humanists.
38. Erasmus, Desiderius, *Folly,* p. 145f: Tyndale, William, *Obedience,* p. 1/149-153: Tyndale, William, *Obedience,* p. 1/157f
39. Erasmus, Desiderius, *Enchiridion,* p. 44, 45; Tyndale, William, *Jonas,* p. 1/449
40. Erasmus, Desiderius, *Colloquies,* vol 1, p. 169; Tyndale, William, *Answer,* p. 3/22
41. Lindberg, Carter, *Sourcebook,* p. 48. Foxe, John, *Acts and Monuments,* vol 5, p. 117
42. Tyndale, William, *Answer,* p. 3/16
43. Brown, Andrew, *William Tyndale on Priests and Preachers.* "It is not unlikely that Colet would have been present at Tyndale's ordination as deacon, which took place at St. Paul's. Whether or not they became personally acquainted is unknown, but it is reasonable to suppose that Tyndale was aware of Colet's emphasis on the need for certain reforms. While in London he may have found opportunity to hear Colet preach. He could also have previously read a copy of Colet's 1512 sermon to Convocation, in which he had rebuked the clergy for their inveterate worldliness and had even ventured to criticise the bishops. . . . Tyndale's later remarks on the shortcomings of priests and prelates contain many echoes of the kind of criticisms that Colet had made." p. 20. These are all suppositions but without any real foundation.
44. O'Day, Rosemary, *The Debate on the English Reformation,* p. 7. Rosemary O'Day has claimed, "William Tyndale (c. 1494-1536), pupil of John Colet..."
45. John Yost is one of the greatest advocates of Tyndale's humanist credentials. Although he found some problems which undermine his theory to a certain extent.
46. Yost, J.K., "The Christian Humanism of the English Reformers 1525-1555", p. 65
47. Richardson, Anne, "Tyndale's Quarrel with Erasmus", p. 55

3

The Covenant Revealed

Introduction

The doctrine of the covenant runs through the whole of Tyndale's theology and binds it into a coherent whole. Tyndale believed that if we are to understand the covenant then we have to turn to the word of God, for it is here and here alone that we can hear what God is saying to us. By *scripture,* Tyndale meant the books of the Old and New Testaments only: he did not follow either Luther or Zwingli in quoting from the Apocrypha in any of his writings.[1] He was probably following John Trevisa (whose work he had read as a boy) who wrote: "The Apocrypha is a writing of no authority."[2]

Sola scriptura (Scripture alone) means that the scriptures were sufficient for us to understand all Christian truth. It was one of the watchwords of the Reformation but it pre-dated the Reformation as a tool of reform. It was fundamental to Wyclif.

> According to Netter, Wyclif as a theologian appeals to Scripture alone, openly defying and rejecting the Tradition of the Church. . . .[3] As grace is not just a condition of dominion but rather its source and cause, so conformity to Scripture is no mere condition but very source and cause, sole source and cause, of the validity and authority of all ecclesiastical acts.[4]

This was also the position taken by Tyndale: "In brief, it is evident that scripture is the sole and exclusive source of faith for Tyndale and also the only standard and rule by which to judge it."[5] And, "The cornerstone of Tyndale's doctrine is that the Scriptures are absolute and sufficient authority in all matters of church dogma and practice."[6]

Whilst Luther treated the word of God quite freely, rejecting parts of it because he felt they were inconsistent with the doctrine of justification by faith, Tyndale accepted the whole Bible as God's word. Luther, famously, called the *Epistle of James* an "epistle of straw;"[7] in his *Preface to the Epistle of James* he wrote, "I do not regard it as the writing of an apostle,"[8] and in his *Table Talk,* that "it contains not a syllable about Christ."[9] Tyndale's response to Luther's criticisms in both the *Epistle of James* and *Epistle to the Hebrews* was that Luther had been biased as he read them. Instead of "looking indifferently upon" what the writers of those two Epistles wrote, Luther believed they disagreed with Paul's doctrine;[10] Luther imagined what he thought Paul might have said about them.

The scholastic method of biblical interpretation was called the *Quadriga,* or the "fourfold sense of Scripture", which were the literal, tropological, allegorical and anagogical senses by which the meaning of scripture was expounded.[11] Tyndale believed that there was no difference between the tropological, allegorical and anagogical senses for they were *all* allegories. He wrote that the only true meaning was the literal one, but that had been lost "for the pope hath taken it clean away, and hath made it his possession."[12] As a result the medieval Church was left with the other "meanings", which are no sense at all.[13]

Tyndale pressed for the literal sense, insisting that we had to recognise the figures of speech the writer used when seeking the literal meaning of a text. Within scripture there were allegories, similitudes, and every other figure of speech; some things were facts or historical statements, whilst other passages were not. The literal sense of the text recognises the meaning of the writer and interprets the text in the context in which it was written.[14]

The danger posed by using other methods of biblical interpretation is that they obscure the true meaning of God's word. John Fisher[15] is a good example of the way the spiritual "pervert" the word of God. Tyndale said, Fisher "playeth bo-peep with the scripture, . . . wresting them unto their abominable purpose, clean contrary to the meaning of the text." One of the examples Tyndale gives is that of Aaron in the *Epistle to the Hebrews.* Fisher takes Aaron to mean the pope, whilst it is obvious that the author meant us to understand that Aaron stood for Christ.[16]

The plain literal meaning was lost because the doctors of the church argued that the scriptures would remain a closed book unless we had a sound knowledge of the teaching of the Greek philosopher Aristotle.[17] The result was chaos. Tyndale wrote:

> when they be admitted to study divinity, because the scripture is locked up with such false expositions, and with false principles of natural philosophy, that they cannot enter in, they go about the outside, and dispute all their lives about words and vain opinions, pertaining as much to the healing of a man's heel, as health of his soul.[18]

The vernacular

The medieval Church taught that without Aristotle's philosophy one could not understand the scriptures. The clergy were trained to understand the word of God and they could teach the laity its meaning; therefore it was unnecessary to translate the Bible into the vernacular.

It was not only the scriptures, but also Tradition, which formed the Church's doctrines. Thomas More states the Catholic Church's position:

> I said, that it was thought reasonable to believe the scripture being God's own words rather than the words of men. You proved that the common faith of the Church was as well God's own words as was Holy Scripture itself; and of as great authority. And that no student in scripture should presume to try, examine, and judge the catholic faith of Christ's Church by the scripture. But, by the catholic faith of Christ's Church should examine and expound the texts of scripture.[19]

Tyndale attacked the position held by the Church of his day with the scriptures. He asked:

> How, I say, couldst thou understand the scripture without philosophy, inasmuch as Paul, in the second to the Colossians, warned them to "beware lest any man should spoil them" (that is to say, rob them of their faith in Christ) "through philosophy and deceitful vanities, and through the traditions of men, and ordinances after the world, and not after Christ?"[20]

Tyndale also pointed out that the scriptures were to be taught to every man so that they could all know them.[21] Tyndale showed that, in *John* 5 and in *Acts* 17, both "Christ and his apostles, for all their miracles, required not to be believed without scripture."[22] For, "all things are profoundly grounded in the scriptures, . . . that a man can here desire no more."[23]

Tyndale listed other reasons why the spiritualty said it was unsuitable for the laity to have the scriptures in their native language. Firstly, the laity "are cumbered with worldly business" and so have neither time nor quietness to understand what they read.[24] Secondly, regarding the Traditions, or Christian doctrines that were not found in the Bible, it was only as the spiritualty were the sole interpreters of scripture could those doctrines go unchallenged.[25] Tyndale wrote:

> That thou mayest perceive how that the scripture ought to be in the mother tongue, and that the reasons which our spirits make

> for the contrary, are but sophistry and false wiles to fear thee from the light, that thou mightest follow them blindfold, and be their captive to honour their ceremonies, and to offer to their belly.[26]

Tyndale believed that if people are to understand God's word and allow their lives to be governed by the scriptures it is important that the translation is clear and easily understood. The English Bible must be an accurate translation free from all the glosses of the medieval Church and the traditions which had been added to God's word. Moreover, it had to be a translation so that the ploughboy could understand it and know more about the word of God than the pope or any priest.[27]

> Which thing only moved me to translate the new Testament. Because I had perceived by experience, how that it was impossible to establish the lay-people in any truth, except the scripture were plainly laid before their eyes in their mother-tongue, that they might see the process, order, and meaning of the text: for else, whatsoever truth is taught them, these enemies of all truth quench it again, partly with the smoke of their bottomless pit, . . . (that is, with apparent reasons of sophistry, and traditions of their own making, founded without ground of scripture,) and partly in juggling with the text, expounding it in such a sense as is impossible to gather of the text, if thou see the process, order, and meaning thereof.[28]

Tyndale knew Greek and was one of the few clergy who knew Hebrew. He was easily able to refute the spiritualty who said that English was too crude a language for the scriptures to be translated into the vernacular, or that the original languages of the Bible did not lend themselves to be translated into English.[29] The Bible had been written in the common language of the people because it was important for the laity to know and understand its meaning.[30] Tyndale said that the English Bible would also enable the laity to see where the spiritualty had corrupted God's word.[31]

Furthermore, if they had not the vernacular Bible, how could the laity obey God's command, given through Moses, that God's word should "stick fast in thine heart," and for them to "whet them on their children." Tyndale then asked the rhetorical question, "How can we whet God's word (that is, to put it in practice, use and exercise) upon our children and household, when we are violently kept from it and know it not?"[32] Or how can fathers teach their children if they are not allowed to read God's word?[33]

Understanding the Scripture

Tyndale believed that the scriptures were the only source of doctrine, and that every theological system had to be tried by the word of God. God's plan for the salvation of mankind was to be found in the whole canon of scripture, and both the Old and the New Testaments were the only source of God's revelation to his people. "Our conjectures of other theological underpinnings for Tyndale's theology remain only conjectures and can be buried with Tyndale, for only scripture bore worth in Tyndale's eyes."[34] This assertion did not mean that the works of other Christians were to be ignored, but they – even Tyndale's – had to be tried against the word of God.[35] For when we are faced by a variety of theologies, Tyndale asked, how do we know which is false and which is true? "Whereby shall I try and judge them? Verily by God's word, which only is true."[36]

Only as we turn to the scriptures and allow them to speak God's words to us can we understand what God is saying. The scriptures reveal God's covenant, and in them we follow the development of the covenant from Adam through to the Christian Church. We can then understand the meaning and the importance of the covenant to God's people.

If we are to understand God's word correctly, we must have an empathy with the writers of the Old and New Testaments. They must not be read in a worldly manner. In order that we can judge the true teacher from the false,[37] we need the Holy Spirit to give us the true meaning of scriptures for only then we can know and understand what God is saying to us. "For without the Spirit it is impossible to understand them."[38] After that the Christian can bring God's message to the world, even as the angels brought the glad tidings to the shepherds at Bethlehem. "And these tidings we bring you with the word of God only, which we received of his Spirit, and out of the mouth of his Son, as true messengers."[39] The *only* in that quotation is important for Tyndale, for any doctrine which is not drawn from "the word of God only" is a false doctrine, and those who have deviated from a strict adherence to God's word "are fallen from Christ, and make an idol of their opinions."[40]

The key to Scripture

Tyndale believed that the unity of the Scriptures showed that God counted children of baptized parents in the same way that God counted the children of Israelites through circumcision.[41] (Unlike the unreformed Church baptism was not a sign of one's salvation; unlike the Anabaptists it was not a statement of one's faith.) It is through the profession of our baptism that we find the key to open the scriptures and are able to discover the true meaning of the word of God. In baptism we are reminded of our sin and of the call to repentance; we are reminded of God's promises to us, and of our promises to God – which we can only keep through a true faith. "Baptism saveth through the word, that is, through faith in the word, according to the covenant made in Christ."[42] For Tyndale, the *word* in baptism is not the formula used when a person is baptized, but the word of God. This is made clear in Christ's *Parable of the Sower* (Luke 8:4-15) where the seed sown (which is the word of God) bears fruit, but only to those who love and keep God's word. It is "a covenant to them that love the word of God to further it, that they shall increase therein, and another that they that love it not, shall lose it again, and wax blind."[43] For those who are baptized, the covenant has a commission to evangelize attached to it, for it is "a covenant to them that love the word of God to win other with word and deed."[44] This evangelistic emphasis is an important part of Tyndale's doctrine, but it has usually been overlooked in studies on his theology.[45] He wrote:

> The right way, yea, and the only way, to understand the scripture unto salvation, is that we earnestly and above all things search for the profession of our baptism, or covenants made between God and us.[46]

These are the promises of God, and they give us the keys to open God's word to our understanding:

> And thus, as the Spirit and doctrine on God's part, and repentance and faith on our part, beget us anew in Christ, even so they make us grow, and wax perfect, and save us unto the end. . . . These things, I say, to know, is to have all the scripture unlocked and opened before thee, so that if thou wilt go in, and read, thou canst not but understand.[47]

Unlocking the Scriptures

The covenant runs through the whole of the Bible, and as we read it we find the covenant unfolding before our eyes. The covenant was developed through several stages in the Old Testament, for example, with Adam, then Noah, Abraham and the Children of Israel.[48] Each stage unfolded something more until in Christ the fullness of the covenant was revealed. Many of the promises in the Old Testament are temporal and relate to the nation of Israel in the Promised Land, and to the material blessings God gives to his people as they keep his commandments.[49] These promises must not be spiritualized and made to apply to Christianity since they are temporal and material promises.

At the same time, through the spiritual promises to Israel, the continuity of the covenant is seen:

> for God had made them of the old testament as great promises, that he would be their God, and that his Spirit and all grace should be with them if they kept his laws, as he hath made to us.[50]

The great promise of the covenant to the Children of Israel has been continued to the Christian Church. God promised the members of the Church, he would be their God and they would be his people. More than that, he will be a Father and they will be his children. The literal understanding of this promise means it must be interpreted in a spiritual manner.[51]

As we unlock the scriptures God's law is revealed to us, and we realise that we are all sinners in his sight.[52] But through the gospel there is forgiveness of sins to those who repent[53] and turn to God with faith in Christ's blood[54] for they are then justified in God's sight.[55] The key to the scriptures then opens up true holiness for us, not a holiness of holy works which are unable to save us, for there is no way to be saved from sin:

> save with the holiness of God's word; which only speaketh unto the heart, and sheweth the soul his filthiness and uncleanness of sin, and leadeth her by the way of repentance unto the fountain of Christ's blood, to wash it away through faith.[56]

When we realise that faith is one of the keys which open up the scriptures[57] we find that we have not the strength to turn it ourselves, for it is only the Holy Spirit who can unlock God's truth for us.

> For though the scripture be an outward instrument, and the preacher also, to move men to believe, yet the chief and principal cause why a man believeth, or believeth not, is within: that is, the Spirit of God teacheth his children to believe.[58]

It was Christ who gave the apostles authority to preach.[59] And as they sow the seed in the hearts of their hearers the Holy Spirit gives life to the seed and keeps them from sin.[60] The early Christians carried on this work of preaching,[61] and, like the apostles, their authority came from Christ and not the Church.[62] The sign that a preacher has been given Christ's authority is seen as he preaches the pure word of God.[63] It is those who are called "heretics" by the spiritualty who show that they have Christ's authority by preaching from the "authentic and manifest scripture."[64]

Tyndale then challenged the spiritualty to defend their authority to preach: "first give us authentic scripture for your doctrine."[65] Tyndale said that the faithful preachers are the good angels of the *Book of*

Revelation,[66] and the profession of their baptism is seen in their lives as well as heard through their words. For unless those who preach visibly show a true Christian life they are "blind leaders of the blind,"[67] and those without faith are hurt and driven from faith in Christ.[68] However, Tyndale wrote, it was not in the lives of the spiritualty[69] that God's word is visibly preached. But it is in the lives of those they called "heretics who "walk in the clear light of God's word,"[70] who "preach nothing save that which our Saviour Jesus Christ preached, and his apostles; adding nought thereto, nor plucking aught therefrom."[71] In this way the people are enabled to learn, to know, and to love the scriptures.[72]

Although these people have no position in the Church they are condemned by the spiritualty (to be burnt) because they cling to the scriptures "whereunto they cleave as burs, so fast that they cannot be pulled away, save with very singeing them off."[73]

The true Christians, even though they are "lay and unlearned people," have the profession of their baptism written in their hearts. They "read the scripture, and understand and delight" in it,[74] finding there a "soul, spirit, and life," for God's word has within it "pith, kernel, marrow, and all sweetness for God's elect, which he hath chosen to give them his Spirit, and to write his law, and the faith of his Son, in their hearts."[75] For it is through the profession of our baptism that we benefit from the scripture:

> If our hearts were taught the appointment made between God and us in Christ's blood, when we were baptized, we had the key to open the scripture, and light to see and perceive the true meaning of it, and the scripture should be easy to understand.[76]

This key opens the door so that we can understand the scriptures, for the Christian finds the first and whole purpose of scripture is to bring him into the true "fellowship of God and Christ, and of them that believe in Christ,"[77] and God the Father reveals to every one he has chosen to be his child that "he is merciful, kind and good, yea, and a father unto me for Christ's sake."[78]

Scripture the judge of all things

"Search the scriptures, for by them may ye try all doctrine."[79] For Tyndale the scriptures are their own interpreter, and they are the only source of truth for the Christian Church. Two things follow from this. Firstly, every doctrine and way of life has to measure up to God's word. Secondly, Christians must be able to read and understand the scriptures for themselves, otherwise they would not be able to judge whether the writings of any doctor of the Church were true or not.[80] Therefore the teaching of every preacher and teacher of the Christian faith needs to be checked against the scriptures, and this applies equally to Tyndale's doctrine as to that of anyone else; he wrote:

> And when I allege any scripture, look thou on the text whether I interpret it right: which thou shalt easily perceive by the circumstance and process of them, if thou make Christ the foundation and the ground, and build all on him, and referrest all to him; and findest also that the exposition agreeth unto the common articles of the faith and open scriptures.[81]

This scriptural test has to be applied to every sermon we hear,[82] and to all human writings.[83] The importance of this testing is because not only can individual Christians fall into error, the history of the Church shows that Councils have erred, and later Councils have corrected the errors of earlier ones. Therefore the teachings of the Church fathers and doctors, and the Church's canons, need to be measured against the scriptures.[84] It is therefore necessary that the Christian has God's word in his own language so that he can make a true judgement.[85]

> Let God's word try every man's doctrine, and whomsoever God's word proveth unclean, let him be taken for a leper. One scripture will help to declare another. And the circumstances, that is to say, the places that go before and after, will give light unto the middle text. And the open and manifest scriptures will ever improve the false and wrong exposition of the darker sentences.[86]

Christ told the Jews to test his teaching by searching the scriptures, and he wants us to do the same. The Christian is not to believe anything he is taught unless he can give "a reason of the scripture and authority of God's word."[87] Only then can the hypocrisy of the spiritualty be seen.[88] Neither should Christians be put off when they are told that the doctrine is too hard for them to understand without the doctors. Even St. Augustine had "followed the opinions of Plato, and the common persuasions of man's wisdom that were then famous" before he understood the scriptures and their teaching.[89] There are sound reasons why Christians should judge and examine the doctrines they are being taught to see if they are grounded on God's word,[90] mainly because there are false prophets who teach lies instead of the truth.[91] The Bishop of Rochester preached against Luther and the Protestant doctrines which were rocking the Church. Tyndale challenged his readers to compare Fisher's sermon and his own writings, and judge them against the scriptures to see who was telling the truth.[92]

Tyndale allowed the argument that doctrine could be proved by miracles, but he reminded his readers that the false miracles of the sorcerers of Egypt had mimicked God's miracles performed by Moses. Only authentic scripture is the true judge of doctrine and miracles cannot prove anything without the support of God's word.[93]

Tyndale sums it all up:

> Compare therefore all manner doctrine of men unto the scripture, and see whether they agree or not. And commit thyself whole and altogether unto Christ; and so shall he with his Holy Spirit, and with all his fulness, dwell in thy soul. Amen."[94]

Scripture and the Christian life

After we have been born again as a child of God, Tyndale believed that one of the first things we realise about the Christian life is that we have a relationship with God. In the Covenant we see that God receives us to be his children, and it is the relationship of a child to its father that binds us to God and God to us.[95]

The true Christian has the law of God written in his heart; he loves the law and does his best to keep it, otherwise his faith is vain "and built upon the sand of his own imagination, and not upon the rock of God's word."[96] He has to study the scriptures carefully "and to search God's word the more diligently" so that his faith may be grounded on scripture alone and not on any false teaching of the Church, even though it may sound reasonable to him.[97]

Tyndale knew that the Christian needed material things, and that they were necessary for life, but the Christian should not "covet inordinately more than sufficient, or but even that I have need of," for that shows a lack of faith in God.[98] What is important for the Christian is a knowledge of God's word; as Jesus said, man does not live by bread alone, but by every word of God, which is "the daily bread of the soul."[99] The Christian, therefore, needs to search the scriptures for the promises God has given him[100] so that he might fulfil his part in the covenant which God has made with him.

> For all the promises throughout the whole of scripture do include a covenant: that is, God bindeth himself to fulfil that mercy unto thee only if thou wilt endeavour thyself to keep his laws.[101]

There is a difference between reading God's word and understanding it, for, as Christ said in *John* 8, we have to be of God to understand his word, and this is the work of the Holy Spirit.[102] As Christians we have the Holy Spirit "to open our eyes, and to make us understand and feel wherefore the scripture was given, that we may apply the medicine of the scripture, every man to his own sores."[103] He will then find that the seed of God's word has been sown in his heart,[104] and that this is the word of health.[105] It is the word of God which brings faith to a man, and Tyndale uses the picture of the sun driving away the darkness of night:

> even so are all men's hearts of themselves dark with lies, . . . the lying heart of man can give the word of God no truth; but contrariwise, the truth of God's word is of herself, and lighteneth the hearts of the believers, and maketh them true, and cleanseth them from lies.[106]

Until the gospel light shines into the Christian's heart, not even the vernacular scriptures can teach him the profession of his baptism.[107]

Tyndale repeatedly calls on Christians to keep the profession of their baptism. Then, through God's word, they are brought to repentance and to the blood of Christ, which alone can cleanse them from sin[108] and lead them in the paths of holiness.

> Yea, and God's word will be alway in his heart, and in his mouth, and he every day perfecter than other. For there can nothing edify man's soul, save that which preacheth him God's word. Only the word of God worketh the health of the soul. And whatsoever preacheth him that, cannot but make him perfecter.[109]

The profession of his baptism also means a Christian has to give up trusting in man's words or stories; his task is "not to believe a tale of Robin Hood, or Gesta Romanorum, or of the Chronicles, but to believe God's word that lasteth ever."[110] For to believe in anything other than God's word is "a false faith, superstitiousness, and idolatry, and damnable sin."[111] The apostles Peter, Paul, and all who preach God's word faithfully, preach Christ alone, "and those everlasting promises and eternal testament that God had made between man and him in Christ's blood."[112] Therefore the Christian is told: "Put your trust in God's words only, and not in Abraham. Let saints be an example unto you and not your trust and confidence. For then you make Christ of them."[113]

The Christian learns from the authentic scriptures all God wants him to know, and, where there is no one to teach him, he finds God is his teacher.[114] He is encouraged to "read God's word diligently and with a good heart, and it shall teach thee all things."[115] God teaches the Christian doctrine[116] and all truth.[117] He is taught God's mercy and shown its truth from the history of God's people revealed in the Bible.[118] The scripture teaches him the way of repentance and faith into the kingdom of God.[119] It also teaches the Christian the service that he has to give to God.[120] The result of all this is that the Christian delights in the word of God.[121]

Tyndale warns us that "We may not be too curious in the searching of God's secrets, but rather study to understand and to do our duty towards God and our neighbour."[122] For neither Christ nor the apostles kept anything back which was needful for us to know, "as Paul testified (Acts xx.), how he had shewed them all the counsel of God, and had kept nought back."[123] Those who seek to fathom the hidden wisdom of God have their eyes blinded by the Devil with "falsehood and lies," which is worldly wisdom. This had happened to the spiritualty and the doctors of the medieval Church, who could not accept the open scriptures, and "they have searched to come to the bottom of his bottomless wisdom".[124]

The scriptures also teach us that our Christian life cannot be divided into separate compartments; the whole of our life must be under the control of the Holy Spirit so that our faith may be seen.

> That good works spring of the Spirit; the Spirit cometh by faith; and faith cometh by hearing the word of God, when the glad tidings and promises, which God hath made unto us in Christ, are preached truly, and received in the ground of the heart, without wavering or doubting, after that the law hath passed upon us, and hath condemned our consciences.[125]

The word of God teaches us that our good works must have an evangelistic purpose:

> For God giveth no man his grace, that he should let it lie still and do no good withal; but that he should increase it, and multiply it, with lending it to other, and with open declaring of it with the outward works provoke and draw other to God.[126]

The reason the Christian does good works is because "one man hath bought us all with his blood, and bound us to help one another."[127]

The Christian must stand firm in the trials of faith. Tyndale exhorts every Christian:

> tie to thy ship this anchor of faith in Christ's blood with the cable of love, to cast it out against all tempests; and so set up thy sail, and get thee to the main sea of God's word.[128]

Again our lives must be built on "the rock of God's word,"[129] for the Christian must

> seek the word of God in all things; and without the word of God do nothing, though it appear never so glorious. Whatsoever is done without the word of God, that count idolatry. The kingdom of heaven is within us.[130]

Scripture and the Church

The spirituality taught that the Church was not subject to the scriptures, but the scriptures were subject to the Church. More in his *Dialogue* makes this position very clear, writing that it was "By the Church we know the scripture."[131] Because More believed that the Church had decided what books were scripture he believed that the Church alone could decide the truth.

> And therefore if ye will in faith or living or avoiding of all damnable error (that you might fall in by misunderstanding of scripture) take a sure and infallible way; you must in all these things hear, believe and obey the Church.

A little later More wrote:

> And therefore are we bound, not only to believe against our own reason, the points that God shows us in scripture, but also that God teaches his Church without scripture; . . . to give diligent hearing, firm credence, and faithful obedience to the Church of Christ, concerning the sense and understanding of Holy Scripture.[132]

Tyndale differed from More by making the scriptures the sole authority and not the Church. "The pope keepeth the scripture . . . to make merchandise of it," but it was by those, who were called "heretics" by the spiritualty, that "we know the scripture, and the true sense thereof."[133] Against the claim of the prelates,

> "We be the church, and cannot err; and therefore," say they, "what we conclude, though there be no scripture to prove it, it is as true as the scripture, and of equal authority with the scripture, and must be believed as well as the scripture under pain of damnation."[134]

But for Tyndale it is only by authentic scripture God's word can be understood and interpreted, for scripture will teach us true doctrine and which "is the right church."[135]

The scriptures are the letter sent by God to his people, and the true preacher is the one who delivers the letter. The truth and validity of the word of God therefore belongs to God who sent it, and not the Church which is the bearer of the message.[136] Therefore the Church's officers must be faithful servants of the word of God[137] who teach the scriptures to their brethren.[138] Furthermore their task is to use the sword of the Spirit, which is the word of God, in the fight against evil – whatever the cost to themselves.[139]

Notes

1. The only time Tyndale translated any of the Apocrypha was where they were read during the Mass so that people could follow them in the Church services.
2. Trevisa, John, "Apocrifa is a wrytynge of none auctoryte." *Polychronicon*, p. clxix
3. Hurley, "*Scriptura Sola:* Wyclif and his critics." p. 278
4. ibid. p. 344
5. Flesseman-van Leer, "The Controversy about Scripture and Tradition between Thomas More and William Tyndale," p. 145
6. Pineas, Rainer, ""William Tyndale's Polemical use of the Scriptures," p. 65
7. Luther, Martin, *Works*, vol 35. p. 362
8. Luther, *Works*, vol 35. p. 395f
9. Luther, *Works*, vol 54. p. 424f
10. Tyndale, *Prologues upon Hebrews, and James*, p. 1/524, 1/525
11. McGrath, Alister, *Reformation Thought*, p147f. "1. The *literal* sense, whereby the text is taken at face value. 2. The *allegorical* sense, . . . to produce statements of doctrine. . . . 3. The *tropological* or *moral* sense, . . . to produce ethical guidance for Christian conduct. 4. The *anagogical* sense, . . . to indicate the grounds of Christian hope."
12. Tyndale, William, *Obedience*, p. 1/303
13. Tyndale, William, *Obedience*, p. 1/343f
14 Duerdon, Richard Y., "Justice and Justification: King and God in Tyndale's *The Obedience of a Christian Man*", p. 78
15. The Bishop of Rochester
16. Tyndale, *Obedience*, p. 1/214f
17. Tyndale, William, *Mammon*, p. 1/107
18. Tyndale, William, *Prelates*, p. 2/291
19. More, Thomas, "I sayd that it was thought reasonable to byleue the scrypture beynge goddys owne wordys rather than the wordys of men / ye therin proued that the comen fayth of the chyrche was as well goddys owne wordys as was holy scypture selfe / and of as greate authoryte / and that no student in scrypture sholde presume to trye / examyn / and iudge the catholyque faythe of Chrystys chyrche by ye scrypture / but by the catholyque fayth of crystys chyrche shold examyn and expowne the textys of scrypture." *A Dialogue .. CWM* vol 6, p. 188
20. Tyndale, William, *Obedience*, p. 1/155f
21. Tyndale, William, *Obedience*, pp. 1/241, 1/249f
22. Tyndale, William, *Answer*, p. 3/111
23. Tyndale, William, *Prologue to Romans*, p. 1/507f
24 Tyndale, William, *Obedience*, p. 1/146
25. Pineas, Rainer, "William Tyndale's Polemical use of the Scriptures," pp. 66, 75
26. Tyndale, William, *Obedience*, p. 1/144
27. Foxe, John, *Acts and Monuments*, vol 5, p. 117
28. Tyndale, William, *Preface Moses*, p. 1/394
29. Tyndale, William, *Obedience*, p. 1/148f: *Preface Moses*, p. 1/392
30. Tyndale, William, *Answer*, p. 3/168f
31. Tyndale, William, *Answer*, p. 47: *Exposition Matthew*, p. 2/16
32. Tyndale, William, *Obedience*, p. 1/145

33. Tyndale, William, *Marginal Note, Exodus, Old Testament,* p. 107
34 Mayotte, Judith, "William Tyndale's Contribution to the Reformation in England." p. 269
35. Tyndale, William, *Preface Moses,* pp. 1/392, 1/396f
36. Tyndale, William, *Obedience,* p. 1/153
37. Tyndale, William, *Pathway,* p. 1/7f
38. Tyndale, William, *Mammon,* pp. 1/88, 1/107: *Prologue 2 Peter,* p. 1/528
39. Tyndale, William, *Exposition 1 John,* p. 2/148
40. Tyndale, William, *Answer,* p. 3/33
41. see page 96f
42. Tyndale, *Marginal Note, Ephesians, New Testament,* p. 286
43. Tyndale, Tyndale, *Marginal Note, Matthew, New Testament,* p. 37
44 Tyndale, Tyndale, *Marginal Note, Mark, New Testament,* p. 67
45. McGiffert, Michael, "William Tyndale's Conception of Covenant", p. 171
46. Tyndale, William, *Prologue Matthew,* p. 1/469
47. Tyndale, William, *Pathway,* p. 1/27 *Jonas,* p. 1/464
48. Genesis 3: Genesis 9: Genesis 17: from Exodus 12 and throughout the Old Testament.
49. Tyndale, William, *Prologue Exodus,* p. 1/415
50. Tyndale, William, *Exposition Matthew,* p. 2/43
51. Tyndale, William, *Jonas,* p. 1/463
52. Tyndale, William, *Prologue Romans,* p. 1/496: *Exposition 1 John,* p. 2/150
53. Tyndale, William, *Obedience,* p. 1/270: *Prologue Numbers,* p. 1/434: *Answer,* p. 3/132
54 Tyndale, William, *Mammon,* p. 1/48: *Exposition Matthew,* p. 2/11: *Exposition 1 John,* p. 2/136f
55. Tyndale, William, *Obedience,* p. 1/267f
56. Tyndale, William, *Jonas,* p. 1/462
57. Flesseman-van Leer, E., "The Controversy about Scripture and Tradition between Thomas More and William Tyndale", p. 158
58. Tyndale, William, *Answer,* p. 3/139
59. Tyndale, William, *Obedience,* p. 1/211
60. Tyndale, William, *Exposition 1 John,* p. 2/190
61. Tyndale, William, *Answer,* p. 3/68
62. Tyndale, William, *Obedience,* p. 1/270
63. Tyndale, William, *Obedience,* p. 1/300: *Exposition Matthew,* p. 2/36
64 Tyndale, William, *Answer,* p. 128
65. Tyndale, William, *Answer,* p. 3/128
66. Tyndale, William, *Marginal Notes, Revelation, New Testament,* p. 376
67. Tyndale, William, *Prelates,* p. 2/242; (see Luke 6:39 etc)
68. Tyndale, William, *Obedience,* p. 1/229f
69. for the meaning of *spiritualty* and *temporalty* see p. 6
70. Tyndale, William, *Answer,* p. 3/115
71. Tyndale, William, *Prelates,* p. 2/242
72. Tyndale, William, *Answer,* p. 3/114
73. Tyndale, William, *Answer,* p. 3/102
74 Tyndale, William, *Pathway,* p. 1/28
75. Tyndale, William, *Jonas,* p. 1/449

76. Tyndale, William, *Exposition 1 John,* p. 2/141
77. Tyndale, William, *Exposition 1 John,* p. 2/147
78. Tyndale, William, *Mammon,* p. 1/84f
79. Tyndale, William, *Marginal Note, Acts, New Testament* p. 189
80. Tyndale, William, *Obedience,* p. 1/153
81. Tyndale, William, *Obedience,* p. 1/167
82. Tyndale, William, *Obedience,* p. 1/241f
83. Tyndale, William, *Mammon,* p. 1/44
84 Tyndale, William, *Answer,* p. 3/99f
85. Tyndale, William, *Obedience,* p. 1/324: *Exposition Matthew,* p. 2/121
86. Tyndale, William, *Obedience,* p. 1/250
87. Tyndale, William, *Obedience,* p. 1/330
88. Tyndale, William, *Answer,* p. 3/137
89. Tyndale, William, *Obedience,* p. 1/153f
90. Tyndale, William, *Exposition 1 John,* p. 2/222f
91. Tyndale, William, *Exposition 1 John,* p. 2/195
92. Tyndale, William, *Obedience,* p. 1/1/208-223
93. Tyndale, William, *Answer,* p. 3/128
94 Tyndale, William, *Prologue Romans,* p. 1/508
95. Tyndale, William, *Exposition Matthew,* p. 2/9
96. Tyndale, William, *Sacraments,* p. 1/363
97. Tyndale, William, *Answer,* p. 3/95
98. Tyndale, William, *Exposition Matthew,* p. 2/111
99. Tyndale, William, *Prologue Romans,* p. 1/484
100. Tyndale, William, *Jonas,* p. 1/464
101. Tyndale, William, *Prologue Genesis,* p. 1/403
102. Tyndale, William, *Mammon,* p. 1/88
103. Tyndale, William, *Prologue Genesis,* p. 1/398
104 Tyndale, William, *Exposition 1 John,* p. 2/190: *Obedience,* p. 1/263
105. Tyndale, William, *Obedience,* p. 1/281
106. Tyndale, William, *Answer,* p. 3/24f
107. Tyndale, William, *Exposition 1 John,* p. 2/144
108. Tyndale, William, *Jonas,* p. 1/466
109. Tyndale, William, *Answer,* p. 3/63
110. Tyndale, William, *Obedience,* p. 1/328
111. Tyndale, William, *Obedience,* p. 1/289f
112. Tyndale, William, *Obedience,* p. 1/288
113. Tyndale, William, *1525 New Testament (The Cologne Fragment),* p. 21. "Put youre truste i*n* goddes wordes only / & not i*n* abraham. Let saynctes be an ensa*m*ple vnto you & not youre truste & co*n*fidence: For then ye make Christ of them."
114 Tyndale, William, *Obedience,* p. 1/156
115. Tyndale, William, *Prologue Numbers,* p. 1/440
116. Tyndale, William, *Prologue Genesis,* p. 1/398f
117. Tyndale, William, *Answer,* p. 3/136ff
118. Tyndale, William, *Obedience,* p. 1/197
119. Tyndale, William, *Prologue Numbers,* p. 1/434: *Obedience,* p. 1/270: *Answer,* p. 3/132

120. Tyndale, William, *Obedience,* p. 1/332
121. Tyndale, William, *Pathway,* p. 1/28
122. Tyndale, William, *Prologue Deuteronomy,* p. 1/444 (Marginal Note)
123. Tyndale, William, *Answer,* p. 3/169
124 Tyndale, William, *Answer,* p. 3/191
125. Tyndale, William, *Prologue Romans,* p. 1/499
126. Tyndale, William, *Mammon,* p. 1/60
127. Tyndale, William, *Exposition Matthew,* p. 2/69
128. Tyndale, William, *Exposition Matthew,* p. 2/15
129. Tyndale, William, *Prologue Matthew,* p. 1/472f
130. Tyndale, William, *Mammon,* p. 1/103
131. More, Thomas, "By ye chyrch we know ye scrypture." *Dialogue, CWM* vol 6, p. 206
132. More, Thomas, "And therfore yf ye wyll in fayth or lyuynge or auoydynge of all dampnable arrour (that ye myght fall in by mysse vnderstandynge of scrypture) take a sure and vnfallyble way / ye must in all these thynges here / byleue & obay the chyrche." "And therfore are we bounden not onely to byleue agaynste oure owne reason / the poyntes that god sheweth vs in scrypture / but also that god techeth his chyrche without scrypture . . . to gyue dylygent herynge / ferme credence / and faythfull obedyence to the chyrche of Cryst / concernynge the sence and vnderstandynge of holy scrypture." *Dialogue, CWM* vol 6, p. 165f
133. Tyndale, William, *Answer,* p. 3/114
134 Tyndale, William, *Prelates,* p. 2/289
135. Tyndale, William, *Answer,* p. 3/44
136. Tyndale, William, *Answer,* p. 3/136
137. Tyndale, William, *Prologue Matthew,* p. 1/479
138. Tyndale, William, *Prelates,* p. 2/251
139. Tyndale, William, *Prelates,* p. 2/247

4

The Covenant Envisaged

Of prime importance for Tyndale was his theology of the covenant. This covenant was to restore creation to its original state; and man could, once again have fellowship with God. "We ought to love and honour God with all our strength and might, from the low bottom of the heart, because he hath created us, and both heaven and earth for our sakes,"[1] is typical of his treatment of the creation. Of secondary importance was the salvation of man through Christ: although this was the key for creation's restoration. "God hath created us and made us unto his own likeness; and our Saviour Christ hath bought us with his blood."[2]

Tyndale's view of scripture ruled out any doctrine of salvation that could not be proved by scripture. This meant that Tyndale rejected both the medieval idea that God required us only to do our best (*facere quod in se est*); and also the idea that there was anything in fallen man which would enable him to respond to the preaching of the gospel until he had been born again by the Holy Spirit.

The Fall

Tyndale's doctrine of the state of man after the Fall is one of the hardest for contemporary man to accept for it takes away all the power from man and ties him completely to the devil's will. Philip Watson wrote that for Luther man

> retains his powers of reason and will, and he still has some knowledge of God and his law. But both his reasoning and his willing are radically corrupt, being governed from the start by the false premises dictated by Satan.[3]

Luther, in his exposition of *Genesis* wrote: "This should be emphasized, I say, for the reason that unless the severity of the disease is correctly recognized, the cure is also not known or desired."[4] This idea of sickness is also found in Zwingli, who wrote, "And he will see that sickness, too, when he realizes that everything that we do has its origin in frailty, lust and temptation."[5] In his commentary on *Ephesians* 2, where Paul wrote that we were "dead in trespasses and sins," Calvin wrote:

> Some kind of life, I acknowledge, does remain in us, while we are still at a distance from Christ; for unbelief does not altogether destroy the outward senses, or the will, or the other facilities of the soul.[6]

Even the Synod of Dort has not left man entirely hopeless and states, "There remain, however, in man since the fall, the glimmerings of natural light, whereby he retains some knowledge of God, . . ."[7]

But for Tyndale the picture is black and white, without the shades of grey seen in other Reformers, and the Synod of Dort. Tyndale's position is clear: man is incapable of knowing God or doing anything good without the power of the indwelling Holy Spirit. Through Adam's disobedience man was totally alienated from God, unable to get any further from God than he already is, and unable to do anything pleasing to God.

> By nature, through the fall of Adam, are we the children of wrath, heirs of the vengeance of God by birth, yea, and from our conception. And we have our fellowship with the damned devils, under the power of darkness and rule of Satan, while we are yet in our mother's wombs; and though we shew not forth the fruits of sin [as soon as we are born], yet are we full of the natural poison, whereof all sinful deeds spring, and cannot but sin outwards, (be we never so young,) [as soon as we be able to work,] if occasion be given: for our nature is to do sin, as is the nature of a serpent to sting.[8]

Tyndale wrote "that we are by inheritance heirs of damnation,"[9] for the Fall has "brought us into captivity and bondage under the devil. And the devil is our lord, and our ruler, our head, our governor, our prince, yea, and our god."[10] It is impossible for man to keep or consent to the law "his wit, reason, and will being so fast glued, yea, nailed and chained unto the will of the devil."[11] Earlier he had described this chaining more graphically: "Our will is locked and knit faster unto the will of the devil, than could an hundred thousand chains bind a man unto a post."[12]

As if that is not enough, Tyndale wrote: "our hearts were as dead unto all good working as the members of him whose soul is departed." He then quotes from *Ephesians* 2:1-10 and continues,

> The text is plain: we were stone dead, and without life or power to do or consent to good. The whole nature of us was captive under the devil, and led at his will. And we were as wicked as the devil now is (except that he now sinneth against the Holy Ghost); and we consented unto sin with soul and body, and hated the law of God.[13]

Thus, for Tyndale, we see that there is not even the slightest glimmer of light in fallen man who has no thoughts or desires to change from serving the devil,

> because that of nature we are evil, therefore we both think and do evil, and are under vengeance, under the law, convict to eternal damnation by the law, and are contrary to the will of God in all our will, and in all things consent to the will of the fiend.[14]

Tyndale teaches that the reason for this total separation between God and fallen mankind rests on a family relationship. Adam and his offspring are now children of the devil, while a Christian belongs to a different family, whose father is God.

> God and the devil are two contrary fathers, two contrary fountains, and two contrary causes: the one of all goodness, the other of all evil. And they that do evil are born of the devil; and first evil by that birth, ere they do evil. . . . [For,] as Christ saith, (John viii.) "Ye are of your father the devil, and therefore will do the lusts of your father."[15]

This brings with it our enmity to God,

> For how can we be at peace with God and love him, seeing we are conceived and born under the power of the devil, . . . that we are by birth and of nature the heirs of eternal damnation, as saith Paul, Eph. ii.? We (saith he) 'are by nature the children of wrath;' which thing the law doth but utter only, and helpeth us not, yea, requireth impossible things of us.[16]

Freewill

This contrast of sonships naturally leads us to the question of freewill, and we need to look at how Tyndale expressed this, for he makes a difference between fallen man and those who have been born again by the Holy Spirit.

The natural man is totally separated from God and his deeds are evil because the devil has blinded him so that he "cannot see the goodness and righteousness of the law of God."[17] Original sin has resulted in man's will being powerless to desire spiritual freedom, nor would he choose it if he could. Tyndale wrote:

> The will of man followeth the wit, and is subject unto the wit; and as the wit erreth, so does the will, and as the wit is in captivity, so is the will; neither is it possible that the will should be free, where the wit is in bondage.

Tyndale recognised that men had a freedom to chose to do different things and make decisions, but man's freewill does not let him choose what is good for he is prevented by his "natural blindness" and one man thinks this is right, and another, that, for "we are all out of the right way, every man his ways: one judgeth this best, and another that to be best." Tyndale continued: "Now when we say, every man hath his free will, to do what him lusteth, I say, verily, that men do what they lust. Notwithstanding, to follow lusts is not freedom, but captivity and bondage."[18]

However, Tyndale is more concerned with the Christian than with the unregenerate man, and so we find that everything he writes about fallen man is but a springboard to show the greatness of God's love to his elect and chosen children. Therefore he quickly turns to the freewill God has given to the Christian.

It is not until God has liberated us from bondage to the devil, and through our new birth he has given us the power to "hate and resist" everything that kept us apart from God, and we are set free "even with the freedom wherewith Christ maketh free." Only then have we the power to do God's will,[19] for it is only after God has "poured the Spirit of his grace into our souls" that we have the freewill to do God's will and keep his law.[20]

Tyndale also raised the problem of the Christian sinning against this spiritual will he has been given: "I mean the will of the Spirit, for after our conversion we have two wills, fighting one against the other."[21] Here Tyndale seems to be agreeing with Luther that the Christian is *simul justus et peccator* (at the same time righteous and a sinner). Quoting *Romans* 7, Tyndale wrote: "Thus we are sinners, and no sinners," but his explanation of this phrase moves him away from Luther. Tyndale regarded sin in the life of the Christian as "frailty" for "we never cast off the yoke of God from our necks, neither yield up ourselves unto sin for to serve it."[22] We are either children of God (*justus*) or children of the devil (*peccator*); we cannot be both at the same time, for the child of God has God's nature and the Holy Spirit so that he "cannot consent to sin."[23] For, if we sin, we are not "judged by the rigorousness of the law; but chastised, if we do amiss, as children that are under no law."[24]

God's plan for man's salvation

Tyndale's theology of the covenant runs through all his writings, from the 1525 *Cologne Fragment* onwards. Yet we still find those who follow William Clebsch in putting Tyndale's covenant theology late in his theological development.[25] The question lying behind the covenant is: "How can God the Father choose and enable those he has elected from fallen mankind to be his children?"

Tyndale uses different words when writing about the covenant. The main ones are "covenant", "testament" and "appointment". In his earlier writings Tyndale uses "testament"; he then in his later writings changes to "covenant". In many of his writings during his transition from "testament" to "covenant" he writes "covenant, that is testament" showing that the change in words does not mean a change in his theology. As we uncover Tyndale's meaning of "testament" and "covenant" it becomes clear that they are two aspects to Tyndale's covenant theology.

We are led into confusion and seeming contradictions if we try to link Tyndale's (natal) covenant with that of the Continental Reformer's (forensic) covenant. For whilst the Continental Reformers considered the covenant was a legal contract between God and the sinner whereby the sinner was counted justified, for Tyndale the covenant was established through birth as a child of God. An analogy of this difference can be seen between the Roman citizenship of the centurion and Paul, "And the captain answered: With a great sum obtained I this freedom. And Paul said: I was free born."[26]

Firstly, for Tyndale, there is the unilateral covenant which sets out the way fallen men are saved from the power of sin and the devil, and born again into God's family as his children. This covenant of salvation is made between the Persons of the Trinity; the Father, the Son and the Holy Spirit covenanting together to make man's salvation possible. It enabled God to destroy the effects of the Fall and restore man into fellowship with himself. God the Father covenanted with the Son and the Holy Spirit to be a Father to those whom they had chosen to become children of God, "In Christ God loved us, his elect and chosen, before the world began, and reserved us unto the knowledge of his Son and of his holy gospel."[27]. On his part, God the Son covenanted to make this sonship possible by becoming the sacrifice for man's sin and shedding his blood on the cross, and thus satisfying God's justice, for "the blood of Christ hath obtained all things for us of God."[28] God the Holy Spirit covenanted to give a new birth through Christ's blood to those who would become the children of God, and, through Christ's blood, keep them safe as God's children and bring them into God's kingdom.

> Note now the order: first God giveth me light to see the goodness and righteousness of the law, and mine own sin and unrighteousness; out of which knowledge springeth repentance. Now repentance teacheth me not that the law is good, and I evil; but a light that the Spirit of God hath given me, out of which light repentance springeth. Then the same Spirit worketh in mine heart trust and confidence, to believe the mercy of God and his truth, that he will do as he hath promised; which belief saveth me.[29]

Paul Laughlin discovered three phases in Tyndale's covenant theology which "corresponded roughly to the three persons of the Trinity and to the particular activity most closely associated with each of them: election by the Father, justification in the Son, and perfection through the Spirit."[30]

Because Tyndale's writings are practical and more concerned with the Christian in relationship with God, this aspect of the covenant is not as easy to find as other doctrines in his writings.

> It is God who takes the believers into the covenant with him for Christ's sake, as it is Christ who gives grace to do the Law and to understand it "and writeth it with his holy Spirit in the tables of the hearts of men; and maketh it a true thing there, and no hypocrisy."[31]

We fail to understand Tyndale's view of the covenant if we make it between God and man, and if we – like the Swiss Reformers – try to make it have a legal framework between God and man. Tyndale's "stress upon the notion of covenant appears to weaken the forensic approach to grace and faith, matters so pronounced and one-sided in Luther and Calvin."[32]

God had foreseen the Fall, and even before the foundation of the world He had made his plans for man's salvation.[33] God would restore rebellious man to fellowship with himself. At the same time God would be just and the justifier of those who had sinned through disobeying the one commandment God had given him in the Garden of Eden. God planned to elect some of those who would be taken captive of the devil,[34] save them from their captivity, and adopt them as children of God.[35] It was an agreement between the Father, Son and Holy Spirit to restore man into the favour of God, "God hath also made us promises, and hath sworn; yea, hath made a testament or a covenant, and hath bound himself, and hath sealed his obligation with Christ's blood, and confirmed it with miracles."[36]

Secondly, God applies the covenant to those elected to become his children, and here Tyndale writes about the covenant being bilateral between God and man. He refers to this aspect of his covenant theology in his *Prologue to Matthew,* and points out that it is not a single covenant, but where God has made a promise to us he has made a covenant.[37] This chapter deals with the unilateral covenant made between God the Father, God the Son and God the Holy Spirit.

The Covenant

There are similarities and differences in the covenant theologies of all the Reformers, and the overlap between them varied. Like Luther's and Calvin's, Tyndale's covenant was unilateral; like Bullinger's it related to election only; like Zwingli's the Holy Spirit played a vital part in its application to man. Unlike Luther's covenant it was not the work of the

Word of God, nor had it any relationship to man's faith for its validity; unlike Calvin's there was no double predestination; unlike Zwingli's there was no pact between God and man; unlike Bullinger's it was not bilateral.[38] The covenant for Tyndale differed from all the other Reformers in the fact that it was between the Persons of the Trinity only and not between God and man. Paul Laughlin wrote of Tyndale's *ordo salutis:* "The *ordo* was of Tyndale's own devising and contained certain terminology, concepts, and emphases that were unusual for Reformation theology and indeed define a slant on soteriology peculiar to him."[39]

As we will see, Tyndale's covenant is straightforward and depends entirely on God, and it relates to our birth as children of God. In the same way that no human child has anything to do with its conception, so the child of God has no part in its election or new birth, which is solely the work of God. The Holy Spirit is active in applying the covenant to those God has chosen from those who are spiritually dead children of the devil, and until the Holy Spirit has given them life, and they are born again, they are spiritually dead and can do nothing. The covenant is fulfilled as the new born child of God lives and grows within the covenant of salvation.[40]

The Trinity

In his thinking Tyndale sought to find in the Bible a consistent theology that did justice to each Person in the Trinity, to the sovereignty of God, and to his righteousness and love. God had to be just and the justifier of sinful man,[41] and his theology had to take into account man's inability to do anything himself towards his salvation. All his findings, Tyndale knew, had to be based on scripture alone, without any outside influences based on Greek philosophy or humanist rationalism.

> Forasmuch as we can do no works unto God, but receive only of his mercy with our repenting faith, through Jesus Christ our Lord and only Saviour: unto whom, and unto God our Father through him, and unto his holy Spirit, that only purgeth, sanctifieth, and washeth us in the innocent blood of our redemption, be praise for ever."[42]

In this passage from the *Prologue of the Prophet Jonas* we see Tyndale's covenant theology in embryonic form.

The Love of the Father

The first problem to be overcome was "How can God the Father be a Father to man after his rebellion against God?" Man had chosen to disobey God and to suffer eternal death and separation from God. God had to punish man's sin with death if he was to be just and righteous. Therefore, if the

Father was to love man as his child, then man had to be made righteous and freed from sin. The only way this problem could be solved was for the effects of the Fall to be undone, and man to have once again a perfect righteousness.

Tyndale constantly ruled out man's involvement in the covenant by stressing that God's plan for man's restoration to fellowship with himself was before creation. "In Christ God loved us, his elect and chosen, before the world began, and reserved us unto the knowledge of his Son and of his holy gospel; . . . and we know him as our Father most merciful."[43] He wrote:

> God is ever fatherly-minded toward the elect members of his church. He loved them, ere the world began, in Christ. (Eph. 1.) He loveth them while they be yet evil, and his enemies in their hearts, ere they be come unto the knowledge of his Son Christ, and ere his law be written in their hearts; as a father loveth his young son, while he is yet evil, and ere it know his father's law to consent thereto.[44]

The love of God the Father shines through all of Tyndale's writings.[45]

The Love of the Son

The certainty of the covenant depends on it being fulfilled before creation. "The treasure of his mercy was laid up in Christ for all that should believe, before the world was made; *ergo,* nothing that hath happened since hath changed the purpose of the invariable God." God's love meant that he gave his Son for the elect.[46] To achieve man's salvation God the Son had to become man and to shed his blood for the elect, for there was no "covenant made that was not confirmed with blood." Throughout the Old Testament the covenant was confirmed with the blood of the animals that were sacrificed, "but this new and gentle testament, . . . as it is a better testament, so is it confirmed with a better blood."[47]

To achieve his part in the covenant God the Son had to become man and shed his blood for the elect so that God the Father could adopt them into his family as his children.

> His blood, his death, his patience in suffering rebukes and wrongs, his prayers and fastings, his meekness and fulfilling of the uttermost point of the law, appeased the wrath of God; brought the favour of God to us again; obtained that God should love us first, and be our Father, and that a merciful Father.[48]

The covenant is certain, for, wrote Tyndale, "Jesus is God and Almighty," he is our "advocate and intercessor. . . . And this advocate, and our Jesus, to save us from our sins," has "an everlasting office, to make atonement for sin."[49] As God the Son fulfils his part of the covenant for the chosen child of God, so "God, for his truth's sake, must put the righteousness of Christ in him, and wash his unrighteousness away in the blood of Christ."[50]

The Work of the Holy Spirit

The Holy Spirit's part in the covenant is to apply the blood of Christ to those chosen to be the children of God. For those "whom God chooseth to reign everlastingly with Christ, him sealeth he with his mighty Spirit."[51] For the Holy Spirit's work in the elect, and all that he does for us "is the deserving of Christ's blood."[52]

The Holy Spirit is active for the whole life of those God has chosen; from bringing the elect to the new birth as God's children, he gives them faith and repentance and enables them to be faithful and obedient children of their heavenly Father.

> So we see that God only, who, according to the scripture, worketh all in all things, worketh a man's justifying, salvation, and health; yea, and poureth faith and belief, lust to love God's will, and strength to fulfil the same, into us, even as water is poured into a vessel; and that of his good will and purpose, and not of our deservings and merits.[53]

The whole of man's salvation as a child of God is the work of the Holy Spirit as he applies the covenant to the elect and enables God to be their Father and the Son to be their Saviour, and for the elect to grow in grace and the knowledge of God. As Carl Trueman wrote,

> According to Tyndale, the presence of the Spirit within the believer has a fourfold effect: first, he frees man from bondage to the Devil. . . . Secondly, he assures man of the love of God towards him. Thirdly, he makes man return this love. Finally he causes man to demonstrate this love in the performance of good works.[54]

In the following chapters we will see how the Holy Spirit is involved in every stage of the life of the elect, from bringing them from death and separation from God to life as God's children, his enabling them to grow and develop as children of God until at length he brings them into God's eternal presence in heaven.

Notes

1. Tyndale, William, *Pathway*, p. 1/18
2. Tyndale, William, *Answer*, p. 3/57
3. Watson, Philip S., *Luther and Erasmus: Free Will and Salvation*. p. 16
4. Luther, Martin, *Lectures on Genesis, 1-5*, Works, 1, p. 142
5. Zwingli, Huldrych, "Of the Education of Youth", Bromiley, G.W., (ed), *Zwingli and Bullinger*, p. 105
6. Calvin, John, *Commentaries, Galatians and Ephesians*, p. 219f

7. *Canons Ratified in the National Synod of the Reformed Church, Dordrecht,* p. 45
8. Tyndale, William, *Pathway,* p. 1/14. Words in [. . .] added to *The Cologne Fragment, 1525*
9. Tyndale, William, *Mammon,* p. 1/64
10. Tyndale, William, *Pathway,* p. 1/17
11. Tyndale, William, *Pathway,* p. 1/18
12. Tyndale, William, *Pathway,* p. 1/17
13. Tyndale, William, *Exposition 1 John,* p. 2/199
14. Tyndale, William, *1525 New Testament,* p. 7. "because that of nature we are evell / therfore we bothe thynke and doo evyll / and are vnder vengeaunce / vnder the lawe / convicte to eternall damnacion by the lawe / and are contrary to the will of god in all oure wyll / and in all thyngs consent to the wyll of the fende."
15. Tyndale, William, *Exposition 1 John,* p. 2/190
16. Tyndale, William, *Mammon,* p. 1/47
17. Tyndale, William, *Answer,* p. 3/191
18. Tyndale, William, *Obedience,* p 1/182f
19. Tyndale, William, *Obedience,* p. 1/183
20. Tyndale, William, *Answer,* p. 3/174
21. Tyndale, William, *Exposition Matthew,* p. 2/76
22. Tyndale, William, *Answer,* p. 3/32: *Obedience,* p. 1/301, In this passage Tyndale quotes Romans 7: *Prologue Romans,* p. 1/492, "Sinners we are, because the flesh is not full killed and mortified," but "God is so loving and favourable unto us, that he will not look on such sin, neither will count it as sin."
23. Tyndale, William, *Exposition 1 John,* p. 2/190
24. Tyndale, William, *Exposition 1 John,* p. 2/158f
25. for example: Day, John, "Tyndale and Frith on Tracy's Will and Justification" (Tracy signed his will October 1530, and Tyndale's Commentary was not printed and published until 1535) wrote, concerning this late work of Tyndale's, "What's relatively new here is the emphasis on covenant." p. 174. Trueman, Carl; *Luther's Legacy,* In dealing with Tyndale's "Later Career: 1533—6" he wrote, "The writings of this period reveal a new emphasis in Tyndale's theology on God's covenant." p. 109
26. Acts 22:28
27. Tyndale, William, *Pathway,* p. 1/14. *1525,* p. 7
28. Tyndale, William, *Pathway,* p. 1/15. *1525,* p. 7.
29. Tyndale, William, *Answer,* 3/195f
30. Laughlin, Paul A. "The Brightness of Moses' Face," p. 69
31. Møller, Jens, "The Beginnings of Puritan Covenant Theology", p. 52
32. Penny, D. Andrew, *Freewill or Predestination,* p. 15. See also p. 49f
33. Tyndale, William, *Pathway,* p. 1/11: *Prologue Ephesians,* p. 1/514: *Answer,* p. 3/111f: etc.
34. Tyndale, William, *Mammon,* p. 1/77
35. Tyndale, William, *Mammon,* p. 1/51: *Prologue Exodus,* p. 1/417
36. Tyndale, William, *Obedience,* p. 1/292
37. Tyndale, William, *Prologue Matthew,* p. 1/471
38. Space does not allow for the explanation of these differences. At the risk of over simplification, 'unilateral' means the covenant is made by God alone;

'bilateral' means it is made between God and man.
39. Laughlin, "The Brightness of Moses" Face", p. 68
40. The doctrine behind Tyndale's covenant theology will be more fully unfolded in later chapters.
41. *Romans* 3:26
42. Tyndale, William, *Jonas,* p. 1/466
43. Tyndale, William, *Pathway,* p. 1/14f
44. Tyndale, William, *Answer,* p. 3/111f
45. As with most theologians Tyndale, when he writes "God", he generally means "God the Father". The context will make clear if Tyndale is referring to "the Trinity", "the Son", or "the Holy Spirit", rather than "the Father".
46. Tyndale, William, *Tracy,* p. 3/275
47. Tyndale, William, *Sacraments,* p. 1/364
48. Tyndale, William, *Pathway,* p. 1/18f
49. Tyndale, William, *Exposition 1 John,* p. 2/152f
50. Tyndale, William, *Mammon,* p. 1/94: *Exposition Matthew,* p. 2/90
51. Tyndale, William, *Obedience,* p. 1/139f
52. Tyndale, William, *Mammon,* p. 1/83
53. Tyndale, William, *Prologue Romans,* p. 1/498
54. Trueman, Carl R., *Luther's Legacy,* p. 90

5

The Means to Achieve the Covenant

For Tyndale the covenant was made before the creation of the world between God the Father, God the Son and God the Holy Spirit. As God had foreseen, man disobeyed his one command, and the punishment for his disobedience had been carried out. Man was spiritually dead and separated from God.

We now need to look at the ways Tyndale believed God made it possible for the covenant to work. Paul Laughlin traced Tyndale's thought from man's depravity to the Christian's lifestyle and wrote: "In so doing, it summarized a soteriology that exhibited a unique character among the theologies of the Reformation."[1] That uniqueness is found in the fact that the covenant is made for God and his glory. The salvation of man is secondary in order that God can achieve his purpose in Creation, and also the defeat of the devil's attempts to destroy that purpose. The covenant is not primarily for the salvation of man, but the salvation of man is a means for God to achieve his purpose and for his glory.[2]

At the same time, Tyndale uses the word 'covenant', often in the plural, when he is writing about the covenant where it relates to man's salvation. Between God and man there are many covenants which relate to the fulfilling of God's purpose to restore creation to its pristine state. In fact, Tyndale wrote,

> Faith now in God the Father, through our Lord Jesus Christ, according to the covenants and appointment made between God and us, is our salvation. . . . Moreover, where thou findest a promise, and no covenant expressed therewith, there must thou understand a covenant.[3]

Unless we keep these two aspects of Tyndale's use of the word *covenant* separate, we cannot find a consistent theology in his writings. In this chapter we are concerned with this second use of the word *covenant* – the salvation of man. Although Tyndale never referred to it, *Revelation* 4, section D, sums up the underlying theme of Tyndale's theology.

> And when those beasts gave glory and honour and thanks to him that sat on the seat which liveth for ever and ever: the twenty-four elders fell down before him that sat on the throne, and worshipped him that liveth for ever, and cast their crowns before the throne saying: thou art worthy Lord to receive glory, and honour, and power, for thou hast created all things, and for thy will's sake they are, and were created.[4]

Election

Once the Persons of the Trinity had made the covenant the practical aspects of it had to be worked out. As far as man is concerned the Bible appears to make statements concerning man's salvation which contradict each other (and this has caused different positions to be taken by Reformers who claimed to rely on *sola scriptura* for their doctrine). Tyndale believed that what, on the surface, appeared irreconcilable in the Bible could be brought together and harmonised within the covenant. The problem of seeming contradictions in the word of God are solved when we accept that God's covenant was for the salvation of creation[5] (of which man is part, and the part responsible for the Fall). Therefore everything depended on God for the fulfilment of the covenant. The salvation of fallen mankind enabled the whole creation to rejoice and bring glory to God. A passage in *Obedience* shows how Tyndale brought together one of the apparent difficulties of scripture.

> For Paul saith, Rom. vi. as it is above rehearsed: "Remember ye not (saith he), that all we which are baptized in the name of Christ Jesus are baptized to die with him? We are buried with him in baptism for to die," that is, to kill the lusts and the rebellion which remaineth in the flesh. And after that he saith, "Ye are dead, as concerning sin, but live unto God through Christ Jesus our Lord." If thou look on the profession of our hearts, and on the Spirit and forgiveness which we have received through Christ's merits, we are full dead: but if thou look on the rebellion of the flesh, we do but begin to die, and to be baptized, that is, to drown and quench the lusts, and are full baptized at the last minute of death. And as concerning the working of the Spirit, we begin to live, and grow every day more and more, both in knowledge and also in godly living, according as the lusts abate: as a child receiveth the full soul at the first day, yet groweth daily in the operations and works thereof.[6]

For Tyndale the covenant is unilateral, and every aspect of man's salvation depends on God. Through the Fall man is dead and powerless to do anything of himself. It is because God has chosen us in Christ that we, the elect children of God, are brought to the new birth and are enabled to respond to our Father's love, for of ourselves we can do nothing.

> By grace (that is to say by favour) we are plucked out of Adam, the ground of all evil, and grafted in Christ, the root of all goodness. In Christ God loved us, his elect and chosen, before the world began, and reserved us unto the knowledge of his Son and of his holy gospel.[7] [For] God chooseth them first, and they not God, as thou readest, John xv. And then he sendeth forth and calleth them, and sheweth them his good will, which he beareth unto them, and maketh them see both their own damnation in the law, and also the mercy that is laid up for them in Christ's blood, and thereto what he will have them do.[8]

We must now turn to the way, in Tyndale's doctrine, by which God, the Father, the Son and the Holy Spirit work together to make man's salvation a reality. Election is the way God has fulfilled his promises to those he has chosen in Christ.

> We have a promise that Christ, and his body, and his blood, and all that he did, and suffered, is a sacrifice, a ransom, and a full satisfaction for our sins; that God for his sake will think no more on them, if we have power to repent and believe.[9]

God's promise of mercy is, therefore, fulfilled in us because of the work of Christ for our salvation,[10] and all God's blessings are ours, "heaven, justifying, forgiveness, all gifts of grace, and all that is promised them, they receive of Christ, and by his merits freely,"[11] and we know that we are "beloved of God as Christ is."[12] It is through this work of Christ that we know God to be a merciful Father, whose Son has done everything for us to make this a reality, for "the blood of Christ has obtained all things for us of God. Christ is our satisfaction, redeemer, deliverer, saviour from vengeance and wrath."[13] All this is applied by the working of the Holy Spirit who leads us to be imitators and followers of God, which is a sign that we "are inheritors of all the promises of God, and elect unto the fellowship of the blood of Christ."[14] Sometimes, however, it seems impossible to truly fulfil our responsibility to imitate God and love with our whole being,

> yet if thou feelest lust thereunto, and thy spirit sigheth, mourneth, and longeth after strength to do it, take a sign and evident token thereby, that the Spirit of life is in thee, and that thou art elect to life everlasting by Christ's blood.[15]

What lies behind the motivation to do good works is most important. Tyndale wrote that the Christian naturally follows Christ and imitates his example because he is a child of God. On the other hand, if our good works are done in order to earn a reward, we are worldly-minded and not part of God's family.[16]

In this way, Tyndale believed, our sonship as God's children lies outside of ourselves and cannot be gained by anything that we do.

> Not that our works make us the sons of God, but testify only, and certify our consciences, that we are the sons of God; and that God hath chosen us, and washed us in Christ's blood; and hath put his Spirit in us.[17]

For Tyndale our election and birth into God's family are entirely of God and his grace, and it is solely the work of the Holy Spirit. "Theologically all the elements in this process are undergirded by the activity of the Spirit."[18] There is, therefore, a mystery about election[19] which is beyond our human understanding: "Why doth God open one man's eyes and not another's? Paul (Rom. ix.) forbiddeth to ask why; for it is too deep for man's capacity."[20] Anyone who tries to find an answer to the problem of predestination has to leave God's word and try to find the answer in man's reason, and that usually means relying on Aristotle or other pagan philosophers.[21] This leads to man having a part (however small) in his salvation.[22] For Tyndale that is a heresy which blinds a man so that he cannot see the "bright beams of the scripture."[23]

Tyndale's theology had no problem with those who had not been chosen by God to become children of God; their eternal state was the result of Adam's Fall. Tyndale did not believe in *double predestination;*[24] those God had not chosen were naturally children of the devil and therefore under the curse of their father. "For where Christ is not, there remaineth the curse, that fell on Adam as soon as he had sinned, so that they are in bondage under damnation of sin, death, and hell."[25] In *Answer,* Tyndale argues against More who believed that God chose those he saw would have a "towardness" to doing good. His argument against More's semi-Pelagianism equally applies against those who believe God has predestined some to damnation. "Are we not robbed of all towardness in Adam; and be by nature made the children of sin, so that we sin naturally; and to sin is our nature?"[26] Election is to life: it was man who had chosen death.

The Fatherhood of God

Behind the covenant lies the Fatherhood of God, and this is the reason for the covenant. It is, therefore, one of the main concepts in Tyndale's theology. It is through Christ's blood and the work of the Holy Spirit that those God had chosen are born again as the children of God. This rebirth also means, for Tyndale, that the family relationship between the Father and his children binds them together with love.[27] It is Christ's sacrifice on the cross, and his blood-shedding, which enabled the Holy Spirit to give life to the elect so that they are born again as children of God the Father. Tyndale shows, through the scriptures, that Christ's death and blood-shedding is not only the start of our Christian life but it is in Christ and through Christ's blood that the whole of man's salvation finds its fulfilment. Christ's blood opens the way for the Father to be merciful to us and for us to live as his children, loving God with our whole being and loving our neighbours as ourselves.

> Christ is the whole cause why we do all thing for our neighbour, even so is he the cause why God doth all thing for us, why he receiveth us into his holy testament, and maketh us heirs of all his promises, and poureth his Spirit into us, and maketh us his sons, and fashioneth us like unto Christ, and maketh us such as he would have us to be. The assurance that we are sons, beloved, and heirs with Christ, and have God's Spirit in us, is the consent of our hearts unto the law of God.[28]

The relationship of the Father to his children within God's family is the first part of the covenant which comes to the elect through their faith in Christ as Saviour. "Faith, or confidence in Christ's blood, without help, and before the works of the law, bringeth all manner remission of sins and satisfaction."[29]

Debora Shugar wrote: "Tyndale in particular specializes in delicate and realistic portrayals of parental love as the single analogue for the unmerited *caritas* of God." She then quotes from *Exposition Matthew* about the promises parents make to their children "and that such as they think should most make it to see love, and to provoke it to be willing to do part of his duty."[30] The validity of her remark is perhaps seen more clearly earlier in Tyndale's work,

> If thou believe in Christ that he is thy Saviour, that faith will lead thee in immediately, and shew thee God with a lovely and amiable countenance, and make thee feel and see how that he is thy Father, altogether merciful to thee, and at one with thee, and thou his son, and highly in his favour and grace, and sure that thou pleasest him.[31]

For the love of God towards the elect is as the love he has for his only begotten Son, so "a Christian man perceiveth that God is his Father, and loveth him even as he loved Christ when he shed his blood on the cross."[32]

Tyndale's view of the Fatherhood of God is wider than our understanding of a father's place in the family. For Tyndale takes into account the totality of parenthood and realises that there is a difference between a father's and a mother's love, and that this difference is perhaps clearer in times of difficulty for a child.

> And as for our pain-taking, God rejoiceth not therein as a tyrant; but pitieth us, and as it were mourneth with us, and is alway ready and at hand to help us, if we call, as a merciful father and a kind mother.[33]

God looks after us and cares for us, and we are "tended as young children are by the care of their fathers and mothers."[34] Sometimes Tyndale refers to God's love to us only as maternal love, "The service that a mother doth unto her child is not grievous, because she loveth it."[35]

Throughout his writings Tyndale stresses the importance of God's fatherly love and care for his chosen people. In the covenant God's promise to his Son and the Holy Spirit has bound himself[36] so that "when we look on the seals of his obligations, wherewith he has bound himself," we consider, meditate on, and keep in mind God's promises and covenants so that we understand God's loving purpose for us.[37]

The covenant is that God will be our Father,[38] and he has bound himself "that he will be a father unto us."[39] In order to "be to us a father " he "hath slain his most dear son Jesus, to confirm his oath,"[40] and has "raised our Saviour Christ up again to justify us."[41] It was through his death and resurrection that Christ enabled God to be a Father to us "for he only maketh God our God, our strength, power, sword and shield, and shortly our Father."[42] Therefore God, for Christ's sake, "will be a father unto them"[43] and "take them for his sons, and to love them as well as though they were full righteous."[44]

God challenged his chosen ones "to be his people" and "the godly challenged him to be their God and Father, and to help and succour them at need, and to minister all things unto them according to all his promises."[45] Then God deals with us as "his children, in whose hearts he writeth the faith of his Son Jesus and the love of his laws,"[46] and he has promised that he "shall write it in their hearts with his Holy Spirit."[47] The elect, therefore, believe in God and "are begotten of God through that belief,"[48] for it is by faith "we be born anew, and made the sons of God, . . . and are translated from death to life."[49]

God's wisdom is found in his promises to us for it is through his law and promises that he reveals himself to us, saying that he will "be a Father almighty to us"[50] who is a Father who cannot lie but keeps his promises to his children.[51] Tyndale therefore wrote that we should "turn thine eyes to Christ, and see there the exceeding mercy of thy most kind and loving Father."[52] For as the gospel is applied to your life "thou . . . shalt feel God as a kind and merciful father."[53] "God is a wise father, and knoweth all the infirmities of his children, and also merciful,"[54]and his love is without limits,

> God receiveth both perfect and weak in like grace, for Christ's sake, as a father receiveth all his children, both small and great, in like love. He receiveth them to be his sons, . . . to bear their weakness for Christ's sake, . . . and how often soever they fall, yet to forgive them.[55]

Tyndale finds God's love almost beyond belief, and against More's arguments that we should pray to saints,[56] he wrote that we have direct access to the Father and do not need others to pray for us, and we can boldly go to God "as of a most loving and merciful father, above all the mercy of fathers."[57]

Tyndale constantly wrote of the ways in which God shows he is a true Father to his children. When the Christian does wrong, God disciplines his child[58] and chastises and pardons him[59] for he "is ever fatherly-minded toward the elect members of his church;"[60] and "pardoneth sinners, and giveth them power to be the sons of God."[61] Throughout the whole of their lives God supports his children so that they see "how fatherly and tenderly, and with all compassion, God entreateth his elect, which submit themselves as scholars, to learn to walk in the ways of his laws, and to keep them of love."[62] God the Father shares in his children's lives and helps them to grow up into maturity as his people. Therefore, wrote Tyndale,

> the God of all mercy, which careth for his elect children, and turneth all unto good to them, and smiteth them to heal them again, and killeth them to make them live again, and playeth with them (as a father doth sometime with his young ignorant children), and tempteth them, and proveth them to make them see their own hearts.[63]

Christ and Man's Salvation

Although we have touched on it already, we must come to the place that Christ has in the covenant of salvation and his covenantal promises to God the Father and God the Holy Spirit. God the Son covenanted to shed his blood and appease the wrath of God for man's sin.[64] Tyndale wrote concerning this work of Christ, "'By whom we have redemption through his blood, even the forgiveness of our sins' (Colos. i. and Ephes. i.)." Tyndale continued, "And that 'there is but one mediator, Christ,' as saith Paul (1 Tim. ii.). And by that word understand an atonemaker, a peacemaker, and bringer into grace and favour, having full power so to do."[65]

God promised Abraham that in his seed all the nations of the world would be blessed, and Tyndale quoted Galatians 3: "Christ is that seed of Abraham."[66] To fulfil this promise God sent Christ, who is the Messiah, the anointed one, to save his people, and deliver them from spiritual death, and to bless them through Christ's blood,[67] for "Christ died for their sins, and that he is their only and sufficient Saviour."[68] This means, wrote Tyndale, that our justification is in Christ alone, without any help from our works, the law, or anything else we might think deserves our justification.[69] Tyndale contrasted the difference between the Christian teaching and that of the pope. "The nearer unto Christ a man cometh, the lower he must descend, and the poorer he must wax. But the nearer unto the pope ye come, the higher ye must climb, and the more riches ye must gather."[70] "The reward is given of the mercy and truth of God, and by the deserving and merits of Christ. Whosoever repenteth, believeth the gospel, and putteth his trust in Christ's merits, the same is heir with Christ of eternal life."[71]

There is another aspect of the relationship between Christ and the Christian, that is the union of the Christian with Christ.

> And from henceforth all is Christ with him; and Christ is his, and he is Christ's. All that he receiveth he receiveth of Christ, and all that he doth he doth to Christ. Father, mother, master, lord and prince, are Christ unto him; and as Christ he serveth them, with all love. His wife, children, servants and subjects, are Christ unto him; and he teacheth them to serve Christ, and not himself and his lusts. And if he receive any good thing of man, he thanketh God in Christ, which moved the man's heart. And his neighbour he serveth as Christ in all his need, of such things as God hath lent; because that all degrees are bought, as he is, with Christ's blood.[72]

The Blood of Christ[73]

Although the "blood of Christ" is part of the covenantal work of God the Son, it has an importance in Tyndale's theology which demands that it must be considered separately. The blood of Christ enables the work of Christ within the covenant to be effective, and without the blood there could be no covenant of salvation. Without the blood of Christ the Fatherhood of God would not be possible, nor would the Holy Spirit be able to do his work in the salvation and life of the elect. The "blood of Christ" occurs over 400 times in a theologically significant sense (as opposed to a sacramental sense) in Tyndale's writings, and it is fairly evenly distributed throughout his works from his first to his last writings.[74] There are three exceptions. *The Practice of Prelates,* has half the frequency of other writings, and this is accounted for by the subject matter of the book, which is concerned more with the development of the papacy and the Roman Church than with theology. There is no easy explanation why the other two works should have a frequency double that of every other work, *The Preface to the 1525 New Testament,* and the *Exposition of Tracy's Testament.* The frequency in *Pathway* is slightly less than in the *1525 Preface.*[75] The theology, the importance and the meaning of the blood of Christ in Tyndale's theology did not change between 1525 and 1536. Most of the references to the blood of Christ relate to the work of the Holy Spirit as he applies Christ's blood to the elect and enables them to become and grow as the children of God.

As we have seen, for Tyndale, man's sin and rebellion against God had built a barrier between God and man, and man was dead to God. Being dead, there was nothing man could do to put things right between God and himself. Whilst man remained a sinner, bound by the devil's chains, there was no way God the Father could show any fatherly love to him, for God the Father could not adopt those the Triune God had chosen until his justice had been satisfied and the debt of man's sin had been paid.

Tyndale wrote, "The blood of Christ hath obtained all things for us of God. Christ is our satisfaction, Redeemer, Deliverer, Saviour, from vengeance and wrath."[76] It was God the Son's part in the covenant to remove the barrier caused by man's sin and make it possible for the Father to adopt the elect and make them his children. Therefore, "Christ, and his body, and his blood, and all that he did, and suffered, is a sacrifice, a ransom, and a full satisfaction for our sins; that God for his sake will think no more on them."[77] It is through Christ "we have fellowship with God, and are his sons and heirs, and are purged from all sin through Christ's blood."[78] The blood of Christ is the key which opens the way for the Father to adopt the elect; it opens the way for us to be counted full righteous in God's sight, because

> the scripture saith, Christ is our righteousness, our justifying, our redemption, our atonement, that hath appeased God, and cleanseth us from our sins, and all in his blood, so that his blood is the satisfaction only,[79]

Christ's blood opens the way for the Holy Spirit to cleanse us from all sin, for "to God-ward is there no satisfaction, save faith in Christ's blood out of a repenting heart."[80]

> When Christ is preached, how that God for his sake receiveth us to mercy, and forgiveth us all that is past, and henceforth reckoneth not unto us our corrupt and poisoned nature, and taketh us as his sons, and putteth us under grace and mercy, and promiseth that he will not judge us by the rigorousness of the law, but nurture us with all mercy and patience, as a father most merciful.[81]

Also the blood of Christ allows the Holy Spirit to fulfil his part of the covenant, which enables the elect to become truly God's children. "We cannot work God's will, till we be his sons, and know his will, and have his Spirit to teach us."[82] For this to happen we have to be "translated from death unto life"[83] and be made anew by God. "We are, in this our second birth, God's workmanship and creation in Christ; so that, as he which is yet unmade hath no life nor power to work, no more had we, till we were made again in Christ."[84] The new birth is the work of the Holy Spirit[85], who gives us faith (although Tyndale, following the scriptures, varies the order between "new birth", "faith" and "repentance", he would have said that without being born again we could neither repent nor have faith). For "right faith is a thing wrought by the Holy Ghost in us, and changeth us, turneth us into a new nature, and begetteth us anew in God, and maketh us the sons of God."[86] This faith "bringeth pardon and forgiveness freely purchased by Christ's blood, and bringeth also the Spirit; the Spirit looseth the bonds of the devil, and setteth us at liberty." After detailing the benefits the blood of Christ means to the Christian, Tyndale continued, "But remember that he is the God of mercy and of truth, and cannot but fulfil his promises. Also remember, that his Son's blood is stronger than all the sins and wickedness of the whole world."[87]

Whilst man is still dead in sin his will is not free to choose what is good, for "all that is done in the world before the Spirit of God come, and giveth us light, is damnable sin; and the more glorious, the more damnable; so that that which the world counteth most glorious is more damnable, in the sight of God, than that which the whore, the thief, and the murderer do."[88] But once the Holy Spirit gives us life through the blood of Christ then Christ, "the lord of free-will; which only through his grace maketh the will free, and looseth her from bondage of sin, and giveth her love and lust unto the laws of God, and power to fulfil them."[89]

The Child of God

Tyndale ignored the division between mankind caused by the Fall and by God's elective grace, and he referred to all mankind as children of God because we are all part of his creation. This fact has caused some (who have not read Tyndale's words closely in their context) to assume

Tyndale was a universalist.[90] Tyndale's equating all mankind as brethren through creation relates to the scope of loving our neighbour which extends to all,

> yea, to the very infidels we be debtors, if they need. . . . Thus is every man that needeth thy help, thy father, mother, sister, and brother in Christ; even as every man, that doth the will of the Father, is father, mother, sister, and brother unto Christ."[91]

Because the covenant enables a man to become a child of God, it is common in Reformed theologies to make the covenant bilateral and to give man a place in the covenantal process, particularly where there is a federal[92] aspect to the covenant. For Tyndale a covenant between God and man, as the ground of man's salvation, was impossible – just as a man cannot make a covenant with a corpse. Not only is fallen man dead in sins, he also has no freewill; he has no power to enter into a covenant with God even if he wanted to, just as a child has no power over its conception or its life until after it has been born.

It is only after God's covenant has enabled the Holy Spirit to bring the elect from death to life as a child of God, and the blood of Christ has given him life, that the Christian has a will set free from bondage to sin and can enter into the covenantal relationship with God which we find in scripture. The "covenant" or "covenants" made between God and man express the way God's promises are conditional (usually in the form, "I will . . . , if you. . . .")[93]

The key which reveals the way God's covenants work is through the promises God makes to his elect, and these promises, for Tyndale, link the covenant to God's children. "Where thou findest a promise, and no covenant expressed therewith, there must thou understand a covenant."[94] It is the promise of God which challenges mankind to make a response, "for though God make a promise, yet it saveth none finally but them that long for it, and pray God with a strong faith to fulfil it, for his mercy and truth only, and knowledge their unworthiness."[95] Nonetheless, Tyndale wrote, "God's mercy in promising, and truth in fulfilling his promises, saveth us, and not we ourselves,"[96] "in which promises I see the mercy, favour, and good-will of God upon me in the blood of his Son Christ."[97]

The problems between God and man raised by the Fall are resolved in Tyndale's covenant theology through man's birth into God's family and not by his justification in a court of law. This aspect of the covenant was another example of the way Tyndale differed from Continental Reformation theology. The Continental Reformers had a federal covenant where God, as Judge, passed judgement on the sinner. Those who pleaded Christ's death for their salvation are justified by their faith and counted as righteous. For them the covenant and man's salvation was a legal process between God and the elect. For Tyndale, however, the legal process took place in heaven and was between the Persons of the Trinity. God the Son covenanted to shed his blood to satisfy God's justice. In this way he enabled creation (damaged by man's sin) to be restored. Man can, therefore, be born again as a child of God, and as God's child he is righteous and justified by faith in Christ's blood. Tyndale expressed this difference between a legalistic covenant and a familial covenant when he wrote, "I say we that believe have no judge of him, but a father; neither shall we come into judgment, as Christ hath promised us, but are received under grace, mercy, and forgiveness."[98]

Because the legal problems regarding man's salvation are between God the Father, God the Son and God the Holy Spirit, God's justice cannot be challenged. This covenant is proclaimed to all,

> because God hath made them after the likeness of his own image, and they are his sons as well as we, and Christ hath bought them with his blood, and made them heirs of everlasting life as well as us.[99]

The promises God makes to man in the gospel are made to every man, and anyone who responds to those promises and accepts their terms will be saved – the responsibility to choose between death and life is man's alone, although he cannot choose until he has been born again by the Holy Spirit.[100] Election is a secondary issue, although those chosen to be God's children will be born again and come to eternal life. In itself, election does not preclude those not chosen from accepting the terms of God's promises in Christ and finding his blood cleansing them from sin and eternal life. Tyndale wrote,

> Against this curse, blesseth now the gospel all the world inasmuch as it crieth openly, unto all that knowledge their sins and repent, saying, Whosoever believeth on the seed of Abraham shall be blessed; that is, he shall be delivered from sin, death, and hell, and shall henceforth continue righteous, and saved for ever.[101]

God made promises to man, and later he confirmed them in a covenant. The promise came to Noah when God called him and before he started to build the ark, but "after the general flood God made a covenant with Noah and all mankind."[102] In he same way God's promise to be our Father and make us his children has to be fulfilled and we have to be born again and made alive unto God before a covenant (signified by baptism) is made between God and ourselves. Therefore, wrote Tyndale,

> The right way, yea, and the only way, to understand the scripture unto salvation, is that we earnestly and above all things search for the profession of our baptism, or covenants made between God and us. As, for an example, Christ saith, (Matt. v.), 'Happy are the merciful, for they shall obtain mercy.' Lo, here God hath made a covenant with us, to be merciful unto us, if we will be merciful one to another."[103]

Our election as a child of God is of God alone and happened long before man had any being. "In Christ God loved us, his elect and chosen, before the world began, and reserved us unto the knowledge of his Son and of his holy gospel." We were then given grace to believe, to have the Holy Spirit, to know God as our Father, to have our sins forgiven, and to love God's law and to fulfil it for "the blood of Christ has obtained all things for us of God. Christ is our satisfaction, redeemer, deliverer, saviour from vengeance and wrath."[104] In his *Answer to Sir Thomas More's Dialogue,* Tyndale wrote,

> Even so goeth it with God's elect, God chooseth them first, and they not God; as thou readest, John xv. And then he sendeth forth and calleth them, and sheweth them his good will, which he beareth unto them, and maketh them see both their own damnation in the law, and also the mercy that is laid up for them in Christ's blood, and thereto what he will have them to do. And then, when we see his mercy, we love him again, and choose him, and submit ourselves unto his laws, to walk in them.[105]

Because we are sons and daughters of God we receive the promises of mercy with "all fatherly love and kindness of God."[106] God "hath promised to care for us"[107] and, as we care for his commandments, to give us all we need.[108] We can put our trust in God, knowing that his promises are sure and certain because he is almighty, and nothing can prevent him from fulfilling them as we come to him through Jesus Christ.[109] Through Christ's death we are heirs, because

> Christ before his death commanded and appointed that such Evangelion, gospel, or tidings should be declared throughout all the world, and therewith to give unto all that repent and believe, all his goods: that is to say, his life, wherewith he swallowed and devoured up death; his righteousness, wherewith he banished sin; his salvation, wherewith he overcame eternal damnation."[110]

The executor of this will is the Holy Spirit, and this work is his part of the covenant of God. The Holy Spirit leads the children of God to "counterfeit and follow God in well-doing," and this is a sign that we "are inheritors of all the promises of God, and elect unto the fellowship of the blood of Christ."[111] But sometimes we are unable to *counterfeit* (that is *copy*), the works of Christ, then our "Spirit sigheth, mourneth, and longeth after the strength to do it." This desire is also a sign that the Holy Spirit is working in our hearts and that we are "elect to life everlasting by Christ's blood."[112] It is the motivation to do good works that is all important. The Christian naturally follows Christ and imitates his example because he is a child of God. Others do their good works in order to earn a reward, and they are worldly-minded and not part of God's family.[113]

There is a mystery about election which is beyond our human understanding, and we should not try to solve it.

> Now may not we ask why God chooseth one and not another; either think that God is unjust to damn us afore we do any actual deed; seeing that God hath power over all his creatures of right, to do with them what he list, or to make of every one of them as he listeth. Our darkness cannot perceive his light.[114]

The nearest Tyndale comes to answering this problem is in his *Exposition of the First Epistle of John.*

> And Christ, which is contrary to the devil, came to destroy the works of the devil in us, and to give us a new birth, a new nature, and to sow new seed in us, that we should, by the reason of that birth, sin no more. For the seed of that birth, that is to wete the Spirit of God and the lively seed of his word sown in our hearts, keepeth our hearts, that we cannot consent to sin; as the seed of the devil holdeth the hearts of his, that they cannot consent to good.[115]

Tyndale argued against More, who believed that God chose those he saw would have a "towardness" to doing good.[116] Tyndale's argument against More's position also stands against those who believe in double-predestination; man's eternal loss and punishment was the free choice of Adam that made us "children of sin". "Are we not robbed of all towardness in Adam; and be by nature made the children of sin, so that we sin naturally; and to sin is our nature?"[117] Election (for Tyndale) was to life; it was man who had chosen death. Those who continue to seek an answer and ask,

> Why doth God open one man's eyes and not another's? . . . They have searched to come to the bottom of his bottomless wisdom; and because they cannot attain to that secret, and be too proud to let it alone, and to grant themselves ignorant, with the apostle, that knew no other than God's glory in the elect; they go and set

> up freewill with the heathen philosophers, and say that a man's freewill is the cause why God chooseth one and not another, contrary unto all the scripture.[118]

This is a heresy which blinds a man so that he cannot see the "bright beams of the scripture".[119]

The Christian's love, that he gives to his Father, is because he knows, through faith, that he is a child of God, "as John saith in the first chapter of his gospel: 'He gave them power to be the sons of God, in that they believed on his name.'"[120] And this power transforms us into God's likeness. "Now, to be the son of God is to love righteousness, and hate unrighteousness, and so to be like thy Father. Hast thou then no power to love the law? So hast thou no faith in Christ's blood."[121]

Tyndale constantly pointed out that the Christian does good works because he loves his Father and not for any reward he might get from doing them. "He neither learneth nor worketh now any longer for pain of the rod, or for fear of bugs or pleasure of apples, but doth all things of his own corage."[122] In *Pathway* Tyndale wrote that the reason a child obeyed his father's will was "of pure love."[123] At the same time a father often encourages his children to obey him with promises of rewards, but the rewards are never the reason why the child obeys his father.[124] The amount of service children give to their father and mother is also unimportant; one may do more than another, "yet is the father free, and may with right reward them all alike."[125] Carl Trueman misses Tyndale's point that a Christian's good works spring from our assurance that we are children of our heavenly Father, when he wrote,

> This idea that works constitute a primary basis for assurance introduces a tension into Tyndale's definition of the causal relationship between faith and works: to make works a basis for assurance effectively negates this relationship.[126]

Many signs of parental love do not depend on the child's behaviour. It is a sign of her love when a mother feeds her child[127] or "when the father giveth his son a new coat."[128] (Tyndale also used this illustration to teach about those who God had not chosen to be his children:

> Ask a little boy, who gave him his gay coat? He answereth, "his father," Ask him why? And he answereth, "Because he is his father, and loveth him, and because he is his son." . . . Ask him, why his father giveth not such and such boys coats too? "Nay, saith he, they be not his sons; their fathers must give them, as mine doth me".[129]

Tyndale reminds us of our responsibilities, the profession of our faith to "keep the covenant of the Lord thy God" remains our duty. Even if we are blown off course, we know that God is faithful and fulfils his promises to us, and he "promiseth to forgive that, and not the less to fulfil his promises of one jot."[130] Sometimes, however, the loving care we receive from God takes the form of chastisement for our disobedience.[131] Jonah discovered this through his experience of God's loving correction that it is "God only that smiteth, and God only that healeth: ascribing the cause of thy tribulation unto thine own sin, and the cause of thy deliverance unto the mercy of God."[132]

No child is always obedient, and there are different reasons that lie behind its disobedience. It may be the child is going to school and sees others playing; he joins them and gets carried away so that he forgets school.[133] His disobedience may be because of ignorance or frailty,[134] or deliberate disobedience,[135] whatever the reason, the child has to be disciplined. Even when "the most obedient child in the world" errs and disobeys his father's commandments he is not excused punishment because of all the good things he has done.[136] Therefore, when a child realises his sin, he is afraid of his father's anger and the punishment he must endure,[137] and his conscience torments him.[138] However, after he has erred "the child submitteth himself unto his father's correction and nurture, and humbleth himself altogether unto the will of his father, then the rod is taken away."[139] A child does not need anyone to plead for him (priests or saints) for he knows his father loves him and he can go straight to him.

> A child, when his father threateneth him for his fault, hath never rest till he hear the word of mercy and forgiveness of his father's mouth again, but as soon as he heareth his father say, Go thy way, do me no more so, I forgive thee this fault, then is his heart at rest, then is he at peace, then runneth he to no man to make intercession for him.[140]

The child's disobedience did not alter the father's love for him, and the punishment is not more than the disobedience deserves for "no natural father punisheth his child because he delighteth in tormenting of him, to take satisfaction for the sin that is past; but first teacheth kindly, and suffereth, and forgiveth once or twice," before punishing him for his fault.[141] It is because a father's love reaches out to his children in this way, even to his wayward ones, that Tyndale condemns the doctrine of purgatory.

> Master More feeleth . . . that God forgiveth the everlasting pain, and will yet punish me a thousand years in the pope's purgatory, that leaven savoureth not in my mouth. I understand my father's words as they sound, and after the most merciful manner.[142]

Whatever their child is like, his parents love it still, for "a kind father and mother love their children even when they are evil, that they would shed their blood to make them better, and to bring them into the right way."[143] And a child which is "the least and weakest" and unable to do what his parents desire receives the greatest care and love from them.[144]

The Family of God

As we have already mentioned Tyndale wrote of God's children in two different ways. Firstly, every person is a child of God through creation.[145] This creation family is the temporal regiment or kingdom. Secondly, for Tyndale, every baptized Christian who, through the washing of Christ's blood, had been born again, was doubly a child of God – "And inasmuch as he is our Lord and God, and we his double possession, by creation and redemption."[146] This second way of writing about the children of God is the spiritual kingdom or regiment.

Although Tyndale wrote about every person being a child of God through creation, after the Fall and man's rebellion against God mankind became children of the devil and part of the devil's family.[147] This fact has not removed them from the temporal kingdom and, therefore, the Christian has the responsibility to care for them as part of the family.

The Creation Family

Tyndale's view of mankind has a very modern ring about it, which we find expressed in the work of Christian relief agencies and those concerned with social issues – although many of them do not take Tyndale's warnings seriously. We have a Christian responsibility to help our brethren in their need,

> Yea, to the very infidels, we be debtors, if they need, as far forth as we maintain them not against Christ, or to blaspheme Christ. Thus is every man, that needeth thy help, thy father, mother, sister, and brother in Christ."[148]

The Christian must show neighbourly love to everyone and not just to those who, like ourselves, have become God's children through faith. For, according to Tyndale, our relationship to God lies in creation for,

> as he hath made all, and is God of all, and all are his sons, even so is he judge over all, and will have all judged by his law indifferently, and to have the right of his law, and will avenge the wrong done unto the Turk or Saracen. For though they be not under the everlasting testament of God in Christ, as few of us which are called Christians be, . . . yet are they under the testament of the law natural."[149]

In fact, as God cares for all mankind, even "Turks and Saracens, and all manner infidels to do them good," so must the child of God. Tyndale continues, "Them that are good I love, because they are in Christ; and the evil, to bring them to Christ."[150]

The only difference between one man and another is that for the one who has been born again, "when we had marred ourself through sin, he forgave us, and created us again, in the blood of his beloved Son" and thus we became God's "double possession, by creation and redemption."[151]

There are many places where Tyndale wrote directly about our duty to those outside of Christ. In fact, this is where we have the real test of our faith. He continues,

> If thou love him that doth thee evil, then is thy love of God, . . . and when thou hurtest not thy neighbours, then art thou sure that God's Spirit worketh in thee, and that thy faith is no dream, nor any false imagination.[152]

People have always asked the question, "Who is my neighbour?" In answer to that question, Jesus told the parable of the "Good Samaritan." Tyndale wrote,

> The Samaritan holp him, and shewed mercy as long as he was present; and when he could be no longer present, he left his money behind him, and if that were not sufficient, he left his credence to make good the rest; and forsook him not, as long as the other had need. Then said Christ, "Go thou and do likewise;" that is, without difference or respection of persons: whosoever needeth thy help, him count thy neighbour, and his neighbour be thou, and shew mercy on him as long as he needeth thy succour; and that is to love a man's neighbour as himself.[153]

Tyndale criticised the way loving one's neighbour was interpreted by the Church:

> He believeth that he loveth God, because he is ready to kill a Turk for his sake, that believeth better in God than he; whom God also commanded us to love, and to leave nothing unsought to win him unto the knowledge of the truth, though with the loss of our lives.[154]

Tyndale continues with this theme "And in like wise, against this law, 'Love thy neighbour as thyself,' I may obey no worldly power, to do aught at any man's commandment unto the hurt of my neighbour that hath not deserved it, though he be a Turk."[155]

The Christian Family

The Christian, as we have seen, is still part of God's creation, and he has the same responsibility to an unbeliever as he has to his fellow Christian. However, there is a difference between those who have faith and those without, for the one who has faith in Christ's blood is reborn as a child of God, and this new birth brings him into a different relationship with God and his fellow Christians.

Loving our neighbour as ourselves applies equally to all through creation, but there is an added responsibility to help our brothers and sisters in Christ. The love which a Christian has for his fellow Christian has a spiritual aspect added to his love to all mankind.

> And whosoever excelleth in the gifts of grace, let the same think that they be given him, as much to do his brother service as for his own self, and as much for the love which God hath to the weak, as unto him unto whom God giveth such gifts.[156]

For we are to

> deal soberly with the consciences of the weak in the faith, which yet understand not the liberty of Christ perfectly enough; and to favour them with christian love; and not to use the liberty of the faith unto hindrance, but unto the furtherance and edifying of the weak.[157]

As Tyndale wrote, "A Christian worketh to make his weak brother perfecter," and this is done of love and not for any reward he may get for his works.[158] The brotherly love a Christian shows is irrespective of the worthiness of the other person, for not only does our love stretch out to the brother who is weak, but to each of our brothers and sisters in Christ. For we are to follow the example of Christ and

> bear with others that are yet weak, as them that are frail, open sinners, unlearned, unexpert, and of loathsome manners, and not cast them away forthwith, but suffer them till they wax better, and exhort them in the mean time.[159]

Conclusion

Because the covenant is between the Persons of the Trinity, we have seen that its fulfilment is the work of God alone. Although Paul's teaching about faith is as important to Tyndale as to any other Reformer, he has an equal regard for John's teaching about the new birth. For Tyndale they are equally important and he brings the two together in a simple harmony. If, as Paul wrote, we are dead in trespasses and sins, it is impossible for us to have faith. But if, through the blood of Christ, we are born again by the Holy Spirit we are raised from death to life, and God is our Father, and we his children. Once we have been given life then faith and repentance become possible for us. But the stress is always away from man and towards God, with the blood of Christ making all possible for the Holy Spirit to achieve, and his greatest achievement is to make us live as children of the Father.

This movement away from man and unto God brings a new relationship into Christianity – the relationship of family love. The way we live and the works we do show we are children of God because they show that we love God and we love our neighbour. Since God had created them to be our neighbour every human being is a neighbour to be loved, for

> love that springeth of Christ seeketh not her own self, 1 Cor. xiii., but forgetteth herself, and bestoweth her upon her neighbour's profit, as Christ sought our profit, and not his own.[160]

As a result, although he believed as strongly as any other Reformer in "justification by faith," Tyndale found in the family relationship that faith had been strengthened by love.[161] For "the order of love or charity" is to be like Christ, who gave his all for us, and we owe our all to him. "The love that springeth out of Christ excludeth no man, neither putteth difference between one and another . . . without respect of persons."[162] "For all other gifts, and the remission in Christ's blood also, are given him of God, to bring him to love his neighbour; which thing had, a man hath all; which not had, a man hath nothing."[163] This, too, is only possible as the Holy Spirit applies the blood of Christ to our lives so that we can love God and love to do his will.[164]

For Tyndale the means to achieve the covenant is not through a legal process; there is no judge justifying the Christian – Christ's blood has made him clean already. The covenant is achieved as the Holy Spirit applies Christ's blood to every part of the Christian's life, enabling him to be a child of God the Father – a fact which he shows as his life is filled and governed by the love of God in every part.

Notes

1. Laughlin, Paul A., "The Brightness of Moses" Face," p. 87f
2. Chapter 4 p. 43
3. Tyndale, William, *Prologue Matthew,* p. 1/471
4. Tyndale, William, *New Testament,* p. 374. (Revelation 4:9-11)
5. *Romans 8*
6. Tyndale, William, *Obedience,* p. 1/261
7. Tyndale, William, *1525,* p. 7. "By grace (that is to saye by favoure) we are plucked oute of Adam the grounde of all evyll / and graffed in Christ the rote of all goodnes. In Christ god loved vs his electe and chosen / before the worlde bega*n*

/ and reserved vs vnto the knowledge of his sonne and of hys holy gospell."
8. Tyndale, William, *Answer,* p. 3/35. This contrasts with Clebsch's statement, Tyndale's "idea of covenant as a bipartite, divine-human contract binding upon both parties, shouts itself from every writing attributable to the period." Clebsch, William A., *England's Earliest Protestants,* p. 181. Penny accurately assessed Tyndale's position, Tyndale's 'stress upon the notion of covenant appears to weaken the forensic approach to grace and faith matters so pronounced and one-sided in Luther and Calvin." Penny, D. Andrew, *Freewill or Predestination,* p. 15
9. Tyndale, William, *Obedience,* p. 1/278: *Exposition Matthew,* p. 2/6
10. Tyndale, William, *Prologue Romans,* p. 1/508f
11. Tyndale, William, *Answer,* p. 3/109
12. Tyndale, William, *Obedience,* p. 1/271
13. Tyndale, William, *1525,* p. 7. "the bloud of Christ hath obteyned all thi[n]gs for vs of god. Christ is oure satisfaction / redemer / delyverer / saveour from vengeaunce and wrath.": *Mammon,* p. 1/54: *Prologue Romans,* p. 1/504f
14. Tyndale, William, *Mammon,* p. 1/72
15. Tyndale, William, *Mammon,* p. 1/85
16. Tyndale, William, *Mammon,* p. 1/73. Trueman, Carl R., *Luther's Legacy,* p. 94f, finds a problem between Tyndale's doctrines of assurance and good works. His remark, "Tyndale himself does not appear to have been aware of the problem. . . ." arises because Trueman assumes the covenant is a legalistic bilateral one between God and man, the problem disappears when covenant is understood as it is expressed in Tyndale's writings.
17. Tyndale, William, *Mammon,* p. 1/72
18. Trueman, Carl R., *Luther's Legacy,* p. 90
19. Penny, D. Andrew, *Freewill or Predestination,* 14-18 discusses Tyndale's and Wyclif's doctrine and compares their doctrine with that of Luther and Calvin. "Thus we seem to be facing the possibility of an extra-continental tradition opposed to the rigours of theological determinism." (p. 17)
20. Tyndale, William, *Answer,* p. 3/191: *Mammon,* p. 1/89
21. Tyndale, William, *Obedience,* p. 1/154f: with *Answer,* p. 3/140
22. Tyndale, William, *Exposition 1 John,* p. 2/190: *Answer,* p. 3/191ff
23. Tyndale, William, *Exposition 1 John,* p. 2/141
24. that is that God predestines some to salvation and some to damnation.
25. Tyndale, William, *Pathway,* p. 1/10
26. Tyndale, William, *Answer,* p. 3/209
27. Trueman's remark, "God is obliged to be a father to his people; and they are bound to obey the law to the best of their ability" (Trueman, Carl R. *Luther's Legacy,* p. 111) puts fatherhood and sonship in an unnatural legalistic relationship, and loses the natural motive of love which exists in Tyndale's father/son relationship.
28. Tyndale, William, *Obedience,* p. 1/300
29. Tyndale, William, *Exposition Matthew,* p. 2/130
30. Shugar, Debora K., *Habits of Thought in the English Renaissance,* p. 220f. Tyndale, William, *Exposition Matthew,* p. 2/74f
31. Tyndale, William, *Exposition Matthew,* p. 2/26
32. Tyndale, William, *Pathway,* p. 1/22
33. Tyndale, William, *Obedience,* p. 1/280: *Mammon,* p. 1/107: *Answer,* p. 3/34

34. Tyndale, William, *Exposition Matthew,* pp. 2/8; 2/74f
35. Tyndale, William, *Exposition 1 John,* p. 2/208: *Exposition Matthew,* p. 2/110f: Shugar, Debora K., *Habits of Thought,* p. 220f
36. Tyndale, William, *Obedience,* p. 1/316
37. Tyndale, William, *Sacraments,* p. 1/362
38. Tyndale, William, *Answer,* p. 3/89
39. Tyndale, William, *Exposition 1 John,* p. 2/166
40. Tyndale, William, *Tracy,* p. 3/282
41. Tyndale, William, *Obedience,* p. 1/167
42. Tyndale, William, *Exposition 1 John,* p. 2/182: *Jonas,* p. 1/464: *Exposition Matthew* p. 2/88f
43. Tyndale, William, *Mammon,* p. 1/123: *Jonas,* 1/466
44. Tyndale, William, *Exposition Matthew,* p. 2/90
45. Tyndale, William, *Sacraments,* p. 1/349
46. Tyndale, William, *Answer,* p. 3/182
47. Tyndale, William, *Answer,* p. 3/51
48. Tyndale, William, *Exposition 1 John,* p. 2/206
49. Tyndale, William, *Answer,* p. 3/30f
50. Tyndale, William, *Prologue Matthew,* p. 1/470: *Mammon,* p. 1/110
51. Tyndale, William, *Answer,* p. 3/30
52. Tyndale, William, *Prologue Romans,* p. 1/510
53. Tyndale, William, *Epistle to the Reader,* p. 1/390
54. Tyndale, William, *Prologue Numbers,* p. 1/439
55. Tyndale, William, *Exposition Matthew,* p. 2/9
56. More, Thomas, *Dialogue, CWM* vol 6, p. 215. "And thynke you than / that he beynge content and gyuynge men occasyon to pray to theym whyle they were wyth hym in erthe / he wyll be angry yf we doo them as moche worshyp whan they be with hym in heuyn? Nay / but I thynke on the other syde syth his pleasure is to haue his sayntes had in honoure and prayed vnto / that they may be for vs intercessours to hys hyghe maiestye / wherevnto ere we presume to approche / it becometh vs & well behoueth vs to make frendes of suche as he hath in fauoure."
57. Tyndale, William, *Answer,* p. 3/120
58. Tyndale, William, *Answer,* p. 3/112
59. Tyndale, William, *Tracy,* p. 3/277
60. Tyndale, William, *Answer,* p. 3/111
61. Tyndale, William, *Obedience,* p. 1/309
62. Tyndale, William, *Jonas,* p. 1/451
63. Tyndale, William, *Jonas,* p. 1/455
64. The doctrine of "propitiation".
65. Tyndale, William, *Tracy,* p. 3/274f
66. Tyndale, William, *Pathway,* p. 1/10
67. Tyndale, William, *Exposition 1 John,* p. 2/205: *Answer,* p. 3/110
68. Tyndale, William, *Mammon,* p. 1/125
69. Tyndale, William, *Prologue Galatians,* p. 1/513
70. Tyndale, William, *Practice,* p. 2/274
71. Tyndale, William, *Mammon,* p. 1/113
72. Tyndale, William, *Answer,* p. 3/109: see also *Pathway,* p. 1/19f, "Christ standeth us in double stead; and us serveth two manner wise. First, he is our Redeemer,

Deliverer, Reconciler, Mediator, Intercessor, Advocate, Attorney, Solicitor, our Hope, Comfort, Shield, Protection, Defender, Strength, Health, Satisfaction and Salvation. His blood, his death, all that he ever did, is ours. And Christ himself, with all that he is or can do, is ours. His blood shedding, and all that he did, doth me as good service as though I myself had done it. . . . Secondarily, . . . then have we Christ an example to counterfeit."

73. See my 1994 paper "Tyndale and the Blood of Christ." Tyndale Society Journal, no 2., June 1995.
74. I believe Tyndale used "the blood of Christ" rather than the Cross to make a break between his doctrine and that of the unreformed Church.
75. Frequency is the number of occurances divided by the number of words in the writing.
76. Tyndale, William, *Pathway,* p. 1/15
77. Tyndale, William, *Obedience,* p. 1/278
78. Tyndale, William, *Exposition 1 John,* p. 2/149
79. Tyndale, William, *Exposition 1 John,* p. 2/157
80. Tyndale, William, *Exposition 1 John,* p. 2/137
81. Tyndale, William, *Exposition 1 John,* p. 2/147
82. Tyndale, William, *Obedience,* p. 1/277
83. Tyndale, William, *1 John 3:14: N.T.* p. 340: see also *Exposition 1 John,* p. 2/192
84. Tyndale, William, *Exposition 1 John,* p. 2/200
85. Tyndale, William, *Mammon,* p. 1/111
86. Tyndale, William, *Prologue Romans,* p. 1/493
87. Tyndale, William, *Mammon,* p. 1/48
88. Tyndale, William, *Obedience,* p. 1/183
89. Tyndale, William, *Prologue Numbers,* p. 1/429
90. Baker, J. Wayne, *Heinrich Bullinger and the Covenant,* p. 209
91. Tyndale, William, *Mammon,* p. 1/99
92. see page 43f
93. McGiffert, Michael, "William Tyndale's Conception of Covenant", p. 172f. However, McGiffert's conclusions are incorrect because he conflates the two ways Tyndale uses the word "covenant" as if they were the same.
94. Tyndale, William, *Prologue Matthew,* p. 1/471
95. Tyndale, William, *Prologue Leviticus,* p. 1/423
96. Tyndale, William, *Prologue Romans,* p. 1/498
97. Tyndale, William, *Pathway,* p. 1/12
98. Tyndale, William, *Answer,* p. 3/143
99. Tyndale, William, *Pathway,* p. 1/18
100. Tyndale, William, *Obedience,* p. 1/183; *Prologue Romans,* p. 1/489
101. Tyndale, William, *Pathway,* p. 1/10
102. Tyndale, William, *Sacraments,* p. 1/348
103. Tyndale, William, *Prologue Matthew,* p. 1/469
104. Tyndale, William, *1525 Prologue to N.T.* p. 7. "In Christ god loved vs his electe and chosen / before the worlde bega*n* / and reserved vs vnto the knowlege of his sonne and of hys holy gospell." "the bloud of Christ hath obteyned all thi[n]gs for vs of god. Christ is oure satisfaction / redemer / delyverer / saveour from vengeaunce and wrath." see footnotes 6 and 12

105. Tyndale, William, *Answer,* p. 3/35
106. Tyndale, William, *Exposition 1 John,* p. 2/136
107. Tyndale, William, *Exposition 1 John,* p. 2/217
108. Tyndale, William, *Exposition Matthew,* p. 2/101
109. Tyndale, William, *Tracy,* p. 3/273
110. Tyndale, William, *Pathway,* p. 1/9
111. Tyndale, William, *Mammon,* p. 1/72
112. Tyndale, William, *Mammon,* p. 1/85
113. Tyndale, William, *Mammon,* p. 1/73
114. Tyndale, William, *Mammon,* p. 1/89
115. Tyndale, William, *Exposition 1 John,* p. 2/190
116. More, Thomas, *Dialogue, CWM* vol 6, Book IV chap xi. p. 401 "For he accepteth not folke for theyr persons but for theyr merytys."
117. Tyndale, William, *Answer,* p. 3/209
118. Tyndale, William, *Answer,* p. 3/191
119. Tyndale, William, *Exposition 1 John,* p. 2/141
120. Tyndale, William, *Obedience,* p. 1/222
121. Tyndale, William, *Tracy,* p. 3/276
122. Tyndale, William, *Prologue Exodus,* p. 1/417
123. Tyndale, William, *Pathway,* p. 1/20
124. Tyndale, William, *Exposition Matthew,* p. 2/74f
125. Tyndale, William, *Obedience,* p. 1/313f
126. Trueman, Carl R., *Luther's Legacy,* p. 95
127. Tyndale, William, *Exposition Matthew,* p. 2/110f
128. Tyndale, William, *Exposition Matthew,* p. 2/127
129. Tyndale, William, *Answer,* p. 3/81
130. Tyndale, William, *Exposition Matthew,* p. 2/110
131. Tyndale, William, *Prologue Exodus,* p. 1/413
132. Tyndale, William, *Jonas,* p. 1/465f
133. Tyndale, William, *Answer,* p. 3/34f
134. Tyndale, William, *Answer,* p. 3/112
135. Tyndale, William, *Exposition Matthew,* p. 2/82
136. Tyndale, William, *Exposition 1 John,* p. 2/167
137. Tyndale, William, *Jonas,* p. 1/456
138. Tyndale, William, *Answer,* p. 3/35
139. Tyndale, William, *Obedience,* p. 1/141
140. Tyndale, William, *Obedience,* p. 1/294: *Answer,* p. 3/35
141. Tyndale, William, *Exposition 1 John,* p. 2/138
142. Tyndale, William, *Answer,* p. 3/143
143. Tyndale, William, *Mammon,* p. 1/107
144. Tyndale, William, *Obedience,* p. 1/314
145. Tyndale, William, *Pathway,* p. 1/18
146. Tyndale, William, *Pathway,* p. 1/24
147. Tyndale, William, *Exposition 1 John,* p. 2/190
148. Tyndale, William, *Mammon,* 1/99
149. Tyndale, William, *Obedience,* p. 1/204
150. Tyndale, William, *Obedience,* p. 1/298f
151. Tyndale, William, *Pathway,* p. 1/24

152. Tyndale, William, *Obedience,* p. 1/193
153. Tyndale, William, *Mammon,* p. 1/85
154. Tyndale, William, *Answer,* p. 3/7f
155. Tyndale, William, *Pathway,* p. 1/26
156. Tyndale, William, *Pathway,* p. 1/24
157. Tyndale, William, *Prologue Romans,* p. 1/506f
158. Tyndale, William, *Prologue Exodus,* p. 1/418
159. Tyndale, William, *Prologue Romans,* p. 1/507
160. Tyndale, William, *Obedience,* p. 1/299
161. see 1 Corinthians 13:13
162. Tyndale, William, *Mammon,* p. 1/98
163. Tyndale, William, *Sacraments,* p. 1/375
164. Tyndale, William, *Mammon,* p. 1/97

6

The Covenant – Law and Gospel

Introduction

Law and gospel were important to the Reformers, but they did not all have the same understanding of their relationship to the Christian faith. There was general agreement over the law condemning fallen man, leaving him without hope of having a positive relationship with God. From that point we find there were divergences between the different Reformers which began to separate their theologies and which led to the divisions between the Lutheran, Anglican and Reformed Churches, the Anabaptists, and also to the split between Calvinist and Arminian.

The relationship between the law and the gospel, and man's salvation, exercised the minds of the Reformers. Through the law God had condemned man, and a barrier had been erected between God and man. How could God's justice be done, and yet the sinner be restored to fellowship with God? Generally the Reformers thought in legal terms, and Christ became man's substitute having died in man's place. Therefore justice had been done, and man could be set free. Bernhard Lohse wrote,

> The distinction between law and gospel is one of the most important themes in Luther's theology. . . . Dealing with any doctrine in a formally correct manner is never enough unless we also express the proper distinction between law and gospel in the double nature of God's activity as well as our twofold relationship to God as people who are both judged and who have experienced mercy.[1]

For Luther there was a tension between the law and the gospel as we see in his comment on *John* 1:17,

> "The Law was given through Moses; grace and truth came through Jesus Christ." . . . The Law, given through Moses, is indeed a Law of life, righteousness, and everything good. But

> far more was accomplished through Christ. He comes and fills the empty hand and purse; He brings with Him the fulfilment of the Law's precepts and demands. He supplies grace and truth, . . .[2]

We find in Zwingli a different emphasis with regard to law and Gospel, "Differences in stress and substance are evident between Zwingli and Luther in the understanding of gospel and law. . . . Zwingli was critical of Luther's negative way of describing the law."[3]

Tyndale was close to Luther's position when he wrote that the Mosaic Law could be divided into three parts. Firstly, the ceremonial laws of the Old Testament "ceased as soon as Christ had offered up the sacrifice of his body and blood for us." Secondly, the civil laws "were given unto the Jews only, and we heathen or Gentiles are not bound unto them." Thirdly, there were the laws of creation and these

> pertain unto faith and love; and that a man believe how that there is but one God, and that he is true, good and merciful in all things; and therefore ought to be believed, trusted and loved with all a man's heart, soul, mind and strength; and that a man love his neighbour as himself, for God's sake, which hath created him and made him. And this is the law of nature and pertaineth unto all nations indifferently.[4]

In other ways, Tyndale would have agreed with Zwingli, who wrote, "The law is a gospel for the man who honours God."[5]

The *law* and *gospel* are both important aspects of the covenant, and they lie as a bridge that links man to God. Regarding man in his separation from God, Tyndale wrote,

> Note the difference of the law and of the gospel. The one asketh and requireth, the other pardoneth and forgiveth. The one threateneth, the other promiseth all good things to them that set their trust in Christ only.[6]

They stand as markers for all mankind that point the way for man to be set free from Satan's bondage and become the children of God. The signposts are there pointing the way back to God for everyone to see, which leads people, like Wayne Baker, to write that for Tyndale, "The covenant idea was implicitly, if not always explicitly, universalist."[7]

As always Tyndale's obedience to the Bible means that he never tries to smooth out seeming difficulties by using reason. Very often these same difficulties resolve themselves when we look at them clearly in the light of God's revelation. The Law has one meaning for the sinner (a burden and restrictive) and another for the saint (a joy and a delight);

we need to keep these different reactions to the law separate. Tyndale commands us, "Seek therefore in the scripture as thou readest it, first the law, what God commandeth us to do; and secondarily, the promises, which God promiseth us again, namely in Christ Jesus our Lord."[8] And in the *Pater Noster*,

> The sinner acknowledges that he is worthy to be put back; nevertheless faith cleaves fast to God's promises, and compels him, for his truth's sake, to hear her petition. Mark this well, and take it for a sure conclusion. When God commands us in the law to do anything, he does not command, therefore, that we are able to do it, but to bring us unto the knowledge of ourselves. That we might see what we are, and in what a miserable state we are in, and to know our lack. That thereby we should turn to God, and to acknowledge our wretchedness unto him. And to desire him that, of his mercy, he would make us what he bids us to be, and to give us strength and power to do that which the law requires of us.[9]

To help us as we read God's word Tyndale pointed out that there are "three things in it: first the law, to condemn all flesh; secondarily, the gospel, that is to say, promises of mercy . . . ; and thirdly, the stories and lives of those scholars. . . ."[10] Paul Laughlin commented on Tyndale's relationship to the law and gospel, "Thus Tyndale, in the Prologue of his Cologne New Testament, already altered the law-gospel distinction of Luther," and he shows two ways in which this is seen. "The net effect of his modification was to present the law and the gospel in a way that obscured and blurred the careful distinction that was for Luther fundamental to their dialectical relationship."[11]

The law and the gospel must be known, and this means the "scripture ought to be in the mother tongue." Tyndale gives us reasons for this: "First, God gave the children of Israel a law by the hand of Moses in their mother tongue; and all the prophets wrote in their mother tongue, and all the psalms were in the mother tongue."

Although Tyndale never numbered the other reasons he did write of them,

> Moreover, Moses saith, Deut. vi. "Hear, Israel; let these words which I command thee this day stick fast in thine heart, and whet them on your children, and talk of them as thou sittest in thine house," Christ commandeth to search the scriptures. John v. Though that miracles bare record unto his doctrine, yet desired he no faith to be given either to his doctrine, or to his miracles, without record of the scripture.[12]

He asked, "how can we teach our children or search the scriptures if they were not in a language we can understand?" The value of the scriptures in the vernacular is seen in both the Old and the New Testaments, "for the keeping of the commandments of God teacheth wisdom, . . . that ye may understand what ye ought to do."[13] In expounding *Matthew* 7:13, 14, Tyndale wrote, "The strait gate is the true knowledge and understanding of the law, and of the true intent of works: which whosoever understandeth, the same shall be driven to Christ, to fetch of his fulness, and to take him for his righteousness and fulfilling of the law."[14] Unless God's word is in the vernacular, the Christian can neither understand the law nor the gospel.

The Law

The Law and Fallen Man

Tyndale wrote that we are to note and understand the contrast found in the first chapters of *Genesis*: "the power of God, in creating all of nought; then mark the grievous fall of Adam, and of us all in him, through the light regarding of the commandment of God."[15] The result of this contrast is that man is powerless to keep God's law for "Paul proves that the whole nature of man is so poisoned and so corrupt, yea, and so dead, concerning godly living or godly thinking, that it is impossible for her to keep the law in the sight of God."[16] Even though man does not think about this, but believes his life is acceptable to God, "yet testifieth the scripture, and it is true, that we are by inheritance heirs of damnation; and that ere we be born, we are vessels of the wrath of God, and full of that poison whence naturally all sins spring." Man's works prove this and "kill our consciences, and shew us what we were . . . and certify us that we are heirs of damnation."[17] The result of man's conscience being killed is that men

> see not their own miserable estate in wickedness, and damnation under the law of God, but the worse they are, the bolder they be, and the surer of themselves, the further from repentance, and the more standing in their own conceits, for the darkness that is in them.[18]

It is a darkness because sin has "blinded the spiritual eye, and perverted the right intent of the law of God, and of the works commanded by God."[19] In their blindness they cannot see that "unto the disobedient, that will not turn, is threatened wrath, vengeance, and damnation, according to all the terrible acts and fearful examples of the bible."[20]

For the natural man "the word of God was sore darkened," and the prelates had introduced penance so that you can

> buy out thy sins. And in their description they have clean excluded the faith in the satisfaction of Christ's blood. . . . And for lack of trust in Christ's blood, our contrition is but a fruitless sorrow in the respect of hell, which maketh us hate the law still, and consequently God that made it.[21]

For God had given "him a law that is impossible for him to do, or to consent to."[22] And so every man (even the elect before they receive the grace of God), "consented unto sin with soul and body, and hated the law of God."[23]

"It is manifest, that they which love not God's commandment can do nothing godly,"[24] for they neither know nor accept God and his laws. Then when he finds that he can only sin he goes further from God,

> And when he is so fallen, then the law looketh upon him with so terrible a countenance, and so thundereth in his ears, that he dare not abide, but turneth his back and to go; and the enemy assaileth him on the other side, to persuade him that God hath cast him away.[25]

Tyndale then asks a question of fallen man, "If we will not know God to keep his laws, how should God know us, and keep us, and to care for us, and to fulfil his promises of mercy unto us?"[26] Therefore,

> as he which feeleth not his disease can long for no health, even so it is impossible for any man to believe in Christ's blood, except Moses have had him first in cure, and with his law have robbed him of his righteousness, and condemned him unto everlasting death, and have shewed him under what damnation they are in by birth in Adam.[27]

It is in their response to the law that the elect are separated from the rest of mankind.

The Law and the Elect

When we look at the gospel, we see that the elect are born again and respond to it as children of God. It is after this new birth that the Christian's attitude to the law changes and we will

> see the difference between the sin of them that believe in the blood of Christ for the remission of sin, and consent and submit themselves unto the law, and the sin of them that yield themselves unto sin, to serve it.[28]

That is, between those who love the law and those who hate it.

It is Christ who has opened up the way for man to escape from his hopeless situation.

> When the law through conscience of sin hath slain the soul, then hope and trust in Christ's blood, through certifying of the conscience that the damnation of the law is taken away, quickeneth her again; and maketh her to love the law.[29]

It is to the Bible we must always turn if we are to understand God's plan and purpose for his creation and the way for man's salvation, for

> The scripture hath a body without, and within a soul, spirit, and life. It hath . . . all sweetness for God's elect, which he hath chosen to give them his Spirit, and to write his law, and the faith of his Son, in their hearts.[30]

God will, therefore, show his mercy to "his elect, which submit themselves as scholars, to learn to walk in the ways of his laws, and to keep them of love."[31] It is from the scriptures, wrote Tyndale, that the children of God "have every one of them the law of God written in their hearts; so that if there were no law to compel, they would yet naturally, out of their own hearts, keep the law of God."[32]

Each person in the Godhead is involved in helping the Christian to know, love and keep the law. The Father's love to us has made us a new creation which has totally changed us,

> If God so loved us, when we were sinners and knew him not, that he gave his Son for us: how much more loveth he us now, when we love again, and would fain keep his commandments![33]

It goes even deeper than that for

> with his children, in whose hearts he writeth the faith of his Son Jesus and the love of his laws, he goeth otherwise to work. His law is their will: and their petitions are his honour and their neighbour's wealth; and that he will provide them of all things necessary unto this life, and govern them that their hearts be not overcome of evil."[34]

Through Christ we have been "delivered from under the damnation of the law,"[35] and with his blood he has "full purged, and made full satisfaction for all the sins of the world," and this is for us individually,

> and I shall never be at peace with God again, until I have heard the voice of his mouth, how that my sin is forgiven me for Christ's blood sake. And as soon as I believe that, I am at peace with God, and love his law again, and of love work."[36]

The Holy Spirit's activity is to apply the law to the Christian's life by making "the law a lively thing in the heart."[37] For

> the Spirit of Christ hath written the lively law of love in their hearts; which driveth them to work of their own accord freely and willingly, for the great love's sake only which they see in Christ, and therefore need they no law to compel them.[38]

The Holy Spirit makes the child of God "feel all things," and part of this feeling is a longing for health and "this longing and consent of the heart unto the law of God is the working of the Spirit."[39]

As God's children we know the mercy God has shown us in Christ, and as we believe in God's mercy and love his laws we can "know him as a Father."[40] As children we need to learn, and it is important for the children of God to learn God's laws so that they "have the law of God written in their hearts, and are taught of the Spirit"[41] and so we are told, "noosel[42] thyself with Christ, and learn to understand what the law and the gospel mean, and the office of both the two."[43] The Christian has two Teachers and under these Teachers, Christ and the Holy Spirit, the true scholars "be truly taught, and know the law truly, and her office, and the office and effect of faith, and know which be good works before God, and what the intent of them is."[44]

The Teaching of the Law

The importance of the law for the child of God lies in the fact that it affects the whole of his life. "We be under the law to learn it, and to fashion our deeds as like as we can," but our obedience to the law is not through fear of being punished if we break it. Christians who are

> graffed into Christ to follow his doctrine, are under the law to learn it only, but are delivered from fear of everlasting death and hell, . . . And we are come in to God through the confidence that we have in Jesus Christ; and are as familiar and bold with him as young innocent children, which have no conscience of sin, are with their fathers and mothers.[45]

For the Christian is "knit and coupled fast to God's will, . . . for the law of God is written and graved in his heart, and his pleasure is therein."[46]

The law teaches God's children humility "and maketh them as bare as Job, of all things whereof a man can or may be moved to pride."[47] Therefore, "we forsake evil and turn to God, to keep his laws, . . . that we may do the will of God every day better and better."[48]

The law teaches the Christian obedience to God's law out of love and not for any reward he might get.

> For Christ only hath purchased the reward; and our pain-taking to keep the commandments doth but purge the sin that remaineth

> in the flesh, and certify us that we are chosen and sealed with God's Spirit unto the reward that Christ hath purchased for us.[49]

It is then we show our obedience to the law as we "prepare ourselves to do the commandment of God, and to love every man his neighbour, as Christ loved him; seeking with our own works God's honour and our neighbour's wealth only." For our works cannot earn any reward because Christ has made "us heirs of eternal life with his works only, and with his blood-shedding, without and before all our works."[50] For "Christ's blood hath hired us already . . . that we may fulfil the commandment from the bottom of the heart."[51]

Love is another aspect of the teaching of the law, and Tyndale uses this in his argument that *The Epistle of James* should be accepted as canonical "because it setteth up no man's doctrine, but crieth to keep the law of God, and maketh love, which is without partiality, the fulfilling of the law, as Christ and all the apostles did."[52] Our love to God sends us out to teach his love to others, for the preacher "through preaching of faith, made all that consented to the law of God feel the mercy of God in Christ."[53] Therefore we are to "expound the law truly"[54] and "teach all men repentance to God and his holy law, and faith unto our Saviour Jesus Christ."[55] The true preacher must teach true doctrine so that the light of the gospel might bring "the right knowledge of Christ's blood,"[56] because

> until God hath prevented us, and poured the Spirit of his grace into our souls, to love his laws, and hath graven them in our hearts by the outward ministration of his true preacher and inward working of his Spirit, or by inspiration only, we know not God as he is to be known, nor feel the goodness or any sweetness in his law.[57]

Summing up Tyndale's thoughts of the Christian's teaching role, he wrote,

> The preacher comforteth them, and sheweth them the testament of Christ's blood; how that for his sake all that is done is forgiven, and all their weakness shall be taken a worth, until they be stronger, only if they repent, and will submit themselves to be scholars, and learn to keep this law.[58]

The Law in the Christian's Life

Michael McGiffert drew attention to this aspect of the covenant,[59] but he failed to grasp Tyndale's real theology. Because he interpreted covenant as a legal contract, he did not see the place of the family, nor that Tyndale used 'covenant' in two different senses in his writings. If

McGiffert had rejected the idea of a legal contract between God and man, the difficulty he found would have been clarified. He wrote,

> But if so much may be said for the contractual interpretation, the greater truth is that it neither exhausts the meanings of Tyndale's idea of covenant nor penetrates to the heart of the piety that informed that idea: in grasping the letter it misses the spirit of his teaching.[60]

"The greater truth" he was seeking is Tyndale's doctrine of the Fatherhood of God and the Christian's relationship to God as his child, which removes the need for a "contractual interpretation" of the covenant if man is to be justified in God's sight.

> Christ gave his disciples the key of the knowledge of the law of God, . . . and the key of the promises, [and] he saith, Go ye therefore, and teach and baptize; that is, preach this power unto all nations, and wash off their sins, through faith in the promises made in my blood."[61]

Faith is important for the Christian's understanding of the law in his life. "And the Christian goeth through repentance toward the law unto the faith that is in Christ's blood."[62] In *The Exposition of Matthew,* Tyndale wrote, "Faith is the trust in Christ's blood, and is the gift of God; whereunto a man is drawn of the goodness of God, and driven through true knowledge of the law," he sees his lusts and his "damnation in the glass of the law."[63] And this faith enhances our love, for

> when the peace is made between God and us, and all forgiven through faith in Christ's blood, and we begin to love the law, we were never the nearer except faith went with us, to supply out the lack of full love.[64]

In many other ways Tyndale wrote of how the law affected our Christian life, "for love and works are under the law,"[65] and of the importance of our works through our deeds of mercy "we ought to seek our Father's glory only, even the wealth of our brethren, and to win them to the knowledge of our Father and keeping of his law."[66] Good works are all important in our Christian life for "faith, which hath no good deeds following, is a false faith, and not the faith that justifieth, or receiveth forgiveness of sins" which God promises to those who keep his laws.[67] However, our works cannot obtain salvation for us; even the most perfect works can only "satisfy the law for the present time," since "To God-ward is there no satisfaction, save faith in Christ's blood out of a repenting heart."[68] Paul Laughlin commented on this aspect of Tyndale's theology in his chapter, "Law in the Later Works":

"Tyndale continued to employ the constellation of terms he had introduced in his earliest works to denote the appropriate attitude of the righteous toward the law." He continued with details of how the Christians " 'love of the law' was the prerequisite to doing anything godly."[69]

The law is enshrined in God's commandments, and the Christian shows his obedience through prayer. Therefore, wrote Tyndale, we are to "go boldly to the Father, seeing thou hast a commandment ever to pray, and promise that he will hear thee, not for thy goodness, but of his goodness, and for his truth."[70] Although God has commanded us to pray, it is our faith and our love that drive us to prayer. For it is not "possible to believe in God, to love him, or to love our neighbour, but that prayer will spring out there-hence immediately."[71]

Thus we see that the law is an intrinsic part of the covenant and that it applies to the whole of our Christian life. The covenant "that we should be saved by Christ" was given to Abraham, and so Tyndale (quoting Paul) wrote, "the law given four hundred years after cannot disannul that covenant."[72] It is here we find Tyndale's second use of the word *covenant* that relates to God and man. In this sense Tyndale speaks of *covenants* because they refer to the promises God has made to man[73] which help his children to grow and develop.

> Seek therefore in the scripture, as thou readest it, chiefly and above all, the covenants made between God and us; that is to say, the law and commandments which God commandeth us to do; and then the mercy promised unto all them that submit themselves unto the law. For all the promises throughout the whole scripture do include a covenant: that is, God bindeth himself to fulfil that mercy unto thee only if thou wilt endeavour thyself to keep his laws; so that no man hath his part in the mercy of God, save he only that loveth his law, and consenteth that it is righteous and good.[74]

For we "know it our duty to keep the law of God, and to love our neighbours for their Father's sake which created them, and for their Lord's sake which redeemed them, and bought them so dearly with his blood."[75]

William Clebsch missed the two ways in which Tyndale spoke of *covenant* and thought that from 1532 "his theology, newly organized around the idea of covenant as a bipartite, divine-human contract binding upon both parties, shouts itself from every writing attributable to the period."[76] Michael McGiffert followed Clebsch when he wrote, "The view of covenant as contract receives support from Tyndale's coupling of the gracious *if/then* with a lethal alternative."[77] Judith

Mayotte, however, in her research had seen the ways in which Tyndale used *testament* and *covenant* and wrote,

> Clebsch either did not see, or else did not consider the fact that Tyndale worked throughout his life from the primary foundation of a 'testament betwene' God and man, freely given by God with the attendant response from man of love of God and neighbor.[78]

Gospel

Within the covenant, law and gospel are closely linked. Tyndale wrote in his *Prologue to 1 Timothy*, Paul "maketh a short conclusion of all Christian learning; whereunto the law serveth, . . . also what the gospel is."[79] We have seen that the law is divided between those outside and those within the covenant of salvation. This same division is found in the work of the gospel.

Tyndale did not believe that God had predestined any to damnation, but the gospel was offered to everyone, but "where the right way is set before us, and we of malice will not walk therein, God cannot but let the devil play with us, and juggle our eyes to confirm us in blindness."[80] Those whom God has chosen and elected to be his children will respond positively to the gospel when it is preached, but the preaching of the gospel to those who will not listen, because they are not chosen, is not vain nor valueless. They have the opportunity, but their rejection of the gospel rests with them and with their father the devil, and not with God, as

> Paul saith, "Evil men and deceivers shall prevail in evil, while they deceive, and are deceived themselves," and have taught them to put their trust in their own merits, and brought them in belief that they shall be justified in the sight of God by the goodness of their own works.[81]

With false arguments they make God's law a "worldly law", and they turn the gospel upside down, saying, "'God now receiveth us no more to mercy, but of mercy receiveth us to penance;' that is to wit, holy deeds."[82]

The fact that the gospel is going to fall on deaf ears must not prevent the true Christian from preaching it to everyone. "Christ before his death commanded and appointed that such Evangelion, gospel, or tidings should be declared throughout all the world."[83] Christ gave the command to his disciples, "Go ye therefore, and teach and baptize; that is, preach this power unto all nations, and wash off their sins, through faith in the promises made in my blood."[84] To help his people to proclaim the gospel the Holy Spirit "gave them understanding of the scripture, and of all that they should preach". However, although God's power to save from sin is offered to all that repent, Tyndale knew that some would not repent "but follow the lusts of their flesh".[85]

Christ's disciples were sent into the world and "The authority that Christ gave them was to preach; yet not what they would imagine, but what he had commanded,"[86] so that men listen only to the gospel and "to men's doctrine not at all".[87] The preacher must be single-minded in his work, for

> If a man put his hand to the plough of God's word to preach it, and look also unto worldly business, his plough will surely go awry. . . . He that will preach the kingdom of God (which is Christ's gospel) truly, must have his heart nowhere else.[88]

Tyndale believed that "There is not so simple a thing in the world, or more despised, than the gospel. And yet it saves and justifies them that believe there on."[89] Paul, after preaching the law, "Then preacheth he Christ, the gospel, the promises, and the mercy that God hath set forth to all men in Christ's blood."[90] The blood of Christ is an important part of the gospel for us and we need to "hearken unto the gospel of glad tidings in Christ's blood".[91] For the blood of Christ is all important for our salvation, for Christ

> bought it of his Father dearly, with his blood. . . . Whatsoever good thing is in us, that is given us freely, without our deserving or merits, for Christ's blood's sake. That we desire to follow the will of God, it is the gift of Christ's blood. That we now hate the devil's will . . . is also the gift of Christ's blood.[92]

We have the "redemption that is in Christ's blood,"[93] the "forgiveness of sins in Christ's blood,"[94] and "Christ's blood hath purchased life for us, and hath made us the heirs of God; so that heaven cometh by Christ's blood."[95] Therefore what is required of us is to

> believe as the gospel, glad tidings and promises of God say unto thee; that for Christ's blood's sake only, through faith, God is at one with thee and thou received to mercy, and art become the son of God.[96]

Therefore we must accept the gospel according to God's eternal purpose and the responsibilities which go with it.

> But look that thine eye be single, and rob not Christ of his honour; ascribe not that to the deserving of thy works, which is given thee freely by the merits of his blood. In Christ we are sons. In Christ we are heirs. In Christ God chose us, and elected us before

> the beginning of the world, created us anew by the word of the gospel, and put his Spirit in us, for because that we should do good works.[97]

Therefore we are taught in the *Epistle to the Ephesians* that

> the gospel and grace thereof was foreseen and predestinate of God from before the beginning, and deserved through Christ, and now at the last sent forth, that all men should believe thereon; thereby to be justified, made righteous, living and happy, and to be delivered from under the damnation of the law.[98]

As we remember that "the fulfilling of the law is a fast faith in Christ's blood, coupled with our profession, and submitting ourselves to do better," then God will keep all his promises "of his goodness and fatherly mercy unto thee".[99]

The gospel is important for us as it teaches us how to live as Christians. Tyndale taught that it is the Holy Spirit who brings us into God's kingdom, gives us the love we need to be true children of God and to care for our weaker brethren and those heathen the Holy Spirit has brought into the kingdom. Then as a "man is strong in that kingdom, so love compelleth him to take the weak by the hand, and to help him, and to take him that cannot go upon his shoulders and bear him"[100] who does "yet understand not the liberty of the gospel".[101] The support and help given to the weak is "a thing that Christ commanded and charged to be had above all things."[102] It was to help all Christians , the weak and the strong, that God gave the sacrament of the Lord's Supper, to preach the gospel and "to thrust it in, not at the ears only . . . , neither at our eyes only . . . , but beat it in through our feeling, tasting and smelling also."[103]

When the gospel is received it brings with it "tribulation and persecution".[104] But in spite of this the gospel is to be preached by the bishops[105] and priests[106] who should be "virtuous and learned".[107] Tyndale explains what this preaching is, "The kingdom of heaven is the preaching of the gospel, unto which come both good and bad." Because the bad are the majority, the few have to "take adversity with Christ for the gospel's sake, and for bearing record unto the truth, that all men may hear it."[108] This persecution falls not only on the true bishops and priests, but on all the "children of the gospel, which believe in the mercy and truth of God and in the testament of his Son Jesus our Lord".[109] Those who teach the faith of Christ must go out trusting only in God "to plant the gospel with all love and meekness, and to water it with their own blood, as Christ did".[110] Therefore as John Frith was waiting his martyrdom in 1533, his friend Tyndale could write, "Your cause is Christ's gospel, a light that must be fed with the blood of faith."[111]

We have seen that in Tyndale's doctrine of the law and the gospel there is a double aspect. Both law and gospel apply to all mankind. Everyone is under the law, and because no man has kept it in its entirety all fall under its condemnation. The gospel is the good news of how men can return to God and be forgiven for breaking the law. Tyndale believed the good news is offered to every man "because God has made them after the likeness of his own image, and they are his sons as well as we,"[112] and everyone, who accepts its terms and conditions, will find God's forgiveness through Christ's blood. At the same time, the law and the gospel are two important aspects of the covenant. The law and the gospel form a bridge between the one and eternal covenant between God the Father, God the Son and God the Holy Spirit to choose, justify and save the elect from fallen humanity: and the promises and covenants made between God, the Trinity, and his elect. It is through this covenant which the Persons of the Trinity have made with each other that the elect will be enabled to respond to the gospel and be saved. Those who have not been chosen by God, and who choose to reject the gospel offered to them, remain in their sin and at enmity with God. It is their decision, and the consequence of rejecting the gospel is theirs and the devil's, seeing that the devil has bound them to himself with chains which can only be broken by the blood of Christ.[113]

For those who, through Christ's blood, have been made children of God through repentance and faith, God the Father has made many promises or covenants. These covenants are conditional on their obedience, an obedience which springs out of their love for their Father and not from any fear of punishment.

Notes

1. Lohse, Bernhard, *Martin Luther, An Introduction to his Life and Work,* p. 158
2. Luther, Martin, *Sermons on the Gospel of St. John, ch. 1-4; Works,* vol 22. p. 144
3. Stephens. Peter, *The Theology of Huldrych Zwingli,* p. 164f
4. Tyndale, William, *Prelates,* p. 2/324
5. Zwingli, Huldrych, quoted in Locher, Gottfried W., , *Zwingli's Thought,* p. 198f
6. Tyndale, William, *Epistle,* p. 1/389
7. Baker, J. Wayne, *Heinrich Bullinger and the Covenant,* p. 209
8. Tyndale, William, *Prologue Genesis,* p. 1/399
9. Tyndale, William, *Pater Noster,* p. cii.r. "The sinner knowlegeth that he is worthy to be put backe / neverthelesse fayth cleveth fast to gods promises / and compelleth hym / for his truethes sake / to heare her peticion. Marke this well

and take it for a sure conclusion / when god commaundeth vs i*n* the lawe to doo any thinge / he commaundeth not therefore / that we are able to do yt / but to bryng vs vn to the knowlege of oureselves / that we might se what we are and in what miserable state we are in / and to knowe oure lack / that thereby we shuld torne to god and to knowledge our wretchednes vn to hym / a*n*d to desyre him that of his mercy he wold make vs that he biddeth vs be / a*n*d to geve vs strength and power to doo that whiche the lawe requireth of vs."

10. Tyndale, William, *Jonas,* p. 1/449
11. Laughlin, Paul A., "The Brightness of Moses' Face", p 153
12. Tyndale, William, *Obedience,* p. 1/144-147
13. Tyndale, William, *Prologue Deuteronomy,* p. 1/444
14. Tyndale, William, *Exposition Matthew,* p. 2/120
15. Tyndale, William, *Prologue Genesis,* p. 1/400
16. Tyndale, William, *Prologue Romans,* p. 1/508
17. Tyndale, William, *Mammon,* p. 1/64
18. Tyndale, William, *Exposition 1 John,* p. 2/213
19. Tyndale, William, *Exposition Matthew,* p. 2/102
20. Tyndale, William, *Prologue Matthew,* p. 1/470f
21. Tyndale, William, *Exposition 1 John,* p. 2/162
22. Tyndale, William, *Pathway,* p. 1/18
23. Tyndale, William, *Exposition 1 John,* p. 2/199
24. Tyndale, William, *Answer,* p. 3/83
25. Tyndale, William, *Sacraments,* p. 1/359
26. Tyndale, William, *Exposition Matthew,* p. 2/53
27. Tyndale, William, *Exposition 1 John,* p. 2/146
28. Tyndale, William, *Exposition Matthew,* p. 2/10
29. Tyndale, William, *Exposition 1 John,* p. 2/187
30. Tyndale, William, *Jonas,* p. 1/449
31. Tyndale, William, *Jonas,* p. 1/451
32. Tyndale, William, *Answer,* p. 3/137
33. Tyndale, William, *Sacraments,* p. 1/364
34. Tyndale, William, *Answer,* p. 3/182
35. Tyndale, William, *Prologue Ephesians,* p. 1/514
36. Tyndale, William, *Exposition 1 John,* p. 2/196
37. Tyndale, William, *Prologue Exodus,* p. 1/417
38. Tyndale, William, *Obedience,* p. 1/297
39. Tyndale, William, *Mammon,* p. 78f
40. Tyndale, William, *Exposition 1 John,* p. 2/183.
41. Tyndale, William, *Answer,* p. 3/99
42. "noosel" – find shelter, as a child with a nurse.
43. Tyndale, William, *Prologue Romans,* p. 1/505
44. Tyndale, William, *Sacraments,* p. 1/375
45. Tyndale, William, *Exposition 1 John,* p. 2/159
46. Tyndale, William, *Mammon,* p. 1/55
47. Tyndale, William, *Exposition 1 John,* p. 2/140
48. Tyndale, William, *Prologue Matthew,* p. 1/471
49. Tyndale, William, *Obedience,* p. 1/314f
50. Tyndale, William, *Prologue Epistles John,* p. 1/530

51. Tyndale, William, *Obedience,* p. 1/280
52. Tyndale, William, *Prologue James,* p. 1/525
53. Tyndale, William, *Exposition Matthew,* p. 2/131
54. Foxe, John, *Acts and Monuments,* vol 5. p. 133: Tyndale, *Exposition Matthew,* p. 2/95
55. Tyndale, William, *Prelates,* p. 2/242
56. Tyndale, William, *Exposition Matthew,* p. 2/34
57. Tyndale, William, *Answer,* p. 3/174
58. Tyndale, William, *Answer,* p. 3/108f
59. McGiffert, Michael, "William Tyndale's Conception of Covenant", p. 172
60. McGiffert, Michael, "William Tyndale's Conception of Covenant", p. 174
61. Tyndale, William, *Prelates,* p. 2/282
62. Tyndale, William, *Answer,* p. 3/193
63. Tyndale, William, *Exposition Matthew,* p. 2/88f
64. Tyndale, William, *Answer,* p. 3/205
65. Tyndale, William, *Pathway,* p. 1/15
66. Tyndale, William, *Exposition Matthew,* p. 2/73
67. Tyndale, William, *Prologue James,* p. 1/525
68. Tyndale, William, *Exposition 1 John,* p. 2/137
69. Laughlin, Paul A. "The Brightness of Moses' Face", pp. 178-182
70. Tyndale, William, *Exposition Matthew,* p. 2/79
71. Tyndale, William, *Exposition Matthew,* p. 2/115
72. Tyndale, William, *Tracy,* p. 3/275
73. Tyndale, William, *Prologue Matthew,* p. 1/471
74. Tyndale, William, *Prologue Genesis,* p. 1/403
75. Tyndale, William, *Prologue Matthew,* p. 1/474
76. Clebsch, William A. *England's Earliest Protestants,* p. 181
77. McGiffert, Michael, "William Tyndale's Conception of Covenant", p. 173
78. Mayotte, Judith M., "William Tyndale's Contribution to the Reformation in England", p.77
79. Tyndale, William, *Prologue 1 Timothy,* p. 1/518
80. Tyndale, William, *Exposition 1 John,* p. 2/168
81. Tyndale, William, *Mammon,* p. 1/45f
82. Tyndale, William, *Prologue Jonas,* p. 1/449f
83. Tyndale, William, *Pathway,* p. 1/9
84. Tyndale, William, *Prelates,* p. 2/282
85. Tyndale, William, *Prelates,* p. 2/283
86. Tyndale, William, *Obedience,* p. 1/211
87. Tyndale, William, *Prologue 2 Peter,* p. 1/528
88. Tyndale, William, *Prelates,* p. 2/253
89. Tyndale, William, *1525 N.T., chapter 13,* p. 44. "There is not so simple a thynge i*n* the worlde / or more despised / then the gospell / & yett yt saveth a*n*d iustifieth the*m* that beleve there on."
90. Tyndale, William, *Mammon,* p. 96f
91. Tyndale, William, *Exposition I John,* p. 2/168
92. Tyndale, William, *Pathway,* p. 1/23
93. Tyndale, William, *Answer,* p. 3/33
94. Tyndale, William, *Exposition 1 John,* p. 2/220

95. Tyndale, William, *Mammon,* p. 1/65
96. Tyndale, William, *Mammon,* p. 1/71
97. Tyndale, William, *Mammon,* p. 1/77
98. Tyndale, William, *Prologue Ephesians,* p. 1/514
99. Tyndale, William, *Prologue Jonas,* p. 1/451
100. Tyndale, William, *Prelates,* p. 2/250
101. Tyndale, William, *Prologue 1 Corinthians,* p. 1/511
102. Tyndale, William, *Prologue Romans,* p. 1/507
103. Tyndale, William, *Sacraments,* p. 1/361
104. Tyndale, William, *Prologue 1 Thessalonians,* p. 1/516
105. Tyndale, William, *Prologue 1 Timothy,* p. 1/517f
106. Tyndale, William, *Prelates,* p. 2/288
107. Tyndale, William, *Prologue Titus,* p. 1/519
108. Tyndale, William, *Obedience,* p. 1/165
109. Tyndale, *Obedience,* p. 1/307
110. Tyndale, William, *Exposition Matthew,* p. 2/68
111. Foxe, John, *Acts and Monuments,* vol 5, p. 131
112. Tyndale, William, *Pathway,* 1/18
113. Tyndale, William, *1525,* p. 10

7

The Covenantal Signs

Sacraments – Old and New Testaments

Tyndale's view of the unity of the covenant between the Old and the New Testaments meant that there was also a unity between the covenantal signs of the Old and the New Testaments. The signs were given to help man remember and understand the covenant,

> Hereof ye see also, that as the Hebrews wrote their stories in covenants and signs, giving their signs such names as could not but keep them in mind; so God the Father did follow the ensample of his people (or they following him) and commanded his promises, covenants and prophecies, to be written in gestures, signs and ceremonies, giving them names that could not but keep his covenants in mind. Even so Christ wrote the covenant of his body and blood in bread and wine, giving them that name, that ought to keep the covenant in remembrance.[1]

Our salvation does not depend on the sacraments, which are signs of the covenant, but God has given them "to have his benefits kept in memory."[2] Tyndale lists many of the signs used by the Israelites to mark the covenants they made with others, and continued,

> And such fashions as they used among themselves, did God also use to themward, in all his notable deeds, whether of mercy in delivering them, or of wrath in punishing their disobedience and transgression, in all his promises to them, and covenants made between them and him.[3]

Tyndale wrote that there were many signs which marked the different covenants between God and man, but they could not be called *sacraments*. The sacraments are not signs attached to those promises or covenants that God makes with man, but only those signs attached to the covenant of salvation whereby the elect are adopted into God's family as his children.

In the Old Testament there were two sacraments, circumcision and the Passover, and these correspond to the two New Testament sacraments, baptism[4] and the Lord's Supper.[5] Tyndale stressed the continuity of God's covenant; therefore, he showed that both circumcision and baptism had the same meaning and expressed the same covenantal relationship in God's plan for man's salvation. The same was true of the relationship of the Passover and the Lord's Supper within the covenant. He also wrote that the differences between the Old and New Testament sacraments were due to the change that took place when Christ fulfilled the covenant in his blood.[6]

Because of his understanding of the signification of the sacraments, Tyndale could not agree with Luther's statement in *The Little Catechism,*

> What gifts or benefits does baptism bestow? Answer: It effects forgiveness of sins, delivers from death and the devil, and grants eternal salvation to all who believe, as the Word and promise of God declare.

For Tyndale the meaning of baptism was "the profession and religion of a christian man, and the inward baptism of the heart, signified by the outward washing of the body."[8] Neither could Tyndale accept Luther's insistence that "This is my body," meant Christ's body was really present in the Lord's Supper, Luther's words were much closer to the Roman Catholic position than Tyndale would allow, and therefore Tyndale wrote that there was no real difference between consubstantiation and transubstantiation in his understanding.[9] We can understand why Thomas More in his *Dialogue Concerning Heresies* included the Bishop of Rochester's remarks: "And over this he said that he had seen of Luther's own words worse than he had ever heard rehearsed. And in Tyndale worse yet in many things than he saw in Luther himself."[10]

Bucer also could write of the effectiveness of the sacraments,

> For by Baptism men must be washed from sins, regenerated and renewed for eternal life, incorporated in Christ the Lord, and clothed with him, and all of these things are reserved only to those chosen for eternal life.[11]

Again he wrote, "Since by these sacraments remission of sins and the holy communion of Christ are imparted, and the covenant of eternal salvation is sealed and confirmed," for "by these sacraments men receive the supreme benefits of God, the forgiveness of sins and inheritance of eternal life."[12]

There is a similarity between Zwingli's and Tyndale's position: Zwingli wrote,

> Circumcision did not confirm the faith of Abraham. It was a covenant sign between God and the seed of Abraham. . . . And in *Genesis* 17 God himself makes it quite clear that circumcision is not a sign for the confirmation of faith but a covenant sign. . . . Similarly, baptism in the New Testament is a covenant sign.[13]

However, there is a difference between Zwingli's and Tyndale's doctrine which stems from their covenantal theologies, and this spreads into every other doctrine they considered. Zwingli's words, "By the first of these signs, baptism, we are initially marked off to God, as we shall see later. In the other, the Lord's Supper or Eucharist, we render thanks to God because he has redeemed us by his Son."[14] It is hard to imagine Tyndale writing those words! For Tyndale there is a real meaning for "inasmuch as the sacraments of the old Testament have significations; and inasmuch as the sacraments of the new Testament . . . have also significations"[15] so that they have a greater depth of meaning than Zwingli allowed.

A Lollard "Sermon" speaks of the sacrament,

> And of this flesh and this blood, in his kind, speaketh the gospel, and of the ghostly eating that men might eat this. The bread of the sacred host is very bread in his kind, and is eaten bodily: but it is God's body in figure. . . . but this host is eaten bodily and ghostly of some men, but Christ's body in his kind is not eaten bodily.[16]

Hudson wrote, "Yet others took up the element of pragmatism inherent in Wyclif's view, and indeed expressed overtly by him: a mouse knows bread when it sees it, even if friars do not. 'Summe folys cummyn to churche thynckyng to see the good Lorde – what shulde they see there but bredde and wyne?'[17] ("Some people coming to church thinking to see the good Lord – what should they see there but bread and wine?")

Tyndale's position is that a sacrament is a sign that represents the covenant "made between God and man, and God's promises." The rainbow for Noah, circumcision for Abraham and the Jewish nation, and for the Christian, baptism which

> signifieth on the one side, how that all that repent and believe are washed in Christ's blood; and on the other side, how that the same must quench and drown the lusts of the flesh, to follow the steps of Christ.[18]

As there was a link between circumcision and baptism, there was also a link between the Passover and the Lord's Supper. In both the Old and the New Testaments the relationship between the two sacraments was very real for the understanding of our relationship with God. With the coming of Christ the signs of the Old Testament were changed to new ones, and the Passover was changed, "in whose stead is the sacrament of the body and blood of Christ come, as baptism in the room or stead of circumcision."[19] For Tyndale this continuity was essential if we were to understand God's covenant of love and mercy towards us.

It is important for us to know the signification of a sacrament "for it is impossible to observe a sacrament, without signification, but unto our damnation."[20] The sacraments when their signification "was away, they were abominable, and devilish idolatry and image-service; as our ceremonies and sacraments are become now."[21] Although Tyndale recognised only Baptism and the Lord's Supper as sacraments, he did not rule out that there might have been others, "for we destroy none, but they destroy which have put out the significations, or feigned some without."[22]

Every God-given sacrament "from Adam to Christ had signification",[23] and Tyndale wrote that the *Epistle to the Hebrews* was of value to help us understand the sacraments, for "there is no work in all the scripture that so plainly declareth the meaning and significations of the sacrifices, ceremonies, and figures of the old Testament, as this epistle." It would also help us to understand "our sacraments."[24]

The Christian in all the sacraments "searcheth the significations, and will not serve the visible things,"[25] for God gave us the "visible signs, to provoke us and to help our weak faith, and to keep his mercy in mind."[26] The "ministers of God preach God's word; and God's signs or sacraments signify God's word also, and put us in remembrance of the promises which God hath made unto us in Christ."[27] Tyndale wrote of the link between God's people in the Old and the New Testament for

> their sacrifices and ceremonies, as far forth as the promises annexed unto them extend, so far forth they saved them and justified them, and stood them in the same stead as our sacraments do us; not by the power of the sacrifice or deed itself, but by the virtue of the faith in the promise, which the sacrifice or ceremony preached, and whereof it was a token or sign.[28]

Sacraments have one important function: they are signs representing the "appointment and promises" God has made with man.[29] Therefore they are "holy signs" and those "which Christ ordained preach God's word unto us," and "Christ's sacraments preach the faith of Christ."[30] A sacrament is only true and teaching true doctrine if it "buildeth thee upon Christ to put thy trust and confidence in his blood."[31] In order that the people could understand the signification of the sacraments, Tyndale wrote that the priest (that is an "elder") had the duty "to teach the younger, and to bring them unto the full knowledge and understanding of Christ, and to minister the sacraments which Christ ordained, which is also nothing but to preach Christ's promises."[32] For the people need to be taught and to understand that they are

> signs that put men in remembrance either of the benefits of God done already, as the Easter lamb; either signs of the promise and appointment made between God and man, as circumcision; or signs that testify unto the people that the wrath of God is peaced, and their sins forgiven, as all manner sacrifices: which all ceased as soon as Christ had offered up the sacrifice of his body and blood for us; and instead of them come the open preaching of Christ, and our signs which we call sacraments.[33]

Although the Old Testament sacrifices and sacraments had ceased, it was not because God's testament had changed, but because Christ had come.

> For the sacrifices which God gave Adam's sons were no dumb popetry or superstitious mahometry, but signs of the testament of God. And in them they read the word of God, as we do in books; and as we should do in our sacraments.[34]

Therefore, "As Tyndale considered the sacraments, he became convinced that in the Old Testament, as in the New, sacraments and ceremonies served as preachers to the people."[35]

Circumcision and Baptism[36]

Tyndale wrote that God had made a covenant with Abraham and with his children to be their God, shield and defender. Abraham promised they would be his people

> to believe and trust in him, and to keep his commandments, . . . which circumcision was the seal and obligation of the said covenant, to keep it in mind, and to testify that it was an earnest thing, whereby God challenged them to be his people, and required the keeping of his laws of them.[37]

In the same way "we be baptized to believe in the death of Christ, and to die with him by the mortifying of the flesh."[38]

Tyndale gave several warnings of the errors we can make as we look at the meaning of baptism, and also the use we make of Biblical illustrations. Firstly, we cannot prove baptism by circumcision; "As though circumcision be a figure of baptism, yet thou canst not prove baptism by circumcision. For this argument were very feeble; the Israelites were circumcised, therefore we must be baptized." Secondly,

Tyndale continued with Peter's example of the flood being a figure of baptism.

> Though that the saving of Noe, and of them that were with him in the ship, through water, is a figure, that is to say an example and likeness of baptism, as Peter maketh it, (1 Pet. iii.) yet I cannot prove baptism therewith, save describe it only. . . . And Paul (1 Cor. x.) maketh the sea and the cloud a figure of baptism; by which, and a thousand more, I might declare it, but not prove it.[39]

However, wrote Tyndale,

> When I have a clear text of Christ and the apostles, that I must be baptized, then I may borrow an example of circumcision to express the nature, power, and fruit, or effect of baptism. For as circumcision was unto them a common badge, signifying that they were all soldiers of God, to war his war, and separating them from all other nations, disobedient unto God: even so baptism is our common badge, and sure earnest and perpetual memorial, that we pertain unto Christ, and are separated from all that are not Christ's."[40]

Whether it is circumcision or baptism, we have to know the meaning of these sacraments.

> For it is the covenant only, and not the sign, that saveth us; though the sign be commanded to be put on at due time, to stir up faith of the covenant that saveth us. And instead of circumcision came our baptism; whereby we be received into the religion of Christ, and made partakers of his passion, and members of his church; and whereby we are bound to believe in Christ, and in the Father through him, for the remission of sins; and to keep the law of Christ, and to love each other, as he loved us.[41]

Tyndale also calls baptism "the washing" because

> The plunging into the water signifieth that we die, and are buried with Christ, as concerning the old life of sin, which is Adam. And the pulling out again signifieth that we rise again with Christ in a new life, full of the Holy Ghost, which shall teach us and guide us, and work the will of God in us, as thou seest, Rom. vi.[42]

The meaning of this washing, the meaning of baptism, is not the cleansing we receive from the water but it is "the inward baptism of the heart, signified by the outward washing of the body."[43] In *The Exposition of 1 John,* some of the things signified by our baptism are explained.

> All that be baptized in Christ are washed in him, to put off pride, wrath, hate and envy, with all their old conversation, by which they oppressed their neighbours; and have promised to become, every man even as Christ himself unto his brethren, in love and kindness both in word and deed."[44]

We approach Tyndale's theology of baptism from the position of fallen man and how it is damnation not to have God's

> law written in our hearts, . . . and how there is no other means to be saved from this damnation, than through repentance toward the law, and faith in Christ's blood; which are the very inward baptism of our souls, and the washing and the dipping of our bodies in the water is the outward sign.[45]

Then we are "to be scholars thereof,"[46] who need to be taught the meaning of baptism,

> As a man can by no means read, except he be first taught the letters of the cross row, even so it is unpossible for a man, of whatsoever degree or name he be of, to understand aught in the scripture unto the honour of God and health of his soul, except he be first taught the profession of his baptism, and have it also written in his heart.[47]

For "if the signification of our baptism, which is the law of God and faith of Christ, were expounded truly unto us, the scripture would be easy to all that exercised themselves therein."[48] Unfortunately, Tyndale wrote, the spiritualty did not understand the profession of our baptism and so did not teach it because "the sentences of the scripture are nothing but very riddles unto them, . . . and all for lack of the right knowledge of the profession of our baptism."[49] Therefore, "The right way, yea, and the only way, to understand the scripture unto salvation, is that we earnestly and above all things search for the profession of our baptism, or covenants made between God and us."[50] The Christian has a certainty as he approaches God's word for

> whosoever hath the profession of baptism written in his heart, cannot but understand the scripture, if he exercise himself therein, and compare one place to another, and mark the manner of speech, and ask here and there the meaning of a sentence of them that be better exercised.[51]

And who better than Tyndale can they turn to? He points to his translation of the scriptures,

> And therefore are there divers introductions ordained for you, to teach you the profession of your baptism, the only light of the

> scripture; one upon the epistle of Paul to the Romans, and another called 'The Pathway into the Scripture.'"[52]

Tyndale teaches that there are three points which are important about our baptism,

> the profession and religion of a christian man, and the inward baptism of the heart, signified by the outward washing of the body. And they be that spiritual character, badge, or sign, wherewith God, through his Spirit, marketh all his immediately and as soon as they be joined to Christ, and made members of his church by true faith.

Those "that have their hearts washed with this inward baptism of the Spirit are of the church, and have the keys of the scripture."[53] The inward baptism is important, and Tyndale explains that this is

> to believe in Christ's blood for the remission of sin, and purchasing of all the good promises that help to the life to come; and to love the law; and to long for the life to come, is the inward baptism of the soul, the baptism that only availeth in the sight of God.[54]

As Christ has done all this for us we make the profession of our baptism by which we have "promised to quench and slay the lusts of the flesh with prayer, fasting, and holy meditation, after the doctrine of Christ, and with all godly exercise, that tame the flesh, and kill not the man."[55] Therefore we desire

> the holiness of God's word; which only speaketh unto the heart, and sheweth the soul his filthiness and uncleanness of sin, and leadeth her by the way of repentance unto the fountain of Christ's blood, to wash it away through faith.[56]

The profession of our baptism means the promises we made when we were baptized must be kept unbroken;

> For what intent? Verily, for the love of Christ which hath bought thee with his blood, and made thee son and heir of God with him, that thou shouldest wait on his will and commandments, and purify thy members according to the same doctrine that hath purified thine heart,[57]

and the Christian must "pay the vow of thy baptism."[58] The vows made to God "when you were first baptized in Christ" are not to keep new laws God has made for his people, but a precept going back to creation, "to love each other as he did you; which is an old commandment, and was given at the beginning of the world, and hath ever since been written in the heart of all that put their hope in God."[59] There are many signs which show that we are keeping the profession of our baptism to love as God loves us. The child of God does not "laugh at another man's sins" because he realises that, however holy he is, he might "through frailty of the flesh be drawn into sin."[60] It also means that he will "care for the poor, and give them all that we may spare, in his name; . . . If the law of Christ be written in thine heart, why distributest thou not unto thy brethren with thine own hands, in the name of thy Saviour Jesus Christ, which died both for them and thee, as thou hast vowed and promised to him in thy baptism?"[61] Tyndale links all these aspects of baptism to the Old Testament circumcision in the *Prologue to Jonas,* "For verily, to confess out of the heart that all benefits come of God, even out of the goodness of his mercy, and not deserving of our deeds, is the only sacrifice that pleaseth God; and to believe that all the Jews vowed in their circumcision, as we in our baptism; which vow Jonas, now being taught with experience, promiseth to pay."[62]

Tyndale believed in infant baptism from the fact that circumcision and baptism had the same meaning in God's covenant. "The covenant made between God and Abraham" was effective for the child "as soon as it was born, yea, as soon as it had life in the mother's womb: for the covenant, that God would be God of Abraham's seed, went over the fruit as soon as it had life; and then there is no reason but that the covenant must needs pertain to the males as soon as the females . . . even so must needs the covenant, made to all that believe in Christ's blood, go over the seed as soon as it hath life in the mother's womb."[63] There was then a need for the baptized infant to accept the covenant for himself, and so "for the succour and help of young children, baptized before the age of discretion, to know the law of God and faith of Christ, was confirmation instituted, that they should not be alway ignorant and faithless, but be taught the profession of their baptism."[64] The children, when they were "six or seven years old," were brought to the parish priest to be taught the profession of their baptism. Then when the children had been taught its meaning "the priests brought the children . . . at eleven or twelve years old" to the archdeacon who questioned them about their faith, knowledge of God's law, and the Christian life. "Then confirmed he their baptism, saying, 'I confirm you; that is, I denounce and declare, by the authority of God's word, and doctrine of Christ, that ye be truly baptized within, in your hearts and in your spirits, through professing the law of God and the faith of our Saviour Jesus, which your outward baptism doth signify; and thereupon I put this cross in your foreheads, that ye go and fight against the devil, the world, and the flesh, under the standard of our Saviour, in the name of the Father, the Son, and the Holy Ghost, Amen.' Which manner, I would to God, for his tender mercy, were in use this day."[65]

The Passover and the Lord's Supper

Both baptism and the Lord's Supper are sacraments, for both of them preach the blood of Christ which was shed once and for all on the cross. Therefore, Christ's sacrifice cannot be repeated without denying the truth of Christ's death at Calvary.[66] When we turn to the three ways the Lord's Supper is interpreted, Tyndale says that both the Catholic and the Lutheran interpretations have lost the true scriptural meaning of the sacrament.

> One part say that these words, "This is my body," "This is my blood," compel us to believe, under pain of damnation, that the bread and wine are changed into the very body and blood of Christ really: as the water at Cana Galilee was turned into very wine.
>
> The second part saith, 'We be not bound to believe that bread and wine are changed; but only that his body and blood are there presently.'
>
> The third say, 'We be bound by these words only to believe that Christ's body was broken, and his blood shed for the remission of our sins; and that there is no other satisfaction for sin than the death and passion of Christ.[67]

Catholics interpreted Christ's words of institution materially. "Bread and wine, say they, cannot be Christ's natural body; therefore the bread and wine are changed, turned, altered, and transubstantiated into the very body and blood of Christ."[68] Then one must believe "that there is no bread in the sacrament, nor wine, though the five wits say all yea."[69] This materialistic interpretation cannot be taken to its logical conclusion without it becoming obvious that it is untrue. Transubstantiation is an impossible, inexplicable mystery because it is not true. "The priest toucheth not Christ's natural body with his hands, by your own doctrine; . . ."[70] If this were true it means a Christian "must believe that it is no more bread, but the very body of Christ, flesh, blood and bone, even as he went here on earth, save his coat: for that is here yet; I wot not in how many places."[71]

The Lutherans did not accept the Roman Catholic position that the sacrament was a sacrifice because the bread and wine were changed into the body and blood of Christ; Tyndale wrote they believed

> Christ dieth no more now, and therefore is no more sacrificed. Neither do we properly offer him to God. But he in his mortal flesh offered himself for us to God the Father, and purchased therewith a general pardon for ever. And now doth God the Father proffer him, and giveth him to us. And the priests, in God's stead, proffer him and give him unto the people."[72]

Tyndale joined these two together, and criticised transubstantiation and consubstantiation in the same way, "The chief hold and principal anchor that the two first have, is these words, 'This is my body: This is my blood.' " They allege Christ's words in John 6,

> which they draw and wrest to the carnal and fleshly eating of Christ's body in the mouth, when it only meaneth of this eating by faith. . . . But truth it is, that the righteous liveth by his faith; ergo, to believe and trust in Christ's blood is the eating that there was meant, as the text well proveth.[73]

Tyndale was firmly in the Reformed position regarding the presence of Christ in the Lord's Supper, but as we will see he does not follow the Zwinglian position. It is his own interpretation of the scriptures which gives this aspect of the Lord's Supper its meaning in Tyndale's theology.

> Zwingli can therefore speak of a sacrament as the sign of a grace that has been given. The signs make their appeal to the senses, but what they signify must already be present to the mind or soul.[74]

Zwingli was concerned with the sacramental meaning of the bread and wine,

> The bread is no longer common, but consecrated. It is called bread, but it is also called the body of Christ. Indeed, it is in fact the body of Christ, but only in name and signification, or, as we now say, sacramentally.[75]

This emphasis is modified slightly in Tyndale who wrote,

> When the priest hath once rehearsed the testament of our Saviour thereon, I look not on bread and wine, but on the body of Christ broken, and blood shed for my sins; and by that faith am I saved from the damnation of my sins.[76]

In other words, the bread and the wine are transformed spiritually in the heart and mind of the true recipient of the sacrament. For

> the words mean no more but only that we believe, by the things that are there shewed, that Christ's body was broken and his blood shed for our sins, if we will forsake our sins and turn to God to keep his law.[77]

For the stress Tyndale puts on the sacraments is that they are "our memorials and signs of remembrance only; and he that giveth in his heart more to them than that, is an image-servant."[78] This is similar to the thought of the writer of *Wycklyffes Wycket* where we read, "The bread is the figure or the remembrance of Christ's body in earth, and therefore Christ said. As oft as ye do this thing do it in remembrance of me. Luke xxii."[79]

We find Tyndale links both the deliverance of the children of Israel from bondage in Egypt, and the Passover, and the Christian's deliverance from bondage to Satan, with the shedding of Christ's blood. The first Passover meal was eaten, before the deliverance of the Children of Israel from bondage in Egypt, as "a seal of the promise to be delivered the same night,"[80] even as at the Last Supper, Christ pointed forward, saying, "My passion that is at hand, and blood that now shall shortly be shed; by the which ye shall be delivered out of the power of Satan, sin, and hell."[81] As we turn to Tyndale's doctrine of the Lord's Supper, we have to go back in time from the events of Good Friday to the Upper Room on the night of his betrayal. It is there on that Thursday evening that we can understand the meaning of the Lord's Supper. Christ was in the room, sharing with his disciples the Passover meal. "And the paschal lamb was a memorial of their deliverance out of Egypt only."[82] Then Christ, on

> the night before his passion, when he had eaten Pesah with his disciples, he said, 'I will no more eat of it henceforth, till it be fulfilled in the kingdom of God.' . . . But it hath yet another signification, hitherto unknown unto you, which must be fulfilled spiritually in the kingdom of God by my passion. . . . Neither was it the lamb's blood that delivered you then: . . . but the blood of Christ (whom that lamb figured, and described his innocence, pureness, and obedience to his Father, and compassion to mankind-ward, . . .[83]

At that Paschal meal in the Upper Room "neither the sacrifices of the old law which prophesied the sacrificing of Christ, neither yet our redemption, was fulfilled that night. For if the scriptures and prophecies were then fulfilled, and we then redeemed, Christ died on the morrow in vain."[84] Therefore Tyndale asked More, "If it were then the very sacrificing of Christ's body, . . . why was he sacrificed so cruelly on the morrow?"[85] The Lord's Supper teaches us the memorial of Christ, our paschal lamb, who shed his blood for us, (1 Corinthians, 5),[86] and Christ commanded his disciples "This do in remembrance of me."[87]

The memorial aspect of the Lord's Supper was important for Tyndale; God ordained it in order that we might remember and not forget what Christ has done for us. Therefore, the sacraments "can be no service to God in his person; but memorials unto men, and a remembrance of the testament, wherewith God is served in the spirit."[88] To give greater signification to it and to help us remember Christ's blood was shed for us we need "red wine, the more lovely to represent it."[89] The fact that we were to remember Christ's death on the Cross was one reason why Tyndale said the papists were wrong in calling the Lord's Supper a sacrifice, for

> a sacrifice is the slaying of the body of a beast, or a man: wherefore, if it be a sacrifice, then is Christ's body there slain, and his blood there shed: but that is not so. And therefore it is properly no sacrifice, but a sacrament, and a memorial of that everlasting sacrifice once for all, which he offered upon the cross now upon a fifteen hundred years ago.[90]

After quoting from 1 Corinthians 11 and Luke 22, Tyndale wrote, "Here ye see again that it was instituted to keep the death of Christ in mind; and to testify wherefore he died, even to save us from sin, death and hell." As the remedy against the serpent's bite was

> to go and behold the brasen serpent; . . . even so, if the sting of death, which is sin, have wounded the soul with the working of the law in the consciences, there is none other remedy than to run to Christ, which shed his blood . . . for the remission of our sins.[91]

Christ "instituted the sacrament of his body and blood, to keep us in remembrance of his body-breaking and blood-shedding for our sins."[92] Therefore, as Christ, at his Last Supper, told his disciples to pray to their loving Father, so we are able to go to him boldly, "as of a most loving and merciful father, above all the mercy of fathers"[93] and "offer for their sins the sacrifice of Christ's blood, and the fat of his mercies in the fire of their prayers; and in the confidence of that sacrifice go in boldly to God their father."[94]

The apostles[95] and Paul[96] received and passed on the Lord's Supper as Christ instituted it, and it is with this simplicity the sacrament should be celebrated. Tyndale believed that it was good

> that men come to the church on the Sundays, to hear God's word, and to receive the sacrament of the body and blood of Christ, in remembrance of his benefits, and so to strengthen thy soul for to walk in his love, and in the love of our neighbour for his sake.[97]

For Tyndale believed that there were benefits for the Christian in the receiving of the sacrament because "true sacraments . . . preach us God's word,"[98] teaching those who partook of the sacrament "the promises and testament" of God.[99]

> And even so our sacraments . . . preach Christ unto us, and lead our faiths unto Christ; by which faith our sins are done away, and not by the deed or work of the sacrament. . . . Nevertheless the sacraments cleanse us, and absolve us of our sins, as the priests do in preaching of repentance and faith."[100]

Faith, as always in Tyndale's theology, is one of the keys to understanding the meaning of the sacraments. God delighted in the faith of his people Israel when they offered sacrifices "for a sure token and earnest of the mercy of God, certified by that sign, that God loved them. . . . as we should be certified by the sacrament of God with us for Christ's death that is past."[101] Although the sacrament is a visible sign for us, the eating and drinking what matters is in the heart and not the mouth, for "where the heart then believeth in Christ, there dwelleth Christ in the heart; though there be no bread in the heart, neither yet in the maw."[102]

"The true worshipping of the sacrament is to believe that it is a true sign that Christ suffered death for us." But Paul, and the other apostles, "say not, Pray to it, neither put any faith therein. For I may not believe in the sacrament, but I must believe the sacrament, . . . which is the only worshipping of the sacrament."[103] This worship must be directed to our Father in heaven, for Christ "taught not his disciples to direct the prayer to the Father in him, . . . neither lift he up his eyes, or prayer, to his Father in the sacrament, but to his Father in heaven."[104]

Our faith makes the sacrament effective for "the sacrament of the body and blood of Christ hath a promise annexed, . . . 'this is my blood, that is shed for many, unto the forgiveness of sins."[105] This means "that the sacrament is an absolution of our sins, as often as we receive it, where it is truly taught and understood, and received aright."[106]

When we partake of the sacrament we "shew the Lord's death until he come."[107] For Paul continues,

> Whosoever shall eat of this bread or drink of the cup of the Lord unworthily, shall be guilty of the body and blood of the Lord. . . . [W]hoso receiveth the sacrament of the body and blood of Christ with an unclean heart, not forsaking the old lusts of the flesh, nor purposing to follow Christ, and to be to his neighbour as Christ was to him, only merciful; the same sinneth against the body and blood of Christ; in that he maketh a mock of the earnest death of Christ, and, as it is written Hebrews the tenth, 'treadeth Christ under foot, and counteth the blood of the testament wherewith he was sanctified as an unholy thing.

This unbelief has led to many ceremonies being invented because of the "unquiet, scrupulous, and superstitious nature of man, wholly given to idolatry."[108]

The Lord's Supper has an important place within the doctrine of the Church to "keep his testament ever fresh in mind" and

> to strength our faith, and to certify our conscience, that our sins were forgiven, as soon as we repented and had reconciled ourselves unto our brethren, and to arm our souls, through the continual remembrance of Christ's death.

Then as a congregation "knit together in one faith and love to eat the Lord's supper, (as Paul calleth it); for the congregation, thus gathered, is called Christ's body and Christ their head."[109]

Tyndale spent much time showing the differences between his doctrine of the sacraments and those of others, supporting his theology by scripture. He showed that the medieval Church had lost the signification of the sacraments and that they "teach a man to trust in dumb ceremonies, and sacraments, in penance, and all manner works that come them to profit; which yet help not unto repentance, nor to faith, nor to love a man's neighbour."[110]

The Five False Sacraments

Tyndale wrote that matrimony,[111] orders,[112] penance and confession,[113] confirmation,[114] and anoiling, "The sacraments, which they have imagined, are all without promise, and therefore help not."[115] In fact, they are not sacraments because the spiritualty "had taken away the signification and very intent of the sacrament, to establish the ear-confession, their merits, deservings, justifying of works, and like invention, unto their own glory and profit."[116]

All the Reformers accepted that Christ had appointed only two sacraments, but they had different views regarding the validity of the other five. In fact, as we will see, Luther accepted Confession as a sacrament.

Marriage

Marriage, for Luther, was one of the "holy orders and true religious institutions established by God."[117] In the same way Tyndale described it as "a state or degree ordained of God, and an office wherein the husband serveth the wife, and the wife the husband."

As, however, it had not a promise attached to it, it ought "not to be called a sacrament."[118] Luther wrote, "Neither is there any need to make sacraments out of marriage and the office of the priesthood."[119] Tyndale and Luther were in complete agreement over the place of marriage in the Church.

Orders

Tyndale wrote, "Subdeacon, deacon, priest, bishop, cardinal, patriarch, and pope, be names of offices and service, or should be, and not sacraments."[120] Here Tyndale and Luther are in agreement.[121]

Confession

Tyndale differed from Luther over confession, which is another of the reasons why More said that Tyndale was more heretical than Luther.[122] Luther wrote,

> I have a high regard for private confession, for here God's word and absolution are spoken privately and individually to each believer for the forgiveness of his sins, and as often as he desires it he may have recourse to it for this forgiveness.[123]

In *The Large Catechism,* Luther wrote, "therefore when I exhort you to go to confession, I am doing nothing but exhorting you to be a Christian."[124]

Tyndale agreed with the statement of Wyclif, "it seems that it is not needful, but brought in late by the fiend;"[125] when he wrote, "Shrift in the ear is verily a work of Satan and that the falsest that ever was wrought and that most hath devoured the faith."[126] Tyndale also wrote, "Through confession they quench the faith of all the promises of God, and take away the effect and virtue of all the sacraments of Christ."[127]

Confirmation

Tyndale believed that, although it is not a sacrament, Confirmation has an importance. It is to "put us in remembrance of the promises which God hath made unto us in Christ."[128] Also, the child who was baptized needed to be taught the Christian faith by the parish priest for about five years, then, after examination by the Archdeacon, have his baptism confirmed and be admitted to the Lord's Supper.[129]

Tyndale's idea of teaching and examination, before the child 'confirms' its baptismal promises, differs from Luther who wrote, "It is sufficient to regard confirmation as a certain churchly rite or sacramental ceremony, similar to other ceremonies."[130]

Unction

Luther wrote, "If unction were practiced in accordance with the gospel, Mark 6[:13] and James 5[:14], I would let it pass. But to make a sacrament out of it is nonsense."[131] Tyndale points out prayer is the important thing stressed and not the ceremony attached to it; "the prayer of faith shall heal the sick.' Where a promise is, there is faith bold to pray, and God true to give her her petition. Putting on of the hands is an indifferent thing."[132] But Tyndale was scathing about *extreme unction,* for it was "without promise, and therefore without the Spirit, and without profit; but altogether unfruitful and superstitious."[133] Here again we find agreement between Tyndale and Luther.

Summary

Tyndale was concerned that the covenantal signs should be restored to their original meaning, purified of man-made changes and additions which took from them their God-given purpose. He wrote of the five so-called sacraments of the unreformed Church, "The sacraments, which they have imagined, are all without promise, and therefore help not. For 'whatsoever is not of faith is sin.' Rom. xiv. Now without a promise can there be no faith."[134] The same is true of the Roman Church's doctrine of baptism and the Lord's Supper where they have "lost the true faith in the covenant made in Christ's blood and body: which covenant is that which saveth."[135]

Tyndale believed that there were only two sacraments instituted by Christ and that proclaimed the covenant of God's love. The two true sacraments were baptism and the Lord's Supper for they preached the promises of God which faith can take hold of and find, through them, God as a loving Father.

> Then come we to the sacraments, where thou seest that the work of a sacrament saveth not; but the faith in the promise, which the sacrament signifieth, justifieth us only. There hast thou that a priest is but a servant, to teach only; and whatsoever he taketh upon him more than to preach and to minister the sacraments of Christ (which is also preaching) is falsehead.[136]

Here we see that Tyndale differed from Luther, who wrote, "Thus two sacraments remain, baptism and the Lord's Supper, along with the gospel, in which the Holy Spirit richly offers, bestows, and accomplishes the forgiveness of sins."[137]

Baptism and the Lord's Supper were signs of the covenant, which had been disfigured and marred by the Church beyond all recognition, and the five so called sacraments were false inventions to deceive the people. Tyndale would have agreed with the words of Peter Martyr Vermigli, published thirty years after Tyndale's martyrdom at Vilvoorde,

> We have parted company with those who have soiled the sacraments and invented others which were never instituted by Christ, lacerating those that he did originate and bequeath, defiling them in many and varied illicit ways.[138]

Notes

1. Tyndale, William, *Sacraments*, p. 1/357
2. Tyndale, William, *Sacraments*, p. 1/359
3. Tyndale, William, *Sacraments*, p. 1/348
4. Tyndale, William, *Sacraments*, p. 1/350
5. Tyndale, William, *Sacraments*, p. 1/354
6. These statements will be justified later in this chapter as we expound Tyndale's theology.
7. Noll, Mark, A., *Confessions and Catechisms of the Reformation*, p. 72
8. Tyndale, William, *Exposition Matthew*, p. 2/12
9. Tyndale, William, *Sacraments*, p. 1/380, 368f
10. More, Thomas, *Dialogue . . . ,CWM-6*, p. 431. "And ouer this he sayd yt he had sene of Luthers owne wordys worse than he had euer herde rehersed / and in Tyndall worse yet in many thyngys than he sawe in Luther hym selfe."
11. Bucer, Martin, *Regno Christi*, in Pauck, Wilhelm, *Melanchthon and Bucer*. p. 236
12. Bucer, Martin, *Regno Christi*, p . 237
13. Zwingli, Huldrych, *Baptism*, in Bromiley, G.W., *Zwingli and Bullinger*, p. 138
14. Zwingli, Huldrych, *Baptism*, p. 131
15. Tyndale, William, *Answer*, p. 3/29
16. Arnold, Thomas, *Select English Works of John Wyclif, Sermon CLXXVII*. p. 2/112. "And of *th*is fleish and *th*is blood, in his kynde, speki*th* *th*e gospel, and of *th*e goostli eetyng *th*at men moten eten *th*is. *Th*e breed of *th*e sacrid oost is verry breed in his kynde, and is eten bodili; but it is Goddis bodi in figure. . . . but *th*is oost is eten bodili and goostli of sum men, but Cristis bodi in his kynde is not eten bodili."
17. Hudson, Anne, *The Premature Reformation*, p. 285
18. Tyndale, William, *Prologue Genesis*, p. 1/409
19. Tyndale, William, *Sacraments*, p. 1/354
20. Tyndale, William, *Answer*, p. 3/30
21. Tyndale, William, *Jonas*, p. 1/459
22. Tyndale, William, *Exposition Matthew*, p. 2/91
23. Tyndale, William, *Answer*, p. 3/29
24. Tyndale, William, *Prologue Hebrews*, p. 1/524
25. Tyndale, William, *Answer*, p. 3/7
26. Tyndale, William, *Exposition Matthew*, p. 2/91
27. Tyndale, William, *Obedience*, p. 1/273
28. Tyndale, William, *Prologue Leviticus*, p. 1/422f
29. Tyndale, William, *Prologue Genesis*, p. 1/409
30. Tyndale, William, *Obedience*, p. 1/283
31. Tyndale, William, *Exposition 1 John*, p. 2/196
32. Tyndale, William, *Obedience*, p. 1/256f
33. Tyndale, William, *Prelates*, p. 2/324
34. Tyndale, William, *Answer*, p. 3/27
35. Mayotte, Judith M., "William Tyndale's Contribution to the Reformation in England," p. 133
36. The importance of Christ's blood in Baptism is more fully covered in my article,

"Tyndale's use of the Blood of Christ in the meaning of Baptism," *Churchman, 1994-3,* pp. 213-221
37. Tyndale, William, *Sacraments,* p. 1/349
38. Tyndale, William, *Sacraments,* p. 1/359
39. Tyndale, William, *Prologue Leviticus,* p. 1/425,426
40. Tyndale, William, *Prologue Leviticus,* p. 1/426
41. Tyndale, William, *Sacraments,* p. 1/350
42. Tyndale, William, *Obedience,* p. 1/253
43. Tyndale, William, *Exposition Matthew,* p. 2/11f (quote 2/12)
44. Tyndale, William, *Exposition 1 John,* p. 2/173
45. Tyndale, William, *Pathway,* p. 1/26
46. Tyndale, William, *Pathway,* p. 1/27
47. Tyndale, William, *Exposition 1 John,* p. 2/136
48. Tyndale, William, *Answer,* p. 3/98
49. Tyndale, William, *Exposition 1 John,* p. 2/140
50. Tyndale, William, *Prologue Matthew,* p. 1/469
51. Tyndale, William, *Exposition 1 John,* p. 2/138f
54. Tyndale, William, *Exposition 1 John,* p. 2/144
53. Tyndale, William, *Exposition Matthew,* p. 2/12
54. Tyndale, William, *Exposition Matthew,* p. 2/13
55. Tyndale, William, *Exposition1 John,* p. 2/160f (quote 2/161)
56. Tyndale, William, *Jonas,* p. 1/462
57. Tyndale, William, *Prologue Numbers,* p. 1/433
58. Tyndale, William, *Jonas,* p. 1/465
59. Tyndale, William, *Exposition 1 John,* p. 2/174
60. Tyndale, William, *Exposition1 John,* p. 2/219
61. Tyndale, William, *Exposition 1 John,* p. 2/216f
62. Tyndale, William, *Jonas,* p. 1/459
63. Tyndale, William, *Sacraments,* p. 1/350
64. Tyndale, William, *Answer,* p. 3/71
65. Tyndale, William, *Answer,* p. 3/71f
66. Tyndale, William, *Answer,* p. 3/149
67. Tyndale, William, *Sacraments,* p. 1/366f
68. Tyndale, William, *Sacraments,* p. 1/367
69. Tyndale, William, *Exposition Matthew,* p. 2/130
70. Tyndale, William, *Answer,* p. 3/162f
71. Tyndale, William, *Obedience,* p. 1/278
72. Tyndale, William, *Sacraments,* p. 1/370
73. Tyndale, William, *Sacraments,* p. 1/368f. Tyndale's statement was possibly more general, and ignored Luther's position, "The sixth chapter of John must be entirely excluded from this discussion, since it does not refer to the sacrament in a single syllable." Luther, *LW-36,* p. 19.
74. Stephens, Peter, *Theology of . . . Zwingli,* p. 188
75. Zwingli, *Exposition of the Faith,* in Bromiley, G.W., *Zwingli and Bullinger,* p. 263
76. Tyndale, William, *Answer,* p. 3/178
77. Tyndale, William, *Sacraments,* p. 1/368
78. Tyndale, William, *Exposition 1 John,* p. 2/216

79. Pantin, Tho. P., *Wycliffes Wycket*, p. xiiii. "The breade is the fygure or mynde of Christes bodye in earth, and therfore Christe sayde. As oft as ye do thys thynge do it in mynde of me. Lu. xxii."
80. Tyndale, William, *Sacraments*, p. 1/354
81. Tyndale, William, *Sacraments*, p. 1/355
82. Tyndale, William, *Answer*, p. 3/65
83. Tyndale, William, *Sacraments*, p. 1/355
84. Tyndale, William, *Sacraments*, p. 1/371
85. Tyndale, William, *Answer*, p. 3/178
86. Tyndale, William, *Answer*, p. 3/85
87. Tyndale, William, *Obedience*, p. 1/252 (Luke 22): *Answer*, p. 3/177
88. Tyndale, William, *Answer*, p. 3/56
89. Tyndale, William, *Sacraments*, p. 1/383
90. Tyndale, William, *Prologue Leviticus*, p. 1/424
91. Tyndale, William, *Sacraments*, p. 1/356f
92. Tyndale, William, *Answer*, p. 3/73
93. Tyndale, William, *Answer*, p. 3/120
94. Tyndale, William, *Exposition 1 John*, p. 2/210
95. Tyndale, William, *Answer*, p. 3/85
96. Tyndale, William, *Answer*, p. 3/96f
97. Tyndale, William, *Exposition 1 John*, p. 2/188
98. Tyndale, William, *Answer*, p. 3/89
99. Tyndale, William, *Prelates*, p. 2/291
100. Tyndale, William, *Prologue Leviticus*, p. 1/423
101. Tyndale, William, *Sacraments*, p. 1/382
102. Tyndale, William, *Sacraments*, p. 1/369
103. Tyndale, William, *Answer*, p. 3/180 (Marginal Note and Text)
104. Tyndale, William, *Sacraments*, p. 1/382f
105. Tyndale, William, *Obedience*, p. 1/252
106. Tyndale, William, *Sacraments*, p. 1/357
107. Tyndale, William, *Sacraments*, p. 1/365
108. Tyndale, William, *Sacraments*, p. 1/366
109. Tyndale, William, *Exposition 1 John*, p. 2/218
110. Tyndale, William, *Answer*, p. 3/194
111. Tyndale, William, *Obedience*, p. 1/254
112. Tyndale, William, *Obedience*, p. 1/254f
113. Tyndale, William, *Obedience*, p. 1/260f
114. Tyndale, William, *Obedience*, p. 1/273
115. Tyndale, William, *Obedience*, p. 1/275f
116. Tyndale, William, *Exposition 1 John*, p. 2/222
117. Luther, Martin, *Works*, vol 37, p. 364. ". . . are these three: the office of priest, the estate of marriage, the civil government."" Tyndale disagreed with Luther's about the civil government being a "true religious institution."
118. Tyndale, William, *Obedience*, p. 1/254
119. Luther, Martin, *Works* vol 37, p. 370
120. Tyndale, William, *Obedience*, p. 1/254f
121. Luther, Martin, *Works*, vol 37, p. 364
122. More, Thomas, *Dialogue . . .* , *CWM-6*, p. 424-6

123. Luther, Martin, *Works* vol 37, p. 368
124. Luther, Martin, *Book of Concord,* p. 479
125. Matthew, F.D., *English Works of Wyclif* . . . , p. 328. "it seme*th th*at it is not nedful, but broug*h*t in late be *th*e fend."
126. Tyndale, *Obedience,* p. 1/263
127. Tyndale, William, *Obedience,* p. 1/337
128. Tyndale, William, *Obedience,* p. 1/273
129. Tyndale, William, *Answer,* p. 3/71f
130. Luther, Martin, *Works,* vol 36, p. 92
131. Luther, Martin, *Works,* vol 37, p. 370
132. Tyndale, William, *Obedience,* p. 1/275
133. Tyndale, William, *Obedience,* p. 1/275
134. Tyndale, William, *Obedience,* p. 1/275f
135. Tyndale, William, *Sacraments,* p. 1/385
136. Tyndale, William, *Obedience,* p. 1/342
137. Luther, Martin, *Works,* vol 37, p. 370
138. *Peter Martyr Vermigli Library,* vol-1, 221

8

The Covenant in Action

Introduction

The covenant, as we have seen, was made between God the Father, God the Son, and God the Holy Spirit, and the Holy Spirit's responsibility in the covenant is to apply God's plan for man's salvation to the elect. It is with the work of the Holy Spirit as he brings life to God's chosen and makes them the children of God that *The Covenant in Action* is concerned. Even if Tyndale does not mention the Holy Spirit in every case, the work of the Holy Spirit underlies every aspect of the Christian's life and bears witness that he is a Child of God. The outworking of the covenant in our lives shows the truth of our Christianity, "The assurance that we are sons, beloved, and heirs with Christ, and have God's Spirit in us, is the consent of our hearts unto the law of God. Which law is all perfection, and the mark whereat all we ought to shoot."[1] For Tyndale the summary of the law contains all that is necessary for our perfect obedience to the commandments of God,

> The kingdom of God is to love God with all thine heart, and to put thy whole trust in him according to the covenant, made in Christ: and for Christ's sake to love thy neighbour as Christ loved thee, and all this is within thee.[2]

The question of man's freewill, which exercised the Reformers, did not create a problem for Tyndale; for Christ is "the lord of freewill; which only through his grace maketh the will free, and looseth her from bondage of sin, and giveth her love and lust unto the laws of God, and power to fulfil them."[3] A man who is dead has no will, whilst a man who is alive has. Therefore, he believed that while our salvation depended on God, it equally depended on us. Both statements are true, and there is no contradiction here if we follow God's word, for what seems irrational to man's reason becomes plain when we listen to God and not to the pagan philosophers, as Tyndale makes clear in his gloss on *Deuteronomy* 4; "Ye shall put nothing unto the word which I command you." "No: nor yet corrupt it with false glosses to confirm Aristotle: but rebuke Aristotle's false learning therewith."[4]

Luther denied that man had freewill; he wrote, "Paul, writing to the Romans, enters upon his argument for the grace of God against 'freewill'." He quotes *Romans* 1:18 then continues,

> Do you hear this general judgement against all men, that they are under the wrath of God? What does this mean, but that they merit wrath and punishment? . . . Where now is the power of 'freewill' to endeavour after some good?[5]

After considering many scriptural passages which appear to require man to have freewill, Luther wrote: "But as 'freewill' is not proved by any of the other words of mercy or promise of comfort, so neither is it proved by this: 'I desire not the death of a sinner', etc."[6]

Tyndale believed that God's word had to be taken at its face value and he would have agreed with Erasmus when he wrote of those texts, (*Matthew* 11.28, etc) "These seem empty and vain if they all refer to necessity. The same is true of the threats in the Gospels, . . ." (*Matthew* 7.16, etc.), "What he means by fruits are works, and he calls them ours. But they are not ours if they all happen by necessity."[7]

It is when we examine the work of the Holy Spirit in applying the covenant to the elect that we see how we change from not having freewill as fallen man to having freewill as the chosen children of God. We will also see how Tyndale breaks with most theologians over the new birth and, at the same time, is enabled to reconcile scriptures which seem to present two different theologies concerning man's freewill.

Tyndale has three areas where we can see the covenant in action. Firstly, in the salvation of God's chosen ones we see God's love and mercy at work. Secondly, in the covenant the Holy Spirit works bringing the elect from death to life, giving them the power to respond to the Father's love so that through repentance and faith they become God's children. Thirdly, the Holy Spirit enables the child of God to show the power of God in his life of love to God and to his neighbour. According to Tyndale every single step in the Christian's journey is marked by the Holy Spirit applying the blood of Christ to his heart and life so that, purified and cleansed, he is able to grow and develop as a child of God. The blood of Christ is all important for "this new and gentle testament, . . . as it is a better testament, so is it confirmed with a better blood, to make men see love, to love again, and to be a greater confirmation of the love promised."[8]

The Mercy of God

For Luther it is God's wrath rather than God's love which opens the way for man to receive God's mercy. "God is still seen as instigating man's humiliation, even if man himself must cooperate with God if this humiliation is to be properly effected."[9] Tyndale believed that the law brought us to know God's wrath, but man was not humiliated by this knowledge before he could find mercy.

> Like wise when God's law hath brought the sinner into knowledge of himself, and hath confounded his conscience, and opened unto him the wrath and vengeance of God: then cometh good tidings. The Evangelion showeth unto him the promises of God in Christ, and how that Christ hath purchased pardon for him, hath satisfied the law for him; and peaced the wrath of God. And the poor sinner believeth, laudeth and thanketh God, through Christ; and breaketh out into exceeding inward joy and gladness, for that he hath escaped so great wrath, so heavy vengeance, so fearful and so everlasting a death.[10]

For Tyndale it is the mercy and the love of God alone which activates the covenant in the hearts and lives of those chosen to be God's children:

> That is to say, for the favour that God hath to his Son Christ, he giveth unto us his favour and good will, as a father to his sons. As affirmeth Paul, saying: which loved us in his beloved before the creation of the world. For the love that God hath to Christ, he loveth us, and not for our own faith. Christ is made Lord over all; and is called in Scripture God's mercy stool: whosoever flieth to Christ can neither bear nor receive of God any other thing save mercy.[11]

Tyndale's doctrine of faith was that salvation did not depend on "our own faith" but on the faith which is given to us by the Holy Spirit: a faith grounded in God's eternal covenant which is ours by God's grace. "The treasure of his mercy was laid up in Christ for all that should believe, before the world was made; *ergo,* nothing that hath happened since hath changed the purpose of the invariable God."[12]

It is, therefore, God's will that decides who is to be chosen for his mercy. In his "Preface" to what is known as *The Cologne Fragment,* Tyndale wrote,

> By grace (that is to say, by favour) we are plucked out of Adam, the ground of all evil; and grafted into Christ, the root of all goodness. In Christ God loved us, his elect and chosen, before the world began, and reserved us unto the knowledge of his Son and of his holy Gospel. And when the Gospel is preached to us, he openeth our hearts, and giveth us grace to believe; and putteth the Spirit of Christ in us; and we know him as our Father most merciful. . . . The blood of Christ hath obtained all things for us of God. Christ is our satisfaction, redeemer, deliverer, Saviour from vengeance and wrath."[13]

Tyndale picks up and develops this in *Mammon,*

> In Adam are we all, as it were, wild crab-trees, of which God chooseth whom he will, and plucketh them out of Adam, and planteth them in the garden of his mercy, and stocketh them, and grafteth the Spirit of Christ in them, which bringeth forth the fruit of the will of God; which fruit testifieth that God hath blessed us in Christ.[14]

The Holy Spirit applies the covenant to the elect and brings God's mercy to him. He raises God's chosen ones from death to life, liberating them from bondage to the devil, and the Holy Spirit gives to the elect a repenting faith. It is to this first work of the Holy Spirit that we now turn.

The New Birth

Man is (as we have seen)[15] nailed, glued and chained to the devil's will. He is dead in sin, separated from God and unable to do anything pleasing to God. As far as doing any good works which are pleasing to God he is powerless and has no freewill to love and obey God's laws. Until he has been given a new life, the passages of scripture which teach that man has no freewill apply. To change man's position is the work of the Holy Spirit.

Tyndale placed the new birth as the first step in man's salvation; man had to be brought from death to life before anything else could happen.[16] This is the work of the Holy Spirit, and Tyndale quotes Christ's words in *John* 3:6, "'That which is born of the flesh is flesh, and that which is born of the Spirit is spirit,' as who should say, He that hath the Spirit through faith, and is born again, and made anew in Christ, understandeth the things of the Spirit, and what he that is spiritual meaneth."[17] Tyndale inserted a passage of over 300 words into his supposed 'translation' of Luther's *Preface to Romans,* to 'correct' Luther's doctrine. After a long passage about man's inability to do anything because of his bondage to Satan, he continues,

> The Spirit must first come, and wake him out of his sleep with the thunder of the law, and fear him, and shew him his miserable estate and wretchedness; and make him abhor and hate himself, and to desire help; and then comfort him again with the pleasant rain of the gospel, that is to say, with the sweet promises of God in Christ, and stir up faith in him to believe the promises. Then, when he believeth the promises, as God was merciful to promise, so is he true to fulfil them, and will give him the Spirit and strength, both to love the will of God, and to work thereafter. So

> we see that God only, who, according to the scripture, worketh all in all things, worketh a man's justifying, salvation, and health; yea, and poureth faith and belief, lust to love God's will, and strength to fulfil the same, into us, even as water is poured into a vessel; and that of his good will and purpose, and not of our deservings and merits.[18]

We see the difference between Tyndale and Luther in an earlier change Tyndale made to Luther's *Preface to Romans*. Tyndale changes Luther's, "Faith, . . . brings with it the Holy Spirit," into "Right faith is a thing wrought by the Holy Ghost in us."[19]

Neither is this stress that Tyndale puts on this initial work of the Holy Spirit found in the Swiss Reformers. Their doctrine of the Fall and the state of fallen man, and their theology of the covenant are different from Tyndale's; furthermore, they had not repudiated Greek philosophy in the way Tyndale had.

The difference between Tyndale and other Reformers is very slight but highly significant, and it depends on whether justification by faith is due to our new birth as a child of God (Tyndale) or through a legal process. It is like the difference expressed in Acts over Roman citizenship, "The chief captain answered, With a great sum obtained I this freedom. And Paul said, But I was free born."[20] It is only after the Holy Spirit has brought the elect to life and that life has been accepted can we find any signs of common ground between Tyndale and the other Reformers.[21] For Christ came

> to give us a new birth, a new nature, and to sow new seed in us, that we should, by the reason of that birth, sin no more. For the seed of that birth, that is to wete the Spirit of God and the lively seed of his word sown in our hearts, keepeth our hearts, that we cannot consent to sin.[22]

> God of his grace only, quickened us in Christ; and raised us out of that death. . . . We are, in this our second birth, God's workmanship and creation in Christ; so that, as he which is yet unmade hath no life nor power to work, no more had we, till we were made again in Christ. The preaching of mercy in Christ quickened our hearts through faith wrought by the Spirit of Christ, which God poured into our hearts, ere we wist.[23]

But there had to be a response on our part to God's mercy, "And thus, as the Spirit and doctrine on God's part, and repentance and faith on our part, beget us anew in Christ."[24] But, for Tyndale, our repentance and faith is also a work of the Holy Spirit, which we take hold of because we have been brought from death to life.

Repentance and Faith

Once one is born again and made alive we find in Tyndale's theology that there is a co-operation between the Holy Spirit and the child of God as one's Christian life begins. Because of this working together between God and the elect, Tyndale sometimes wrote as if repentance and faith were ours alone, and sometimes as if it were the work of the Holy Spirit alone. It is in the context of Tyndale's covenant theology that both are seen to be equally true. Also, we find that Tyndale often changes the order of faith and repentance because they are so entwined that it is not possible to separate repentance from faith – although faith covers every aspect of our Christian life and not just repentance.

Luther formulated the doctrine of *justification by faith* as the basis for the Reformation of the Church. While this doctrine was followed by Tyndale and the other Reformers, we find that their underlying theologies of man's salvation gave them different understandings of the meaning of that phrase. By giving justification a legal meaning Luther and the Continental Reformers put it into opposition to the wrath of God, as Luther wrote, "One ought to remember that repentance and law belong to the common faith. For one must of course first believe that God is the one who threatens, commands, and frightens, etc."[25] For Tyndale our justification came through being born into God's family, and we see God the Father with "a lovely and amiable countenance."[26]

Unlike Tyndale the other Reformers did not have the same emphasis on the blood of Christ. Luther usually linked repentance and faith with Christ's death on the Cross and the sacrament of Holy Communion. Tyndale's emphasis on Christ's blood is not found in Zwingli or the Swiss Reformers although Calvin (some ten years after Tyndale's martyrdom) wrote on Hebrews 9:20:

> The promises of God are then only profitable to us when they are confirmed by the blood of Christ. For what Paul testifies in 2 Cor. i.20, that all God's promises are yea and amen in Christ – this happens when his blood like a seal is engraven on our hearts, or when we not only hear God speaking, but also see Christ offering himself as a pledge for those things which are spoken.[27]

In his *Answer to Sir Thomas More's Dialogue* there is a detailed passage where Tyndale told his reader to "Mark therefore, the way toward justifying, or forgiveness of sin, is the law." As the law is revealed to the sinner he would despair if God did not help him, but God "setteth his son Jesus before me, and all his passion and death." God pointed out that through Christ's death the sinner has been saved, and Christ has prayed for him so that the sinner's heart softens and begins to submit and love God's law.

Tyndale then explains the order of these events. Out of our knowledge of the law and our sin comes repentance which is

> a light that the Spirit of God hath given me. . . . Then the same Spirit worketh in mine heart trust and confidence, to believe the mercy of God and his truth. . . . And immediately out of that trust springeth love toward the law of God again.

But it is not repentance, faith or love which justify us

> For we love not God first, to compel him to love again; but he loved us first, and gave his Son for us, that we might see love and love again. . . . Hereof ye see what faith it is that justifieth us. The faith in Christ's blood, of a repenting heart toward the law, doth justify us only.[28]

This justifying faith comes to us from the Holy Spirit, for "Faith is the work of God only, even as was the raising up of Christ."[29] It is in his *Prologue to Romans* that we find Tyndale writing of faith being both our work and also the work of the Holy Spirit.

> Now is the Spirit none otherwise given, than by faith only, in that we believe the promises of God without wavering, how that God is true, and will fulfil all his good promises towards us for Christ's blood's sake, . . . even as we believe the glad tidings preached to us, the Holy Ghost entereth into our hearts, and looseth the bonds of the devil, . . . All our justifying then cometh of faith, and faith and the Spirit come of God, and not of us. When we say, faith bringeth the Spirit, it is not to be understood, that faith deserveth the Spirit, or that the Spirit is not present in us before faith: for the Spirit is ever in us, and faith is the gift and working of the Spirit.[30]

What seems in that passage to be confusing can be understood as we put it in the context of Tyndale's theology and the power of the gospel.

> The gospel is every where one, though it be preached of divers, and signifieth glad tidings; that is to wit, an open preaching of Christ, and the holy testament and gracious promises that God hath made in Christ's blood to all that repent and believe.[31]

For Tyndale the beginning of repentance occurs when we admit that we are sinners and that we are unable to do anything about our sinfulness unless God makes a way of escape for us. To acknowledge our sin is foreign to our nature and repugnant to us[32] until our conscience is awakened by the Holy Spirit. Then the Holy Spirit empowers us to respond to the Father's love, revealed through the preaching of the gospel, as Tyndale wrote,

> When a true preacher preacheth, the Spirit entereth the hearts of the elect, and maketh them feel the righteousness of the law of God, and by the law the poison of their corrupt nature; and thence leadeth them, through repentance, unto the mercy that is in Christ's blood; and as an ointment healeth the body, even so the Spirit, through confidence and trust in Christ's blood, healeth the soul, and maketh her love the law of God.[33]

Tyndale believed the unwillingness of fallen man to accept his position led the Church to invent all kinds of means to allow man to find his own righteousness. Confession, the sacraments, idolatry, ceremonies, and good works are some of the ways people have sought to make God propitious to them.

> All these are faithless; for they follow their own righteousness, and are disobedient unto all manner righteousness of God; both unto the righteousness of God's law, wherewith he damneth all our deeds . . . and also unto the righteousness of the truth of God in his promises, whereby he saveth all that repent and believe them.[34]

In *Jonas* Tyndale expressed man's inability to become righteous by his own efforts in an uncompromising way:

> And with whatsoever holiness thou wilt, save with the holiness of God's word; which only speaketh unto the heart, and sheweth the soul his filthiness and uncleanness of sin, and leadeth her by the way of repentance unto the fountain of Christ's blood, to wash it away through faith. By the reason of which false righteousness they were disobedient unto the righteousness of God, which is the forgiveness of sin in Christ's blood, and could not believe it. And so, through fleshly interpreting the law, and false imagined righteousness, their hearts were hardened, and made as stony as clay in a hot furnace of fire, that they could receive neither repentance nor faith, or any manner of grace at all.[35]

Peter with the other disciples had come to realise that Jesus was more than a man, that he was the Christ, the Son of God; however, they did not understand what this sonship meant.

> But now it is opened throughout all the world, that, through the offering of his body and blood, that offering is a satisfaction for the sin of all that repent, and a purchasing of whatsoever they can ask, to keep them in favour; and that they sin no more. And Christ answered, "Upon this rock I will build my congregation:"

> that is, upon this faith. And against the rock of this faith can no sin, no hell, no devil, no lies, nor error prevail."[36]

It was only after his death and resurrection that the disciples realised the truth of Christ's life and his purpose in becoming man.

> He took our nature upon him, and felt all our infirmities and sicknesses, and in feeling learned to have compassion on us, and for compassion cried mightily in prayers to God the Father for us, and was heard. And the voice of the same blood that once cried, not for vengeance as Abel's, but for mercy only, and was heard, crieth now and ever, and is ever heard, as oft as we call unto remembrance with repenting faith, how that it was shed for our sins.[37]

The faith that justifies us in the sight of God is not our own but is given to us by God through the working of the Holy Spirit. "Now doth the scripture ascribe both faith and works, not to us, but to God only, to whom they belong only, and to whom they are appropriate, whose gift they are, and the proper work of his Spirit."[38] Faith is not a mere belief but it is active to change us, to give us life, and motivate us to serve God. As Tyndale wrote,

> Right faith is a thing wrought by the Holy Ghost in us, which changeth us, turneth us into a new nature, and begetteth us anew in God, and maketh us the sons of God, as thou readest in the first of John; and killeth the old Adam, and maketh us altogether new in the heart, mind, will, lust, and in all our affections and powers of the soul; the Holy Ghost ever accompanying her, and ruling the heart. Faith is a lively thing, mighty in working, valiant, and strong, ever doing, ever fruitful; so that it is impossible that he who is endued therewith should not work always good works without ceasing.[39]

In this way we see God's covenant at work within our lives as the Holy Spirit gives us both repentance and the saving faith we need to begin our new life as God's children. Then we can do those good works that are pleasing to God for

> the Spirit of him that hath made us safe is in us: yea, and as God, through preaching of faith, doth purge and justify the heart, even so through working of deeds doth he purge and justify the members, making us perfect both in body and soul, after the likeness of Christ.[40]

In fact the Holy Spirit opens the heart to receive Christ.[41] Tyndale quotes *Ephesians* 3, "That he would give them his riches to be strengthened with his Spirit, that Christ may dwell in their hearts through faith." He then continues, "Where the heart then believeth in Christ, there dwelleth Christ in the heart."[42] For Tyndale the Holy Spirit changes the heart, not only in respect of our faith and as a measure of our repentance, but also he gives the Christian a love for all the laws and commandments of God; he also makes the elect righteous in God's sight. For as

> the Spirit entereth the heart, and looseth the heart, and giveth lust to do the law, and maketh the law a lively thing in the heart. Now as soon as the heart lusteth to do the law, then are we righteous before God, and our sins forgiven.[43]

However, our righteousness as Christians is not our own, but the righteousness of Christ who dwells in our hearts, for "Christ is also called our righteousness, to certify us that when we have no righteousness of our own, yet that his righteousness is given us, to make satisfaction for our unrighteousness."[44]

Love to God and our Neighbour

When God has attributed Christ's righteousness to us, we are confirmed in our faith and the outworking of our faith in our lives can be seen. "The assurance that we are sons, beloved, and heirs with Christ, and have God's Spirit in us, is the consent of our hearts unto the law of God." Then the law of God becomes a target for us to aim at with the whole of our being, heart, soul, power, and might,[45] and our love becomes the true love of a child to his father, and to his family.

> When we love God and his law, then we love the sons of God. Which is this-wise proved: The love of God is to keep the law of God: by the text, before and after, the law of God is to love our neighbours; and therefore if we love God, in keeping his laws, we must needs love the sons of God.[46]

Our faith takes hold of all God's promises and realises our Father's love and all that it means to us, and so Tyndale was able to write about the "faith in Christ's blood":

> Another conclusion is this: to believe in Christ for the remission of sins, and, of a thankfulness for that mercy, to love the law truly: that is to say, to love God that is the Father of all and giveth all; and Jesus Christ, that is Lord of us all, and bought us all, with all our hearts, souls, power, and might; and our brethren for our Father's sake (because they be created after his image), and for our Lord and master Christ's sake, because they be the

> price of his blood; and to long for the life to come, because this life cannot be led without sin. These three points (I say) are the profession and religion of a christian man, and the inward baptism of the heart, signified by the outward washing of the body. And they be that spiritual character, badge, or sign, wherewith God, through his Spirit, marketh all his immediately and as soon as they be joined to Christ, and made members of his church by true faith.[47]

This passage shows Tyndale's realism in that "this life cannot be lived without sin," which is why we need continually to repent and to rely on Christ's righteousness alone. It also teaches that it is through loving God with our whole being, and loving our neighbour for God's sake we fulfil the law and show our faith. "If we felt the love of God in Christ's blood, we could not but love again, not only God and Christ, but also all that are bought with Christ's blood."[48]

It is as the Holy Spirit applies the covenant of God to our lives that we are able to do those good works which are pleasing to God.

> Christ's Spirit is poured into us, to bring forth good works, and our works are the fruits of the Spirit; and the kingdom is the deserving of Christ's blood; and so is faith, and the Spirit, and good works also."[49]

These good works are a sign that we love God and his commandments.

> For scripture teacheth, first repentance, then faith in Christ, that for his sake sin is forgiven to them that repent; then good works, which are nothing save the commandment of God only. And the commandments are nothing else save the helping of our neighbours at their need, and the taming of our members, that they might be pure also, as the heart is pure through hate of vice and love of virtue, as God's word teacheth us: which works must proceed out of the faith; that is, I must do them for the love which I have to God for that great mercy which he hath shewed me in Christ, or else I do them not in the sight of God.[50]

Our Christian love is demonstrated by the works that we do. Tyndale taught the true meaning of Christian works as they reflected, through us, the love of God for others.[51] "The works declare love: and love declareth that there is some benefit and kindness shewed, or else would there be no love."[52] For this reason Tyndale laid a great stress on loving our neighbour. As we show this love in our deeds, we bring glory to God. "We do our duty unto our neighbour therewith, and help their necessity unto our own comfort also, and draw all men unto the honouring and praising of God."[53]

Tyndale's answer to the lawyer's question in *Luke* 10, "And who is then my neighbour?" was as revolutionary as Christ's reply in the "Parable of the Good Samaritan."[54] Anyone in need is a neighbour, whoever he is, the poor or rich; another Christian or a heathen; friend or enemy, even a "Turk"[55] or anyone who did not believe in the blood of Christ for salvation was, for Tyndale, a neighbour who needed our help.

Loving our neighbours is not always convenient for us, and there can be many reasons we give as excuses for not loving them. It can also appear to be inappropriate for us to show a love to our neighbour because they do not believe in Christ, or they do not live in our neighbourhood. Tyndale is quite firm in his statements that everyone created by God is our neighbour.[56]

Firstly, "Thy friends are the poor, which are now in thy time, and live with thee; thy poor neighbours which need thy help and succour."[57] By loving them we are showing that we are following our Saviour's example:

> Christ became poor to make other men rich, and bound to make other free. He left also with his disciples the law of love. Now love seeketh not her own profit, but her neighbour's: love seeketh not her own freedom, but becometh surety and bond to make her neighbour free.[58]

Loving one's neighbour also means that the Christian has the responsibility to witness to his neighbour of God's love and the power of Christ's blood for the forgiveness of sins and to correct our lives.

> For if thou study not to amend thy neighbour, when he sinneth, so are thou partaker of his sins; and therefore, when God taketh vengeance and sendeth whatsoever plague it be, to punish open sinners, thou must perish with them."[59]

Secondly, Tyndale had a worldwide view of the neighbourhood which reached out to all in need. It was a vision which reached across all barriers which separate one man from another. He wrote about those who did not have faith in God through Christ and those who worshipped other gods, for our neighbour is not only our fellow Christian, or those we like. Tyndale wrote,

> If thy neighbours which thou knowest be served, and thou yet have superfluity, and hearest necessity to be among the brethren a thousand miles off, to them art thou debtor. Yea, to the very infidels we be debtor, if they need, as far forth as we maintain them not against Christ, or to blaspheme Christ.[60]

"What faith receiveth of God through Christ's blood, that we must bestow on our neighbours, though they be our enemies."[61] This love, shown towards our enemies, also means we cannot obey "any man's commandment unto the hurt of my neighbour that hath not deserved it, though he be a Turk."[62] (This commandment did not mean that a Christian was not to oppose aggression by an enemy, but that a Christian should not be an aggressor.[63]) Lying behind all this stress, on neighbourly love, is the fact that "a man ought to love his neighbour equally and fully as well as himself, because his neighbour (be he never so simple) is equally created of God."[64]

Loving our neighbour had, for Tyndale, an evangelistic purpose. He would not have a Christian show neighbourly love from a humanitarian point of view because that would not be to the glory of God.

> I am bound to love the Turk with all my might and power; yea, and above my power, even from the ground of my heart, after the ensample that Christ loved me; neither to spare goods, body, or life, to win him to Christ. And what can I do more for thee, if thou gavest me all the world? Where I see need, there can I not but pray, if God's Spirit be in me.[65]

God makes his sun to shine on the good and the evil, and the rain to fall on the righteous and unrighteous;[66] and as God shows his love in this way it must be the same with his children who should be able to say, "Them that are good I love, because they are in Christ; and the evil, to bring them to Christ."[67] For Tyndale, the task of the Christian is to follow our Father's example.

Tyndale sums up what it means to love our neighbour in these words:

> Lift up thine eyes unto thy heavenly Father, and as thy Father doth, so do thou love all thy Father's children. He ministereth sun and rain to good and bad; by which two understand all his benefits: for of the heat and dryth of the sun, and cold and moist of the rain, spring all things that are necessary to the life of man. Even so provoke thou and draw thine evil brethren to goodness, with patience, with love in word and deed; and pray for them to him that is able to make them better and to convert them. And so thou shalt be thy Father's natural son, and perfect, as he is perfect."[68]

Because there are those who want to put a terminal point to our showing love to our neighbour, Tyndale went along with their request and placed it beyond any hope of reaching it.

> When thy neighbour hath shewed thee more unkindness than God hath love, then mayest thou hate him, and not before; but must love him for God's sake, till he fight against God, to destroy the name and glory of God."[69]

Good Works

The Continental Reformers, because of their federal understanding of justification, found a link between God's law and good works. Although Tyndale would agree with the Continental Reformers that without faith we cannot do good works and that they brought glory to God, the legal aspect of the law was replaced with the child's obedience to its Father's will. We have already seen that Tyndale disagreed with Luther's judgement on the *Epistle of James* that it was "really an epistle of straw."[70] Tyndale gave it the same importance, regarding good works, in his writings that we find in Lollardy. Behind this disagreement lies their understanding of the covenant. The forensic covenant of the Lutheran and the Swiss Reformers gave a totally different and more formal approach to good works than we find in Tyndale. Tyndale's familial covenant showed that the Christian, as a child of God, does good works naturally because he has been born anew into God's family.

Tyndale disagreed with those who considered some works to be more important than others, and in his Marginal Notes to *Matthew* 10, he wrote, "Compare deed to deed, so is one greater than another: but comapre them to God; so are they all like, and one as good as another. Even as the Spirit moves a man, and time and occasion allows."[71] It is from God's viewpoint that we have to consider the value of the works which a man does. Therefore, the real test of works lies in whether we are true children of God and our works are empowered by the Holy Spirit.

> Moreover, put no difference between works; but whatsoever cometh into thy hands that do, as time, place, and occasion giveth, and as God hath put thee in degree, high or low. For as touching to please God, there is no work better than another. God looketh not first on thy work as the world doth, as though the beautifulness of the work pleased him as it doth the world, or as though he had need of them. But God looketh first on thy heart, what faith thou hast to his words, how thou believest him, trustest him, and how thou lovest him for his mercy that he hath shewed thee: . . . Set this ensample before thine eyes. Thou art a kitchen-page, and washest thy master's dishes; another is an apostle, and preacheth the word of God. Of this apostle hark what Paul saith, in the 1st Cor. ix. 'If I preach,' saith he, 'I have nought to rejoice in, for necessity is put unto me;' as who should say, God hath made me so."[72]

Tyndale continues with this theme,

> Now if thou compare deed to deed, there is a difference betwixt washing of dishes, and preaching of the word of God; but as touching to please God, none at all: for neither that nor this pleaseth, but as far forth as God hath chosen a man, hath put his Spirit in him, and purified his heart by faith and trust in Christ.[73]

For Tyndale every work that we do must be done in obedience to God's will for nothing else can be acceptable to God. We will also see that Tyndale takes this same position in his doctrine of Christian worship.

At the same time Tyndale allowed Christians to do things that he believed to be wrong, provided they were done with the right motive and in ignorance. He applied this principle to most of the ceremonies and objects of the worship in the Roman Church and to pilgrimages – which Tyndale condemned as false. One of the examples Tyndale gives us is:

> If (for an example) I take a piece of the cross of Christ, and make a little cross thereof, and bear it about me, to look thereon with a repenting heart at times when I am moved thereto, to put me in remembrance that the body of Christ was broken, and his blood shed thereon, for my sins; and believe stedfastly that the merciful truth of God shall forgive the sins of all that repent, for his death's sake, and never think on them more: then it serveth me, and I not it; and doth me the same service as if I read the testament in a book.[74]

But a use (which might be acceptable in that way) easily degenerates into misuse, for "how is it possible that the people can worship images, relics, ceremonies and sacraments, save superstitiously?"[75] Tyndale believed that true teaching which would enable the people to know the right use of these aids to worship would, at the same time, make them unnecessary.[76]

As we consider Tyndale's attitude to the use of aids to worship, we must always bear in mind that for Tyndale the relationship between God and man is not a judicial one, but the relationship between a Father and his child. Loving parents do not punish their children who thought they were doing something good and helpful, even when it had the opposite effect. But in their acceptance of their child's actions they use it to teach their child the right way. It is in this way that God teaches Christians so that they can grow and move away from those false props of a Christian life.

Although when thinking about good works we are concerned with Christ's words, "love your neighbour," we cannot separate this commandment from loving God with our heart, soul, strength and mind.

For unless we love God with the whole of our being we cannot love our neighbour as we love ourselves. Tyndale quotes Luke 10:27 – which leads into the "Parable of the Good Samaritan". In discussing the important teaching of this parable, Tyndale wrote, "Neighbour is a word of love; and signifieth that a man should be ever nigh, and at hand, and ready to help in time of need."[77] He showed the falseness of interpreting the "two pence" as "*opera supererogationis*" (that is, a work which is greater than God requires of us). Tyndale continued,

> A greater perfection than to love God and his will, which is the commandments, with all thine heart, with all thy soul, with all thy strength, with all thy mind, is there none: and to love a man's neighbour as himself, is like the same.[78]

As we will see when dealing with the errors of the Church, Tyndale had strong grounds for rejecting the view that works, especially the rites and actions of the Church, merited anything from God. Those who thought that their works merited anything or were, in themselves, righteous acts, were deceived. Tyndale wrote,

> Thou mayest not think that our deeds bless us first, and that we prevent God and his grace in Christ; as though we, in our natural gifts, and being as we were born in Adam, looked on the law of God, and of our own strength fulfilled it, and so became righteous, and then with that righteousness obtained the favour of God.[79]

Therefore Tyndale asked, "Are these works not against Christ? How can they do more shame unto Christ's blood?"[80]

Firstly, Tyndale pointed out that the idea of a works-righteousness, "wherein philosophers put their felicity and blessedness," stemmed from the pagan philosophy of Aristotle.[81] Secondly, that it does not recognise that the law is spiritual and demands perfection.[82] Thirdly, it trusts in self and not in God.[83] Fourthly, "It were too great a shame, rebuke and wrong unto the faith, yea, to Christ's blood, if a man would work any thing to purchase that, wherewith faith hath endued him already."[84] Tyndale sums it all up as follows:

> Now is this a plain conclusion, that both they that trust in their own works, and they also that put their confidence in their own opinions, be fallen from Christ, and err from the way of faith that is in Christ's blood, and therefore are none of Christ's church, because they be not built upon the rock of faith.[85]

Yet there are many places in the scriptures which appear to support the idea that good works are meritorious in the way the medieval Church believed. There are many places where Tyndale raises the issue,

> What shall we say then to those scriptures which go so sore upon good works? As we read Matt. xxv., 'I was an hungred, and ye gave me meat,' &c. and such like. Which all sound as though we should be justified, and accepted unto the favour of God in Christ, through good works. Thiswise answer I: Many there are, which when they hear or read of faith, at once they consent thereunto, and have a certain imagination or opinion of faith: . . . They think no farther than that faith is a thing which standeth in their own power to have, or do other natural works which men work; but they feel no manner working of the Spirit, neither the terrible sentence of the law, the fearful judgements of God, the horrible damnation and captivity under Satan.[86]

Tyndale quotes *James* 2:17, "Faith, without deeds is dead, in itself." He then expounds this, "He meaneth none other thing than all the scripture doth; how that faith, which hath no good deeds following, is a false faith, and not the faith that justifieth, or receiveth forgiveness of sins."[87] More had quoted James as support for the medieval Church's position, and Tyndale's reply was, "And as for that he allegeth out of the epistle of James, for the justifying of works, I have answered in the Mammon, against which he cannot hiss and will speak more in the fourth book."[88]

There are positive reasons behind Tyndale's doctrine of works, and, as we would expect, these all depend on Tyndale's covenant theology. We have to start with the Fatherhood of God if we are to understand what good works are.

> For the favour that God hath to his Son Christ, he giveth unto us his favour and good-will, and all gifts of his grace, as a father to his sons. As affirmeth Paul, saying, "Which loved us in his Beloved before the creation of the world." So that Christ bringeth the love of God unto us, and not our own holy works.[89]

Therefore, we realise that it is

> not that our works make us the sons of God, but testify only, and certify our consciences, that we are the sons of God; and that God hath chosen us, and washed us in Christ's blood; and hath put his Spirit in us."[90]

It is in obedience to God's law that the Christian does good works for,

> The right Christian man consenteth to the law that it is righteous, and justifieth God in the law, for he affirmeth that God is righteous and just; which is Author of the law. He believeth the

> promises of God, and so justifieth God; judging him true and believing that he will fulfil his promises. with the law he condemneth himself and all his deeds; and giveth all the praise to God. Thus everywhere justifieth he God and praiseth God.."[91]

Although the law demands perfection, the Christian is imperfect and in our works we sin

> of infirmity and frailty of our flesh; which flesh not only letteth us, that our works cannot be perfect, but also now and then, through manifold occasions and temptations carrieth us clean out of the right way, spite of our hearts.[92]

However, when we, as God's children, return to our Father with repenting hearts and "we call unto remembrance with repenting faith, how that" Christ's blood "was shed for our sins,"[93] then those sins are forgiven.

> So that, according unto this present text of John, if it chance us to sin of frailty, let us not despair; for we have an advocate and intercessor, a true attorney with the Father, Jesus Christ, righteous towards God and man, and [he] is the reconciling and satisfaction for our sins.[94]

For "Whatsoever is our own, is sin. Whatsoever is above that, is Christ's gift, purchase, doing and working."[95] Having got that straight we can now understand Tyndale's position regarding works.

If we are to be able to understand what God understands about good works, we must turn from Aristotle and other pagan philosophers and turn to the scriptures for the answer. Tyndale wrote: "many have enforced to draw the people from the true faith, and from putting their trust in the truth of God's promises, and in the merits and deserving of Christ, our Lord." They have "brought them in belief that they shall be justified in the sight of God by the goodness of their own works,"[96] and turn to the scriptures for the answer.

> They that do good are first born of God, and receive of his nature and seed; and, by the reason of that nature and seed, are first good ere they do good, by the same rule. And Christ, which is contrary to the devil, came to destroy the works of the devil in us, and to give us a new birth, a new nature, and to sow new seed in us, that we should, by the reason of that birth, sin no more. For the seed of that birth, that is to wete the Spirit of God and the lively seed of his word sown in our hearts, keepeth our hearts, that we cannot consent to sin.[97]

It is from this new birth comes our love to God and to our neighbour – out of which love our good works spring.

There are many different ways in which good works show themselves in the Christian's life. The clergy should teach the laity about

> alms, prayer, and fasting, which are the whole life of a christian man, and without which there is no christian man alive. And let them preach the true use of their alms, which is to help thy neighbour with counsel, with body and goods, and all that is in thy power; and the true use of prayer, which is to bring his necessity and thine own before God, with a strong faith in his promises; and the true use of fasting, which is to tame the flesh unto the spirit, that the soul may attend to the word of God and pray through faith.[98]

In the normal course of events, prayer and works are combined because both spring out of our love to God and his law. However, there are times when we cannot work and we are prevented from showing our love to our neighbour, but we are still able to pray. "As love maketh thee help me in my need; so when it is past thy power to help, it maketh thee pray to God."[99] And so our faith and our love are not real if we cease to pray for our neighbour especially when we cannot physically help them in their need.

It did not matter who we were, what rank or position in society we held, God's command to love our neighbour as we love ourselves applied. Tyndale was aware of the continuing power of fallen human nature and of the temptations which fall upon us, especially of those who have positions of authority, and he warned that they must not exceed the authority God has given to them. Even though "the king, in the temporal regiment, be in the room of God, and representeth God himself," he must love his subjects as God requires,

> remembering that the people are God's, and not theirs: yea, are Christ's inheritance and possession, bought with his blood. The most despised person in his realm is the king's brother, and fellow-member with him, and equal with him in the kingdom of God and of Christ.[100]

Tyndale emphasised the responsibility God had given to rulers. God had appointed them to govern his world as God's servants. Those who have positions of authority have to pass judgement on those who have done wrong, but they must remember that their judgements must be true.

> Moses (Deut. xvii.) warneth judges to keep them upright, and to look on no man's person; that is, that they prefer not the high before the low, the great before the small, the rich before poor, his acquaintance, friend, kinsman, countryman, or one of his own

> nation, before a stranger, a friend or an alien, yea, or one of their own faith before an infidel; but that they look on the cause only, to judge indifferently.[101]

Here again the reason given is that they are acting on God's behalf. Even though the "Turk or Saracen" is not "under the everlasting testament of God" does not mean they can be treated differently to others, for with all mankind we are "under the testament of the law natural."[102]

Tyndale was not a pacifist, and sometimes the good works a Christian had to do involved violence, but he must never act out of hatred or lack of love. There are three levels which Tyndale recognises. Firstly, we must defend people who are being attacked: "If any man would force thy wife, thy daughter, or thy maid, it is not enough for thee to look on, and say, 'God amend you.'" Secondly, the Christian must defend property which is being attacked.[103] Thirdly, he may have to use violence in the king's service, whether it is helping the king's officer to arrest someone or to help the king defend his realm.[104] The Prince is to be a peacemaker and not start any war, but in defending his land and subjects against aggression he is a peacemaker.[105] The Christian who is called up to serve the king against his enemies must "remember what thou art in the first state with them against whom thou must fight, how that they be thy brethren, and as deeply bought with Christ's blood as thou, and for Christ's sake to be beloved in thine heart."[106]

There are times when a Christian, as he seeks to do good works, is placed in a situation where absolute honesty would either do more harm than good, or where he has to break his word. Tyndale gives examples of both these types of actions. The law of charity must take precedence over our actions if we are being, strictly speaking, untruthful.

> To bear a sick man in hand that wholesome bitter medicine is sweet, to make him drink it, it is the duty of charity, and no sin. To persuade him that pursueth his neighbour to hurt him or slay him, that his neighbour is gone another contrary way, it is the duty of every Christian man by the law of charity, and no sin; no, though I confirmed it with an oath.

However, unless the law of charity dictated that we lie for our neighbour's good, we must be truthful, for "to lie for to deceive and hurt, that is damnable only."[107]

Tyndale also mentions various occasions when promises must be broken because duty or loving our neighbour requires it.

> Howbeit though I vow, and swear, and think on none exception, yet is the breaking of God's commandments except, and all chances that hang of God: as if I swear to be in a certain place at

a certain hour, to make a love-day, without exception, yet if the king in the meantime command me another way, I must go by God's commandment, and yet break not mine oath. And in like case, if my father and mother be sick and require my presence, or if my wife, children, or household be visited, that my assistance be required, or if my neighbour's house be a fire at the same hour, and a thousand such chances; in which all I break mine oath, and am not forsworn, and so forth.[108]

For Tyndale there was only one reason for the Christian to do good works and that was the fact that we are servants of Christ. Our love to our father and mother must be because of the love Christ has shown to us. It is the same with our service to those in authority over us, and we must be able to say to them, "I serve thee, not because thou art my master, or my king, for hope of reward, or fear of pain, but for the love of Christ."[109]

Tyndale gives many examples of good works, often contrasting them with the works the Church thought were good.

Good works are things of God's commandment, wrought in faith; and to sew a shoe at the commandment of God, to do thy neighbour service withal, with faith to be saved by Christ, as God promiseth us, is much better than to build an abbey of thine own imagination, trusting to be saved by the feigned works of hypocrites.[110]

Tyndale differed from Luther and the other Reformers about good works in one respect, and that is found in the relationship we have with our neighbours. Luther wrote, "They are called good works . . . because *God has commanded them, and so they also are well pleasing to God.*"[111] Whilst, for Tyndale the emphasis is different,

If a king minister his kingdom in the faith of this name, *because his subjects be his brethren and the price of Christ's blood, he pleaseth God highly;* and if this faith be not there, it pleaseth him not. And if I sew a shoe truly, in the faith of his name, *to do my brother service, because he is the price of Christ's blood, it pleaseth God.*[112]

God's commandment in Luther has disappeared to be replaced by Tyndale with "the price of Christ's blood."

We have seen that behind Tyndale's concern to love our neighbour lay his evangelistic spirit, and the same is true of our good works.

Now all works done to serve man, and to bring him to this point, to put his trust in Christ, are good and acceptable to God; but, done for any other purpose, they be idolatry and image-service, and make God an idol or bodily image.[113]

Here we see clearly what constantly comes through Tyndale's theology: a clear division between what is right and what is wrong without any blurring of the edges. This clarity would make Christianity impossibly hard and cruel were there not, on the other side, the tender affectionate love of a Father towards his children, and the need to show our filial love to our brothers and sisters who are created by God.

Summary

The covenant in action is the work of the Holy Spirit as he applies the blood of Christ to the hearts and lives of the elect, bringing them from death to life and enabling them to realise they are truly the children of God. Because he has been born again, the Christian is responsible for his actions which spring out of love – loving God with the whole of his being and loving his neighbour as he loves himself. All this is possible through the Holy Spirit applying the blood of Christ to every action he does, both toward God and also neighbour. To the world his faith shows in love and good works, but the motive behind our good works is to glorify God his Father, which leads him to desire the conversion of his neighbour (who is anyone of whatever race, creed or unbelief). Tyndale's evangelistic desire was uppermost in his thoughts, and this was an important aspect of the life of the Church and of a Christian's prayers.

Notes

1. Tyndale, William, *Obedience,* p. 1/300
2. Tyndale, William, *Marginal Notes – Luke 17,* p. N.T./119
3. Tyndale, William, *Prologue Numbers,* p. 1/429
4. Tyndale, William, *Marginal Notes – Deuteronomy 4,* OT/262
5. Luther, Martin, *Bondage,* 273f
6. Luther, Martin, *Bondage,* 167
7. Erasmus, *Freedom,* 60
8. Tyndale, William, *Sacraments,* p. 1/364
9. McGrath, Alister E., *Theology,* 154
10. Tyndale, William, *1525,* p. 9. "Lyke wyse when goodds lawe hath brought the synner into knowlege of him sylfe / and hath co*n*founded his conscience / and opened vnto him the wrath and vengeaunce of god / then co*m*meth good tydings / the Eva*n*gelion sheweth vnto him the promyses of god in Christ / and howe that Christ hath purchesed perdon for him hath satisfied the lawe for him / and peased the wrath of god / and the povre synner beleveth / laudeth and thanketh god / throwe Christ / and breaketh oute into exced*in*ge inward ioy and glad nes / for that he hath escaped so greate wrath / so hevy ve*n*geaunce / so fearfull and so everlastinge a dethe."
11. Tyndale, William, *1525,* p 4.. "That is to saye / for the favoure that god hath to his sonne Christ / he geveth vnto vs his favour / and good will / as a father to his

sonnes. As affirmeth Paul sayinge: whych loved vs in his beloved before the creation of the worlde. for the love that god hath to Christ / he loveth vs / and not for oure awne faith. Christ is made lorde over all / and is called in scripture godds mercy stole whosoever flyeth to Christ / can nether beare nor receave of god eny other thinge save mercy."

12. Tyndale, William, *Tracy,* p. 3/275
13. Tyndale, William, *1525,* p. 7. "By grace (that is to saye by favoure) we are plucked oute of Adam the grounde of all evyll / and graffed in Christ the rote of all goodnes. In Christ god loved vs his electe and chosen / before the worlde beg*an* / and reserved vs vnto the knowlege of his sonne and of hys holy gospell / and when the gospell is preached to vs he openeth oure herrts / and geveth vs grace to beleve and putteth the spirite of Christ in vs / and we knowe hime as oure father moost mercyfull. . . . The bloud of Christ hath obteyned all thi*ngs* for vs of god. Christ is oure satisfaction / redemer / delyverer / saveour from vengeaunce and wrath."
14. Tyndale, William, *Mammon,* p. 1/113
15. see *The Covenant Envisaged,*
16. compare with: Calvin, John, "Catechism of the Church of Geneva", *Tracts and Treatises,* vol 2, p. 55. "But this reward springs from the freee love of God as its source; for he first embraces us as sons, and then burying the remembrance of the vices which proceed from us, he visits us with his favour." Bullinger, Henry, *The Decades . . . Parker Society* vol 3, p. 100f. "he new man, that is, the man which is regenerate by the Spirit of God through the faith of Jesus Christ. Now regeneration is the renewing of the man, by which through the faith of Jesus Christ, we which were the sons of Adam and of wrath, are born again the sons of God."
17. Tyndale, William, *Mammon,* p. 1/111
18. Tyndale, William, *Prologue Romans,* p. 1/498
19. Luther, Martin, *Works,* vol 35, p. 370: Tyndale, William, *Prologue Romans,* p. 1/493
20. Acts 22:28; see also, "While we embrace the promises of the gospel with sure heartfelt confidence, we in a manner obtain possession of the righteousness of which I speak." Calvin, John, "Catechism of the Church of Geneva", *Tracts and Treatises,* vol 2. p. 54.
21. Study along the lines of Trueman, Carl R. and Clark, R.S., *Protestant Scholasticism,* would be profitable comparing the early Reformers' position regarding scholasticism, humanism, Greek philosophy, and scripture from their writings.
22. Tyndale, William, *Exposition 1 John,* p. 2/190
23. Tyndale, William, *Exposition 1 John,* p. 2/199f
24. Tyndale, William, *Pathway,* p.1/27
25. Luther, Martin, "Instructions for the Visitors of Parish Pastors," *Works,* vol 40, p. 274f
26. Tyndale, William, *Exposition Matthew,* p. 2/26
27. Calvin, John, *Hebrews,* 212, see also, "Catechism of the Church of Geneva", *Tracts and Treatises* vol 2. p. 50, "God . . . will also by his Spirit make us capable of this redemption and salvation. . . . As we have purification in the blood of Christ, so our consciences must be sprinkled by it in order to be washed."

28. Tyndale, William, *Answer,* p. 3/195-197
29. Tyndale, William, *Marginal Note, Ephesians 1,* p. N.T./283
30. Tyndale, William, *Prologue Romans,* p. 1/488
31. Tyndale, William, *Obedience,* p. 1/213
32. Tyndale, William, *Exposition 1 John,* p. 2/168
33. Tyndale, William, *Exposition 1 John,* p. 2/183f
34. Tyndale, William, *Mammon,* p. 1/122f
35. Tyndale, William, *Jonas,* p. 1/462
36. Tyndale, William, *Answer,* p. 3/31
37. Tyndale, William, *Exposition 1 John,* p. 2/153
38. Tyndale, William, *Mammon,* p. 1/56
39. Tyndale, William, *Prologue Romans,* p. 1/493
40. Tyndale, William, *Obedience,* p. 1/281
41. The heart has an importance in Tyndale's theology and deserves a fuller treatment than can be given in this dissertation – see Auksi, Peter, "Reason and Feeling", pp. 16-20.
42. Tyndale, William, *Sacraments,* p. 1/369
43. Tyndale, William, *Obedience,* p. 1/308
44. Tyndale, William, *Sacraments,* p. 1/377
45. Tyndale, William, *Obedience,* p. 1/300
46. Tyndale, William, *Exposition 1 John,* p. 2/206, (Comment of ! John 5:1-3)
47. Tyndale, William, *Exposition Matthew,* p. 2/11f
48. Tyndale, William, *Exposition 1 John,* p. 2/200
49. Tyndale, William, *Mammon,* p. 1/83
50. Tyndale, William, *Prologue Numbers,* p. 1/434
51. Mayotte, Judith M., "William Tyndale's Contribution to the Reformation in England", p. 102, Although she wrote of a 'just God' and not a 'Father'.
52. Tyndale, William, *Mammon,* p. 1/59
53. Tyndale, William, *Pathway,* p. 1/24
54. Tyndale, William, *Mammon,* p. 1/85
55. The Turks were the Muslim invaders of Eastern Europe, and the Pope was trying to raise a crusade against them.
56. As we will see later in this chapter, Tyndale would have been happy with our modern phrase, "Global Village."
57. Tyndale, William, *Mammon,* p. 1/66f
58. Tyndale, William, *Obedience,* p. 1/333
59. Tyndale, William, *Exposition Matthew,* p. 2/47
60. Tyndale, William, *Mammon,* p. 1/99.
61. Tyndale, William, *Pathway,* p. 1/20
62. Tyndale, William, *Pathway,* p.1/26
63. Tyndale, William, *Exposition Matthew,* p. 2/26f
64. Tyndale, William, *Pathway,* p. 1/25f
65. Tyndale, William, *Mammon,* p. 1/96
66. Matthew, 5:45
67. Tyndale, William, *Obedience,* p. 1/299
68. Tyndale, William, *Exposition Matthew,* p. 2/71
69. Tyndale, William, *Exposition Matthew,* p. 2/47
70. Luther, Martin, *Works,* vol 35, p. 362

71. Tyndale, William, *1525*, Matthew 10, Margin. "Compare dede too dede / so ys one greater then another: but co*m*pare them to god / so are they all lyke / a*n*d one as good as another. even as the spyrite movyth a ma*n* / & tyme & occasio*n* gevyth."
72. Tyndale, William, *Mammon,* p. 1/100
73. Tyndale, William, *Mammon,* p. 1/102
74. Tyndale, William, *Answer,* p. 3/59f
75. Tyndale, William, *Answer,* p. 3/62
76. Tyndale, William, *Answer,* p. 3/59-64
77. Tyndale, William, *Mammon,* p. 1/85
78. Tyndale, William, *Mammon,* p. 1/86
79. Tyndale, William, *Mammon,* p. 1/112
80. Tyndale, William, *Obedience,* p. 1/284
81. Tyndale, William, *1525,* p. 8; "werein philosophers put there felicitie and blessednes" : *Obedience,* p. 1/155
82. Tyndale, William, *Pathway,* p. 1/15f
83. Tyndale, William, *Pathway,* p. 1/22
84. Tyndale, William, *Mammon,* p. 1/63
85. Tyndale, William, *Answer,* p. 3/33f
86. Tyndale, William, *Mammon,* p. 1/52f
87. Tyndale, William, *Prologue James,* p. 1/525
88. Tyndale, William, *Answer,* p. 3/97. This is further discussed in *The Covenant Broken,*
89. Tyndale, William, *Pathway,* p. 1/11
90. Tyndale, William, *Mammon,* p. 1/72
91. Tyndale, William, *1525,* p. 6. "T[h]e right cristen man consenteth to the lawe that hit is rightwes / and iustifieth god in the lawe / for he affyrmeth that god is rightwes and iuste / which is autor of the lawe / he beleveth the promyses of god / and so iustifieth god / iudgynge hym trewe and beleuinge that he will fulfyll hys promyses. With the lawe he conde*m*neth hym sylfe and all his deds / and geveth all the prayse to god. he beleueth the promyses / and ascribeth all trouth to god / thus every where iustifieth he god and prayseth god." (two misspellings in the text have been corrected.)
92. Tyndale, William, *Exposition 1 John,* p. 2/152
93. Tyndale, William, *Exposition 1 John,* p. 2/153
94. Tyndale, William, *Exposition 1 John,* p. 2/156
95. Tyndale, William, *Pathway,* p. 1/23
96. Tyndale, William, *Mammon,* p. 1/45f
97. Tyndale, William, *Exposition 1 John,* p. 2/190
98. Tyndale, William, *Exposition Matthew,* p. 2/93f
99. Tyndale, William, *Exposition Matthew,* p. 2/42
100. Tyndale, William, *Obedience,* p. 1/202
101. Tyndale, William, *Obedience,* p. 1/203f
102. Tyndale, William, *Obedience,* p. 1/204
103. Tyndale, William, *Exposition Matthew,* p. 2/67
104. Tyndale, William, *Obedience,* p. 1/206
105. Tyndale, William, *Exposition Matthew,* p. 2/26f.
106. Tyndale, William, *Exposition Matthew,* p. 2/63

107. Tyndale, William, *Exposition Matthew,* p. 2/57f
108. Tyndale, William, *Prologue Numbers,* p. 1/440
109. Tyndale, William, *Obedience,* p. 1/296f
110. Tyndale, William, *Prologue Genesis,* p. 1/407
111. Luther, Martin, "Instructions for the Visitors of Parish Pastors" *Works* vol 40, p. 277 *italics, mine*
112. Tyndale, William, *Exposition Matthew,* p. 2/126 *italics mine,*
113. Tyndale, William, *Sacraments,* p. 1/373

9
The Covenant People

Introduction

Although the doctrine of the two kingdoms (the temporal and spiritual regiments) is generally associated with Luther, the separation between Church and State as two parallel authorities goes back to the New Testament. Both Paul and Peter wrote of our Christian duty to obey and pray for kings and rulers. Franz Lau wrote, "The doctrine of the two kingdoms is not specifically a doctrine of Luther's. Other Reformers such as Melanchthon, Zwingli and Calvin have ideas similar to Luther's, but also depart from him in characteristic ways."[1] A common factor binding these together is that the temporal regiment's purpose is to control man's sinfulness. If we compare Luther's and Zwingli's doctrine, "Both maintained that the need for such government is the result of sin. As Zwingli put it, 'If everyone rendered to God what they owed him, we should need neither prince nor ruler – indeed, we should never have left paradise.'"[2] But for Tyndale, the temporal regiment is a creation ordinance because, every society needs some form of government.[3] Unlike the medieval Church, which subordinated the temporal regiment to the spiritual, Tyndale understood them as parallel aspects of the Christian world. All who lived on earth were part of the temporal regiment and were brothers and sisters through creation. The spiritual regiment comprised everyone (laity as well as clergy) who called themselves Christian – whether they were part of God's chosen people or not. The Christian, therefore, belongs to both the temporal regiment (through creation) and the spiritual regiment (through salvation). The authority of the officers in one regiment does not give authority in the other regiment.

> Ye must understand that there be two states or degrees in this world: the kingdom of heaven, which is the regiment of the gospel; and the kingdom of this world, which is the temporal regiment. . . . Now is every person a double person; and under both the regiments. In the first regiment, thou art a person for

> thine own self, under Christ and his doctrine. . . . In the temporal regiment, thou art a person in respect of other; thou art an husband, father, mother, master, mistress, lord, ruler, or wife, son, daughter, servant, subject, &c. And there thou must do according to thine office.[4]

Cargill Thompson highlighted the problem of those who considered Tyndale was a Lutheran, and he followed Clebsch's thesis of supposed changes in Tyndale's theology. In his article, "The Two Regiments", he set out to prove Tyndale's Lutheran credentials, but found many places where fact did not fit his theory. For instance, "Tyndale could well have gained his ideas from any of the French, Swiss or Rhineland reformers."[5] Again, "Nor did he ever act as a slavish disciple, but could be independently minded."[6] Tyndale "probably accepted the Lutheran distinction between the two regiments."[7] "There are problems in the relation of Tyndale's work to Luther's"[8]

We do not have to go to the Continental Reformers for Tyndale's doctrine of the two regiments. There are close similarities between Tyndale's doctrine and that of John Trevisa. In *Dialogus inter Militem et Clericum,* Trevisa wrote that the "first state" is the "temporalte" and the "secunde state" is the "spiritualte". Therefore concerning the pope's rule, "This is not understood for the first state but for the second. For in the first state Christ used no such power, but put it away from him and used only that belongs to the governance of our salvation." For the pope to claim

> that he may take of princes, and of kings, principalities and kingdoms at his own will, and give them to those he likes. But take heed how wrongful it is to do that. . . . Then it is true that he did not receive such great temporal power as Christ, but only the power that Christ used and taught in his earthly life.[9]

The medieval Church had confused these two powers. A large part of *The Practyse of Prelates* deals with the way in which the pope seized power, first in the spiritual regiment and then in the temporal. The pope claimed headship of both the spiritual and temporal regiments. Bishops were officers of the Church and of the State; there was no way of knowing if there was any difference between spiritual and secular. The spiritualty had downgraded God's laws and made them into directions for living,

> They have interpreted here the words of Christ, wherewith he restoreth the law again, to be but good counsels only, but no precepts that bind the consciences. And thereto they have so ruffled and tangled the temporal and spiritual regiment together, and made

> thereof such confusion, that no man can know one from the other: to the intent that they would seem to have both by the authority of Christ, which never usurped temporal regiment unto him.[10]

In fact Christ "ordained rulers, both spiritual and temporal, to teach them and exhort" the people.[11] In doing this, Tyndale wrote, there was made a "clear difference between the spiritual regiment and the temporal."[12] Although the temporal regiment has priority in time, I will begin with the spiritual kingdom and the covenant people.[13] The reason behind this reversal of order is to bring it in line with the common theological position, and to help us understand the full impact of Tyndale's thought in both the spiritual and temporal regiments.

The Spiritual Regiment

The spiritual regiment was, for Tyndale, the people of God; therefore, he translated the Greek word *ekklesia* as congregation. Sir Thomas More accused him of mistranslating *ekklesia* in order to confuse the people. More wrote,

> Now where he calls the church always the congregation, what reason had he in this? For every man clearly sees that although the church is in deed a congregation; yet is not every congregation the church, but a congregation of Christian people. Which congregation of Christian people has always been in England called and known by the name of the church.[14]

Tyndale was, however, concerned that the meaning attached to the word *church* should be understood, for it was used in different ways. People understood the word *church* first of all as a building in which the congregation could meet to worship God. Secondly, the word *church* "is abused and mistaken for a multitude of shaven, shorn, and oiled; which we now call the spiritualty and clergy."[15] By using the word *congregation* Tyndale was pointing out that every Christian was part of the spiritual regiment, clergy and laity alike. Thus the church was the congregation and therefore "the lay people be as well of the church as the priests."[16]

The congregation is the spiritual regiment, and it is divided between those who are and those who are not children of God. "So now the church of God is double, a fleshly and a spiritual: the one will be, and is not; the other is, and may not be so called, but must be called a Lutheran, an heretic, and such like."[17] For, as Christ and Paul taught, there are always the false mixed with the good.[18]

Tyndale picked up the biblical terms of the true church being the remnant, (*Joel* 2:32) or the little flock (*Luke* 12:32) who were faithful to God; in fact "little flock" was one of Tyndale's favourite terms for the elect. He was aware that the majority within the visible Church were not the elect children of God.

> The kingdom of heaven is the preaching of the gospel, unto which come both good and bad. But the good are few. Christ calleth them therefore a "little flock," Luke xii. For they are ever few that come to the gospel of a true intent, seeking therein nothing but the glory and praise of God.[19]

It is in the keeping of the profession of their baptism the little flock is different from the many who nominally follow Christ.[20] It is in the *Prologue* to the *1525 New Testament* that we find the beginning of Tyndale's teaching about the little flock who are chosen and taken out of the mass of fallen mankind. The elect are "plucked oute of Adam."[21] Then when the gospel is preached "the hearts of them which are elect and chosen, begin to wax soft, and to melt at the bounteous mercy of God, and kindness shown of Christ."[22]

However, the spiritual regiment is much wider than the little flock, and it consists of all who belong to the visible Church. The context in Tyndale's writings always reveals whether it is the universal Church or the elect to which he is referring. The word Church

> is sometimes taken generally for all them that embrace the name of Christ, though their faiths be naught, or though they have no faith at all. And sometimes it is taken specially for the elect only; in whose hearts God hath written his law with his holy Spirit, and given them a feeling faith of the mercy that is in Christ Jesu our Lord.[23]

Tyndale does not try to separate the true from the false (although he frequently points out the difference between them). But as everyone who has received the sign of the covenant has been committed to serve God, he stresses the importance of the profession of our baptism as a sign of our election as God's children.[24]

In chapter Seven, we saw the importance and meaning of the sacraments. In the Old Testament the sign of the covenant was circumcision, and this has, since Christ shed his blood for us, been changed to baptism. "And instead of circumcision came our baptism; whereby we be received into the religion of Christ, and made partakers of his passion, and members of his church."[25] Although Tyndale teaches that through baptism we become members of the Church and therefore the spiritual regiment, he understands this membership in a totally different way from the medieval Church. Israel consisted of everyone circumcised, but not all had a true faith in God, and Tyndale quotes

Romans 9:6 and Matthew 22:11,12 to prove that there is a difference between the "carnal" and the "spiritual" Christian.[26]

As we would expect from Tyndale, Christ's blood is important for the Church, and "faith in Christ's blood . . . is also the rock whereon Christ's church is built,"[27] so that the Christian's "rejoicing is that Christ died for him, and that he is washed in Christ's blood."[28] Having been cleansed the Christian can, therefore, go direct to God "in the confidence of Christ's blood."[29]

It is clear that in Tyndale's theology we can never get away from the covenant – the covenant in Christ's blood. Although the spiritual regiment has a greater emphasis on the work of God the Son in man's salvation and God the Holy Spirit in man's spiritual growth and development, behind this is the elective love of God the Father who has chosen them to be His children within the Church.[30]

Contrary to the papists, Tyndale's understanding of "the rock" was, therefore, not Peter but his confession of faith when he said,

> "Thou art Christ, the son of the living God," which art come into this world. This faith is the rock whereon Christ's church is built. For who is of Christ's church, but he only that believeth that Christ is God's Son, come into the world to save sinners? This faith is it, against which hell-gates cannot prevail. This faith is it, which saveth the congregation of Christ.[31]

Tyndale turns to Peter's confession in his *Answer*, after explaining how Christ brought about man's salvation he returns to the text.

> And Christ answered, "Upon this rock I will build my congregation:" that is, upon this faith. And against the rock of this faith can no sin, no hell, no devil, no lies, nor error prevail. . . . For this knowledge maketh a man of the church. And the church is Christ's body (Col. i.); and every person of the church is a member of Christ (Eph. v.). Now it is no member of Christ that hath not Christ's Spirit in it (Rom. viii.), as it is no part of me, or member of my body, wherein my soul is not present and quickeneth it."[32]

The spiritual regiment is the kingdom of Christ, and in every way the rule of Christ is different from the rule of kings in the temporal regiment. Tyndale wrote that "the pope's kingdom is of the world"[33] and was like the kingdoms of the world's rulers.

> But in the kingdom of God it is contrary. For the Spirit that bringeth them thither maketh them willing, and giveth them lust unto the law of God; and love compelleth them to work, and

> love maketh every man's good, and all that he can do, common unto his neighbour's need. And as every man is strong in that kingdom, so love compelleth him to take the weak by the hand, and to help him, and to take him that cannot go upon his shoulders and bear him. And so to do service unto the weaker is to bear rule in that kingdom.[34]

It is in ways like this we see "that Christ's kingdom is altogether spiritual; and the bearing of rule in it is clean contrary unto the bearing of rule temporally."[35]

Prayer and the preaching of God's word are essential marks of the spiritual regiment, or kingdom of Christ, and it is through Christ and the power of the Holy Spirit that the "little flock" is able to grow as children of God in Christ's kingdom.

Christ is the King who reigns and who stirs up the elect to pray and hears their prayers, and "ere they ask, he sendeth his Spirit into their hearts to move them to ask: so that it is his gift that we desire aught in his name."[36] Yet Christ's method of working is that through the preaching of the word of God the Holy Spirit comes upon God's people[37] and does his great work in their lives. "For if the Spirit of Christ," wrote Tyndale,

> with which God anointeth us and maketh us kings, and sealeth us and maketh us his sure and several kingdom, and which he giveth us in earnest (2 Cor. i.), and with which he changeth us into the image of Christ (2 Cor. iii.), dwell in our souls through faith, the same Spirit cannot but quicken the members also, and make them fruitful, (Rom. viii.).[38]

It is as Head of the Church that Christ has given authority to preach the gospel, and their obedience to Christ's commands should be seen in the lives of those who have authority in the spiritual regiment.

> The authority that Christ gave them was to preach; yet not what they would imagine, but what he had commanded "Lo," saith he, "I am with you always, even unto the end of the world." He said not, I go my way, and lo, here is Peter in my stead; but sent them every man to a sundry country, whithersoever the Spirit carried them, and went with them himself.[39]

Officers in the Spiritual Regiment

There has to be order in the spiritual regiment. Therefore, Christ has appointed officers in the Church who must be faithful to the charge they have been given.

> The apostles, following and obeying the rule, doctrine, and commandment of our Saviour Jesus Christ, their master, ordained in his kingdom and congregation two officers; one called, after the Greek word, *bishop,* in English an over-seer; which same was called *priest* after the Greek; elder in English. . . . Another office they chose, and called him *deacon* after the Greek, a *minister* in English., to minister the alms of the people unto the poor and needy.[40]

> Tyndale contended that congregations must have publicly ordained preachers, called by the common ordinance of the congregation. The formal office of ministry does not belong to everyone.[41]

The apostles chose men who were anointed by the Holy Spirit to be bishops or priests, and their job was "to preach God's word."[42] In his First Epistle, Peter taught how "they should love and feed Christ's flock."[43] Whilst Paul wrote to Timothy, "be an ensample to all bishops, what they should teach, and how they should teach; and how they should govern the congregation of Christ in all degrees." The bishop should also "cleave to the gospel of Christ and true doctrine."[44] The choice of bishop or priest was, therefore, important and "the apostles chose priests to preach Christ only, all other things laid apart, and chose none but learned and virtuous."[45] The deacon was chosen by the congregation "to help and assist the priest, and to gather up his duty, and to gather for the poor of the parish."[46]

The important work that the bishop or priest had to do was to preach, and we find Tyndale constantly writing about preaching and the appointment of preachers. The appointment of a preacher lay with the congregation who knew him,[47] for "no man may yet be a common preacher, save he that is called and chosen thereto by the common ordinance of the congregation, as long as the preacher teacheth the true word of God."[48] The preacher, therefore, has to be faithful to God's word if he is not to be rejected by both God and the congregation. Tyndale's commentary on Matthew 5:13 says, "If the preacher, which for his doctrine is called salt, have lost the nature of salt, that is to say, his sharpness in rebuking all unrighteousness, all natural reason, natural wit and understanding, and all trust and confidence in whatsoever it be, save in the blood of Christ; he is condemned of God, and disallowed of all them that cleave to the truth." Tyndale continued that those who do not preach God's word truly, "though they stand at the altar, yet are they excommunicate and cast out of the living church of almighty God."[49] The preacher must not just be salt; another aspect of his work, through his preaching, is that he "comforteth them, and sheweth them the testament of Christ's blood; how that for his sake all that is done is forgiven, and all their weakness shall be taken a worth, until they be stronger, only if they repent, and will submit themselves to be scholars, and learn to keep his law." Then for the true Christian "all is Christ with him, and Christ is his, and he is Christ's."[50]

Here we find Tyndale is echoing the words of Wyclif about the importance of preaching.

> Christ ordained three things to be fulfilled by his apostles. First, that they should go forth into the world and preach his gospel: and, that this should be fruitful to convert very many people. This fruit should remain both in this world and the next.
>
> And therefore Jesus Christ spent most of his time in the work of preaching, and left other works. The apostles followed Christ in preaching, and therefore God loved them.[51]

It is not only through the sermon that preaching takes place; the sacraments also preach the word of God, "Now as a preacher, in preaching the word of God, saveth the hearers that believe; so doth the washing, in that it preacheth and representeth unto us the promise that God hath made unto us in Christ."[52] It is through faithful preaching of the word of God that the Holy Spirit does his work in the hearts and lives of those chosen to be the children of God.

> When a true preacher preacheth, the Spirit entereth the hearts of the elect, and maketh them feel the righteousness of the law of God, and by the law the poison of their corrupt nature; and thence leadeth them through repentance, unto the mercy that is in Christ's blood; and as an ointment healeth the body, even so the Spirit, through confidence and trust in Christ's blood, healeth the soul, and maketh her love the law of God.[53]

Worship

Tyndale believed that Christians should restore the Church building to the importance it had in the past, and to its true purpose.

> First it signifieth a place or house; whither christian people were wont in the old time to resort at times convenient, for to hear the word of doctrine, the law of God, and the faith of our Saviour Jesus Christ, and how and what to pray, and whence to ask power and strength to live godly. For the officer, thereto appointed, preached the pure word of God only, and prayed in a tongue that all men understood: and the people hearkened unto his prayers, and said thereto Amen.[54]

Tyndale constantly stressed that services, as well as the scriptures, should be in the mother tongue so that the people are able to understand what is being said. Tyndale turns to the scriptures to justify this position and wrote, "Paul commandeth that no man once speak in the church, that is, in the congregation, but in a tongue that all men understand, except that there be an interpreter by."[55] In the *Exposition of Matthew,* Tyndale brings all these meanings of *church* together, showing the importance of the building, the task the officers have to perform, and the scope of the worship of God's people.

> For we must have a place to come together, to pray in general, to thank and to cry to God for the common necessities, as well as to preach the word of God in: where the priest ought to pray in the mother tongue, that the name of God may be hallowed, and his word faithfully taught and truly understood, and faith and godly living increased; and for the king and rulers, that God will give them his Spirit, to love the commonwealth; and for peace, that God will defend us from all enemies; for wedering and fruits, that God will keep away pestilence and all plagues.[56]

However, the building itself was not so important, as if God were tied to a particular building or place, for "God so loveth no church, but that the parish have liberty to take it down, and to build it in another place: yea, and if it be timber, to make it of stone, and to alter it at their pleasure."[57] For the real importance of the building is to be a shelter for the congregation when they come together. Tyndale believed that true worship is in the heart, for "the temple wherein God will be worshipped, is the heart of man."[58] Tyndale expresses this aspect more fully in his *Exposition on 1 John,* where he wrote,

> The true believers have the testimony of God in their hearts, and they glorify God, witnessing that he is true. They have the kingdom of God within them; and the temple of God within them; and God in that temple; and have the Son of God, and life through him. And in that temple they seek God, and offer for their sins the sacrifice of Christ's blood, and the fat of his mercies in the fire of their prayers; and in the confidence of that sacrifice go in boldly to God their father.[59]

"Prayer is God's commandment; and where faith is, there must prayer needs be, and cannot be away."[60] This link between faith and prayer is a constant theme with Tyndale, and it is one of the signs of true faith.

> Faith prayeth alway. . . . But blind unbelief prayeth not alway, . . .
> Faith, when she prayeth, setteth not her good deeds before her, . . .

> nor bargaineth with God, . . . But she setteth her infirmities and her lack before her face, and God's promises, . . .[61]

Tyndale's belief that the Old and the New Testaments are one is seen clearly in his teaching on prayer. Before we start to pray, we need a priest to offer a sacrifice to God, even as Aaron did for the Children of Israel.

> Of that manner is Christ a priest for ever; and all we priests through him, and need no more of any such priest on earth, to be a mean for us unto God. For Christ hath brought us all into the inner temple, within the veil of forehanging, and unto the mercy-stool of God, and hath coupled us unto God; where we offer, every man for himself, the desires and petitions of his heart, and sacrifice and kill the lusts and appetites of his flesh, with prayer, fasting, and all manner godly living.[62]

Christ is our advocate who has made "an atonement for sin" and shed his blood for us.

> And the voice of the same blood that once cried, not for vengeance as Abel's, but for mercy only, and was heard, crieth now and ever, and is ever heard, as oft as we call unto remembrance with repenting faith, how that it was shed for our sins.[63]

Thus, a Christian does not need a human intermediary between himself and God; although that did not mean there was no place for the clergy within the Church. Apart from Christ being the Mediator between God and man, there is another reason why the Christian can go directly to God without the help of a human priest – God is our Father, and we are his children.[64] Therefore,

> thou must go to him as a merciful Father; which of his own goodness and fatherly love, that he beareth to thee, is ready to do more for thee than thou canst desire, though thou have no merits, but because he is thy Father.[65]

God has promised to love all his children equally,

> therefore, as every man believeth God's promises, longeth for them, and is diligent to pray unto God to fulfil them, so is his prayer heard; and as good is the prayer of a cobbler as of a cardinal, and of a butcher as of a bishop; and the blessing of a baker that knoweth the truth is as good as the blessing of our most holy father the pope.[66]

It is because God is the Almighty Creator and also our Father that Tyndale could write, "God is no vain name; but signifieth one that is almighty, all merciful, all true and good; which he that believeth will go to God, to his promises and testament, and not follow his own imaginations."[67] When our faith grasps this and we turn to God and claim his promises, and his mercy which is given us for Christ's blood's sake, then we "feel God as a kind and merciful father."[68] This stirs up the Christian to pray, for "where a promise is, there is faith bold to pray,"[69] because "prayer is the longing for God's promises."[70] Christ has promised to all who trust in him for their salvation that "whatsoever we ask in his name, the Father giveth us."[71] In one of his letters written to John Frith, who was in prison waiting to be burnt at the stake, Tyndale wrote, "If the pain be above your strength, remember, 'Whatsoever ye shall ask in my name, I will give it you.' And pray to your Father in that name, and he shall cease your pain, or shorten it."[72] Commenting on this verse (*John* 16:23), Tyndale wrote,

> To ask in the name of Jesus Christ, and according to his will, be both one; and are nothing else but to ask the things contained in the promises and testament of God to us-ward, that God will be our father, and care for us both in body and in soul.[73]

Even though the church building exists to bring all God's people together, the Christian is not tied to certain times nor places in which to pray. In saying "Wheresoever," Christ did not place any restrictions on our prayers. After quoting that verse in *The Answer,* Tyndale wrote, "he saith not in this or that place, or this or that day; but wheresoever and whensoever, as well in the fields as in the town, and on the Monday, as on the Sunday." For God's Spirit dwells in the "hearts of men that love his laws and trust in his promises. And wheresoever God findeth such an heart, there he heareth the prayer, in all places and times indifferently." The one proviso Tyndale adds to that statement is that we need a place "more quiet and still from the rage of worldly businesses."[74]

Although Christ spoke of Christians gathering together for prayer, Tyndale believed that God was as attentive to the prayers of one person as much as he was to the prayers of the congregation. Christ had promised

> that when two or three, or more, agree together in any thing, according to the will of God, God heareth us. Notwithstanding, as God heareth many, so heareth he few, and so heareth he one, if he pray after the will of God, and desire the honour of God.[75]

We are to cast on God our earthly cares, and after quoting many biblical passages to support his argument, Tyndale wrote,

> Whether, therefore, we complain of intolerable oppression and persecution that we suffer, or of the flesh that cumbreth and resisteth the Spirit, God is merciful to hear us and to help us. Seest thou not also, how Christ cureth many, and casteth out devils out of many, unspoken to? how shall he not help, if he be desired and spoken to?[76]

Christ constantly stressed the need of prayer to his disciples, and of Matthew 7:7 this

> heaping of so many words together, 'ask, seek, and knock,' signify that the prayer must be continual; and so doth the parable of the widow, that sued to the wicked judge: and the cause is, that we are ever in continual necessity.[77]

However, Tyndale gives a warning to the Christian, "As for your prayer, it must be according to God's word: ye may not desire God to take vengeance on him whom God's word teacheth you to pity and to pray for."[78] Neither, when we turn to God in prayer, must we prejudge the way God will answer our prayers. As we cast our cares on God, God will fulfil his promise.

> And though it seem never so unlikely, or never so impossible unto natural reason, yet believe stedfastly that he will do it: and then shall he (according to his old use) change the course of the world, even in the twinkling of an eye, and come suddenly upon our giants, as a thief in the night, and compass them in their wiles and worldly wisdom.[79]

Tyndale is also concerned about the different kinds of prayer which we should make to God and that there should be a balance in the prayer life, both of the individual and of the Church.

Since sin is a reality in the Christian's life, there is a need for us to confess our sins. Tyndale was opposed to auricular confession to a priest (as we will see when we examine the errors of the Church[80]), because the Christian has access to God in the same way that a child has to his father, for God "is alway ready and at hand to help us, if we call, as a merciful father and a kind mother."[81] In the Lord's Prayer, Christ "teacheth us daily to repent, and to reconcile ourselves together, and daily to ask God forgiveness. Seeing he commandeth us to ask, we may be bold so to do, and to believe that he will forgive us."[82] For when we have sinned, wrote Tyndale,

> there is none other salve for remedy, than to run to Christ immediately, and to the Father through him; and to say, 'Father I have sinned against thee, and thy godly, holy, and righteous law,

> and against my brother, whom I ought of all right to love, for thy sake, as well as myself: forgive me, O Father, for thy dear son Jesus Christ's sake, according to thy most merciful promises and testament.[83]

There is, however, a condition God places on his forgiving us our sins, "that a man must forgive if he will be forgiven of God."[84] Therefore the only way we can have the assurance of God's forgiveness is by being forgiving ourselves. "Christ maketh thee sure of pardon; for if thou canst forgive thy brother, God hath bound himself to forgive thee."[85] Tyndale links this with mercy, for "to be merciful is lovingly to forgive them that offended thee, as soon as they knowledge their misdoing and ask thee mercy."[86]

This leads the Christian to pray for others, for

> of his own experience he feeleth other men's need, and no less commendeth to God the infirmities of other than his own, knowing that there is no strength, no help, no succour, but of God only. And as merciful as he feeleth God in his heart to himself-ward, so merciful is he to other; and as greatly as he feeleth his own misery, so great compassion hath he on other. . . . And whensoever he seeth occasion, he cannot but pray for his neighbour as well as for himself.[87]

It does not matter who the person is, we are "to pray for all degrees,"[88] and as we seek to help our neighbour we must "pray and trust in God that he will assist thee," then, "when it is past thy power to help, it maketh thee pray to God."[89] Unlike the spiritualty who were paid for their prayers, our prayers must be freely given, wrote Tyndale, for

> to pray one for another are we equally bound, and to pray is a thing that we may always do, whatsoever we have in hand; and that to do may no man hire another, Christ's blood hath hired us already.[90]

Finally, as we pray for others, we must pray for those who do not know the power of Christ's blood to save them. "To be merciful is patiently to long to abide the conversion of sinners with a lusty courage, and hope that God will at the last convert them, and in the mean time to pray instantly for them," and to do what we can to witness to them.[91] And our prayers are not to be limited to those around us,

> For Paul commandeth, 1 Tim. ii. 'to pray for all men and all degrees,' saying that to be 'acceptable unto our Saviour God, which will have all men saved and come to the knowledge of the truth;' that is, some of all nations and all degrees, and not the Jews only.[92]

An important part of prayer is the praise we give to God. The Christian, "with the law he condemneth himself, and all his deeds, and giveth all the praise to God. He believeth the promises, and ascribeth all truth to God: thus, everywhere, justifieth he God, and praiseth God."[93] The grounds for our praise is because God has forgiven us, given us life and made us his people.

> He bought it of his Father dearly, with his blood, yea, with his most bitter death, and gave his life for it. Whatsoever good thing is in us, that is given us freely, without our deserving or merits, for Christ's blood's sake. That we desire to follow the will of God, it is the gift of Christ's blood. That we now hate the devil's will (whereunto we were so fast locked, and could not but love it), is also the gift of Christ's blood; unto whom belongeth the praise and honour of our good deeds, and not unto us.[94]

We need also, wrote Tyndale, to praise God for those who are brought to faith and salvation and acknowledge they are equal to us in God's kingdom.

> If I had wrought the will of God these thousand years, and another had wrought the will of the devil as long, and this day turn and be as well willing to suffer with Christ as I, he hath this day overtaken me, and is as far come as I, and shall have as much reward as I: and I envy him not, but rejoice most of all, as of lost treasure found. For if I be of God, I have these thousand years suffered to win him, for to come and praise the name of God with me. These thousand years I have prayed, sorrowed, longed, sighed, and sought for that which I have this day found; and therefore rejoice with all my might, and praise God for his grace and mercy.[95]

Closely linked with praise is thanksgiving, and there are many things for which we have cause to thank God, for "prayer is, to give God thanks for the benefits received."[96] Then when we have been through great danger, and have been in spiritual turmoil, "when the rage of thy conscience is ceased, and quieted with fast faith in the promises of mercy, then offer with Jonas the offering of praise and thanksgiving."[97]

We pray for ourselves, that God will send us help when needed,[98] for a true faithfulness, and for everything we need in our Christian life. Peter

> exhorteth to fly sin, and to tame the flesh with soberness, watching, and prayer; and to love each other, and to know that all good gifts are of God; and every man to help his neighbour with such as he hath received of God.[99]

Tyndale stressed also the importance of the congregation, and so Christians come together to help and strengthen one another.

> It is a good law that men come to church on the Sundays, to hear God's word, and to receive the sacrament of the body and blood of Christ, in remembrance of his benefits, and so to strengthen thy soul for to walk in his love, and in the love of our neighbour for his sake, &c.[100]

"And on the Sundays God's word should be truly preached."[101]

However important our Sunday worship is (and no one should avoid going to Church if possible), there are occasions when this commandment is overruled. Therefore,

> of the holy day: he knoweth that the day is servant to man; and therefore, when he findeth that it is done because he should not be let from hearing the word of God, he obeyeth gladly; and yet not so superstitiously, that he would not help his neighbour on the holy day, and let the sermon alone for one day.[102]

It is Scripture which tells us the way we should worship God and give him the honour due to him. "The words which the scripture useth, in the worshipping or honouring of God, are these: Love God, cleave to God, dread, serve, bow, pray and call on God, believe and trust in God, and such like."[103] Tyndale believed that we should kneel in prayer and so he wrote,

> worshipping, whether it be in the old Testament or new, understand the bowing of a man's self upon the ground: as we ofttimes, as we kneel in our prayers, bow ourselves, and lie on our arms and hands, with our face to the ground.[104]

The important thing about worship, whether as the congregation or as individuals, is the rightness of our faith and of our lives. "It is the heart, and not the place, that worshippeth God. The kitchen-page, turning the spit, may have a purer heart to God than his master at Church."[105] For our heart must be right with God if our worship is to be acceptable to God. "Christ is now a spiritual substance with his Father, having also a spiritual body; and with the Father to be worshipped, in spirit only."[106]

Conclusion

Although Tyndale dealt with those in the spiritual regiment who were not part of God's family, I have only dealt with the positive side in this section. The negative side will be covered in the next chapter, *The*

Covenant Broken. This *Conclusion*, to a certain extent, is a bridge between the spiritual and the temporal regiments.

Ideally both regiments should be perfect; the breakdown has come through man's sin.[107] As a result, Tyndale, following John (in his *First Epistle*), was exercised about sin and our approach to open sinners.

> Whatsoever sin we see in the world, let us pray, and not despair; for God is the God of mercy. But for the sin to death, which is resisting grace, and fighting against mercy, and open blaspheming of the Holy Ghost, . . . I think that no christian man, if he perceive it, can otherwise pray than as Paul prayed for Alexander the coppersmith, (the 2 Tim. the last,) "that God would reward him according unto his works."[108]

At the same time we must not make too quick or a wrong judgement, for

> Christ commanded, Matt. v. saying, "Love your enemies. Bless them that curse you. Do good to them that hate you. Pray for them that do you wrong and persecute you; that ye may be the children of your heavenly Father."[109]

Therefore Tyndale wrote to the Christian, You must

> after the ensample of Christ humble thyself, forsake and deny thyself, and hate thyself, and cast thyself away, and be meek and patient, and let every man go over thee, and tread thee under foot and do thee wrong; and yet love them, and pray for them, as Christ did for his crucifiers. For love is all; and what is not of love, that is damnable, and cast out of that kingdom.[110]

The outworking of love in our lives is the perfection which Christ calls for.

> Even so provoke thou and draw thine evil brethren to goodness, with patience, with love in word and deed; and pray for them to him that is able to make them better and to convert them. And so thou shalt be thy Father's natural son, and perfect, as he is perfect. The text saith not, Ye shall be as perfect as God; but perfect after his example."[111]

The Temporal Regiment

"It is a curious fact that although Tyndale's importance as the first English protestant political thinker of the sixteenth century has been widely recognised," wrote Cargill Thompson in 1979, "there has been little detailed investigation of his political thought."[112] This judgement has largely remained true over the intervening years. Robert Bast wrote, "In 1523 Luther had defined the relationship between sacred and secular authority by differentiating between Two Kingdoms or Regiments, mutually supportive but each autonomous in its own sphere."[113] Tyndale, however, had a different view of the two regiments; the separation was not as clear cut as it was for Luther. This obscurity means that sometimes in Tyndale's writings it is difficult to discover whether his remarks relate to the spiritual or temporal regiments – or, perhaps more likely, to both. This apparent ambiguity occurs not because Tyndale's thinking was confused, but because the lines between the temporal and the spiritual regiments are not clear cut. If my non-Christian neighbour has need of my help, then, *(in the temporal regiment)* I serve God and go to his aid because we are both created by him; and *(in the spiritual regiment)* I serve God and hope to win my neighbour for Christ. Every action of a Christian is done in both the temporal and the spiritual regiment, and we cannot separate them into two watertight compartments.

Against those who "credit Tyndale with laying the groundwork for the Royal Supremacy," Bruce Boehrer wrote,

> Here again we return to what was for Tyndale the ultimate arbiter of ethics: the word of God as revealed in scripture. Over and above all ordained authorities stood God's word, demanding ultimate obedience. . . . Thus we find that Tyndale's political philosophy, superficially so congenial to the Henricians, diverges from their views at four important points. First, it denies the sanctity of the royal person as distinct from the royal office. Second, it forbids conflation of the spiritual and temporal jurisdictions. Third it authorizes passive resistance to royal decrees that enlightened scriptural interpretation has concluded are sinful. And finally, it elevates such resistance to the status of a Christian duty.[114]

In The Lord's Prayer, Tyndale expounded *Thy kingdom come,*

> That is, seeing thou art king over all, make all to know thee; and make the kings and rulers, which are but thy substitutes, to command nothing but according to thy word, and to them make all subjects obey.[115]

Tyndale continues the same theme at the end of the Lord's Prayer when commenting on *For the kingdom, and the power and the glory, is thine for ever*;

> Let kings, rulers, and officers remember that God is the very king, and refer the honour that is given to them for their offices' sake to him, and humble themselves to him, and knowledge and confess in their hearts, that they be but brethren, and even no better before God, than the worst of their subjects.[116]

The fact that God is the universal king affects the whole of Tyndale's theology of the temporal regiment. In his thinking, God's kingship brings the two regiments together, and we see them running side by side. From his point of view, God is King of the temporal regiment, and headship stems from the creation of man.[117]

> God therefore hath given laws unto all nations, and in all lands hath put kings, governors, and rulers in his own stead, to rule the world through them. . . . Such obedience . . . requireth God of all nations, yea, of the very Turks and infidels.[118]

In considering the temporal kingdom, "Luther's question was what a Christian was supposed to do, whether he had to abandon the world in order to be perfect, or whether and how he also might live out his being a Christian in the world coram deo."[119] In other words, Luther was looking at a post-Fall temporal regiment.

Both regiments are part of God's plan: the spiritual regiment is covenantal; the temporal regiment goes back to creation. As long as there were people on earth, they needed to be governed. It was

> for their sakes also he [the Father] hath ordained rulers, both spiritual and temporal, to teach them and exhort them; to warn them, and to keep occasions from them, that with custom of sin they fall not from their profession.[120]

And God has given rulers an importance since they bear rule for God. "Mark, the judges are called gods in the scriptures, because they are in God's room, and execute the commandments of God."[121] But it was in the Sermon on the Mount where Tyndale found much of his theology of the two regiments.

> Read here the words of Christ with this exposition following, and thou shalt see the law, faith, and works, restored each to his right use and true meaning; and thereto, the clear difference between the spiritual regiment and the temporal; and shalt have an entrance and open way into the rest of all the scripture.[122]

Although both regiments are part of God's creation, the spiritual and temporal regiments fulfil different functions in the covenant; therefore, we are able to consider them separately. At the same time in a Christian commonwealth there is an overlap because men are in both regiments at the same time. Christ told Pilate that his kingdom was not of this world,[123] and "because he had no temporal kingdom, even so he meant of no temporal power, but of power to save sinners."[124] We will, in this section, only consider the temporal regiment in the context of a Christian nation where both regiments are alongside each other and a Christian prince is the ruler.

When Christ seemed to be undermining the temporal regiment in *Matthew* 5:38f, Tyndale wrote,

> Christ here intended not to disannul the temporal regiment, and to forbid rulers to punish evil doers, no more than he meant to destroy matrimony when he forbade to lust and to covet another man's wife in the heart. But as he there forbade that which defileth matrimony, even so he forbiddeth here that which troubleth, unquieteth, and destroyeth the temporal regiment, and that thing which to forbid the temporal regiment was ordained.[125]

Those in Authority

Apart from fathers, Tyndale writes more about the position and duties of kings than of any other officer in the temporal regiment. This priority occurs because the king has his authority directly from God whereas other rulers are subordinate to the king and their duties are delegated by him. No one can take any authority to oneself "till God have chosen him; that is to wit, till he be chosen by the ordinance that God hath set in the world, to rule it."[126]

The king has been given the sword as a sign of his authority and his power to ensure that justice prevails. "No man should avenge himself, or seek wreak, no, not by the law. But the ruler, which hath the sword, should do such things of himself; or when the neighbours, of love, warn him and require him"[127] For it is the office of the king to maintain justice, for "the sword, and full power to punish evildoers indifferently, is given of God to every king for his time."[128] Tyndale quotes, to support this position, *Romans* 13:1, "'Let every soul submit himself unto the authority of the higher powers.' . . . The higher powers are the temporal kings and princes; unto whom God hath given the sword, to punish whosoever sinneth."[129]

The sword is also given to the king for the defence of his realm and subjects, and therefore should be honoured; for man's laws are "ordained for the furtherance of the commonwealth, to maintain peace, to punish the evil, and to defend the good. Therefore ought the good to honour the temporal sword, and to have it in reverence."[130] The king must also be obeyed in his commands, but in More's *Dialogue*

Concerning Heresies, More wrote of the laws of the Church and of temporal laws, and that both Peter and Paul command us "obedience to our superiors and rulers."[131] However, Tyndale accused the pope of disobedience as far as the temporal power was concerned, "And when he saith, Peter and Paul commanded us to obey our superiors; that is truth, they commanded us to obey the temporal sword, which the pope will not."[132] But Tyndale hedged the king's power with his responsibility to God and Tyndale stated that those the king governed were his brothers and sisters through God's creation.[133]

Tyndale draws our attention to the history of Israel in the Bible, pointing out the importance of obedience to God's commandments if we want peace and security and receive God's blessings on our nation.

> As God there warneth ere he smite, and suffereth long ere he take extreme vengeance, so shall he do with us. As they that turn are there received to mercy, and they that maliciously resist perish utterly, so shall it be with us. As they that resist the counsel of God perish through their own counsel, so shall it be with us until the world's end. As it went with their kings and rulers, so shall it go with ours. As it was with their common people, so shall it be with ours.[134]

As we will see when we consider *The Errors of the Spiritualty,* Tyndale accused the pope of taking possession of the temporal sword from the king. This is a false possession for,

> Though that all power were given unto Christ in heaven and in earth, yet had he no power over his Father, nor yet to reign temporally over temporal princes, but a commandment to obey them. How hath the pope then such temporal authority over king and emperor?[135]

The spiritualty are under the temporal sword of the king and neither free from it nor having power to wield it themselves.

> God did not put Peter only under the temporal sword, but also Christ himself; as it appeareth in the fourth chapter to the Galatians. . . . If the head be then under the temporal sword, how can the members be excepted? If Peter sinned in defending Christ against the temporal sword, . . . who can excuse our prelates of sin, which will obey no man, neither king nor emperor?[136]

Tyndale said that we need to restore to the king his authority so that the Church might be cleansed, for "When temporal kings were in their high authority, then the general council repressed the enormities of the spiritualty."[137]

Tyndale has a lot of practical material about the ways the king should govern and his subjects obey his rule. I can only briefly touch upon some of these. As we would expect from Tyndale, the base from which good government sprang was the word of God.[138] Tyndale wrote of the law and justice,[139] warfare,[140] taxes,[141] and many other aspects of governance. Above all, the help the king needs to govern his people must come from the laity and not from those of the spiritualty, for it is impossible to serve two masters.[142] "Let kings take their duty of their subjects, and that that is necessary to the defence of the realm. Let them rule their realms themselves, with the help of lay-men that are sage, wise, learned, and expert."[143]

Many of Tyndale's remarks about the duty of the king also apply to the temporal officers whom the king appoints: "As a king sendeth forth his judges, and giveth them his authority, saying, 'What ye do, that do I; I give you my full power.'" But they are not to exceed that power.[144]

The duty of the ruler is to punish sin and correct the wrongdoer;[145] therefore, "Let, I say, the governors take heed how they let sin be unpunished, and how they bring the wrath of God upon their realms."[146] For Tyndale realised that not every ruler was good, and that there were evil rulers and tyrants, but he was against rebellion to overthrow them. It was the people who received the king they deserved, and that is why God allowed the people to suffer from a tyrant's rule. Tyndale wrote, "Evil rulers then are a sign that God is angry and wroth with us."[147] It is for this reason that the Christian should not oppose a tyrant, for "A christian man is bound to obey tyranny, if it be not against his faith nor the law of God, until God deliver him thereof."[148] Tyndale illustrates this precept with the example of David.

> How mighty was David when he came to fight; and how overcame he through faith! And how mightier was he when he came to suffering, as in the persecution of king Saul! Inasmuch that when he had his most mortal enemy, king Saul, . . . in his hands, to have done what he would with him, through faith he touched him not, nor suffered any man else to do.[149]

In *Obedience,* Tyndale relates all those incidents, when David cut part of Saul's garment when he came into the cave where David was hiding; and when David and Abishai entered Saul's camp and took Saul's "spear and a cup of water from his head."[150] Tyndale answers the question "Why did not David slay Saul?" with

> For if he had done it, he must have sinned against God; for God hath made the king in every realm judge over all, and over him is there no judge. He that judgeth the king judgeth God; and he

> that layeth hands on the king layeth hand on God; and he that resisteth the king resisteth God, and damneth God's law and ordinance."[151]

Tyndale believed that relief from tyranny lay with the people,

> as when the child submitteth himself unto his father's correction and nurture, and humbleth himself altogether unto the will of his father, then the rod is taken away; even so, when we are come unto the knowledge of the right way, and have forsaken our own will, and offer ourselves clean unto the will of God, to walk which way soever he will have us, then turneth he the tyrants; or else . . . he putteth them out of the way, according unto the comfortable ensamples of the scripture.[152]

He showed not only the cause and the answer, but also his evangelical zeal, when he wrote,

> Of all the subjects of England this I crave – that they repent; for the cause of evil rulers is the sin of the subjects, as testifieth the Scripture. And the cause of false preachers is, that the people have no love unto the truth, saith Paul, in 1 Thess. ii. We be all sinners a hundred times greater than all that we suffer. Let us, therefore, each forgive others, remembering the greater sinners the more welcome, if we repent; according to the similitude of the riotous son. For Christ died for sinners, and is their Saviour, and his blood is their treasure, to pay for their sins . . .[153]

Subjects

The king's subjects are bound to obey him, and Tyndale points out that this duty is taught by Peter in his First Epistle: "And first he teacheth them, in general, to obey the worldly rulers; and then in special, he teacheth the servants to obey their masters, be they good or bad, and to suffer wrong of them, as Christ suffered wrong for us."[154] Tyndale (as is commonly found in theological writers) applied the fifth commandment to the duties of subjects to their rulers. "'Child, obey father and mother, that thou mayest long live on the earth.' And by father and mother is understood all rulers, which if thou obey, thy blessing shall be long life; and contrary, if thou disobey, short life."[155] Tyndale in his writings is very practical, and he gives us other reasons for obedience to those in authority. For us to obey those in authority over us is not only the fact that it is God's commandment.

> And that it is right that we obey father and mother, master, lord, prince and king, and all the ordinances of the world, bodily and ghostly, by which God ruleth us, and ministereth freely his

> benefits unto us all: and that we love them for the benefits that we receive by them, and fear them for the power they have over us to punish us, if we trespass the law and good order.[156]

When it comes to our obedience to evil rulers, we know that we have God's Spirit with us, and that our obedience is pure.[157] But God has placed a limit on our obedience to our rulers, which is true whether they are good or bad. Tyndale continues in *Pathway*, "So far yet are the worldly powers or rulers to be obeyed only, as their commandments repugn not against the commandment of God."[158] For if the king's command is against God's law (here Tyndale's understanding of *neighbour* in a wider sense surfaces), civil disobedience is right. "And in like wise, against this law, 'Love thy neighbour as thyself,' I may obey no worldly power, to do aught at any man's commandment unto the hurt of my neighbour that hath not deserved it, though he be a Turk."[159]

Tyndale was not against people taking oaths, although no one must be put in an impossible situation. He gives examples in the long quote below, because for everyone there must be justice. Commenting on Matthew 5:33-37, Tyndale wrote,

> Howbeit all manner of swearing is not here forbidden, no more than all manner of killing, when the commandment saith, 'Kill not;' for judges and rulers must kill. Even so ought they, when they put any man in office, to take an oath of him that he shall be true and faithful and diligent therein; and of their subjects it is lawful to take oaths, and of all that offer themselves to bear witness. But if the superior would compel the inferior to swear that [which] should be to the dishonour of God, or hurting of an innocent, the inferior ought rather to die than to swear: neither ought a judge to compel a man to swear against himself, that he make him not sin and forswear.[160]

Apart from being a witness for or against another in a lawsuit, there were other ways in which the subject had to serve to maintain the king's laws. This obedience to the king did not break the command to love our neighbour as ourself, even if it involved physical action against another person.

> And so hath the ruler power over thee, to send thee to use violence upon thy neighbour, to take him, to prison him, and haply to kill him too. And thou must ever love thy neighbour in thine heart, by the reason that he is thy brother in the first state; and yet obey thy ruler and go with the constable or like officer, . . . And look, what harm he getteth, yea, though he be slain, that be on his own head. For thine heart loved him.

Tyndale wrote that it is the same when the king sends one to fight against his enemies. "And like is it, if thy lord or prince send thee a warfare into another land; thou must obey at God's commandment, and go, and avenge thy prince's quarrel, which thou knowest not but that it is right." However, there must be no hatred in our heart for the Christian must remember that those he fights against "be thy brethren, and as deeply bought with Christ's blood as thou, and for Christ's sake to be beloved in thine heart." [161]

The temporal regiment is part of God's creation. Within it everyone is our brother or sister whom we should love because we have all been created by God.[162] But as Christians we are doubly God's, and as the covenant people we can say, "I love thee . . . because of the great love that Christ hath shewed me. I serve thee, not because thou art my master, or my king, for hope of reward, or fear of pain, but for the love of Christ."[163]

Tyndale was concerned with social justice, and his thinking was ahead of his time – we see this from his attitude to the "Turks" and others who were not Christians. They are God's children by creation, and we must love them because they are our neighbours. This love to all mankind stems from the fact that we are to be like our heavenly Father. Tyndale tells us to "lift up thine eyes unto thy heavenly Father, and as thy Father doth, so do thou love all thy Father's children. He ministereth sun and rain to good and bad; by which two understand all his benefits."[164]

Conclusion

Unlike Luther, Tyndale did not make a separation between the temporal and the spiritual regiments as if they were in watertight compartments. Neither did Tyndale, like Roman Catholicism and Calvin, make the spiritual regiment superior to the temporal.

Tyndale did not believe the temporal regiment was, in effect, an answer to the Fall and instituted to control sin. The temporal regiment was an ordinance of creation and was needed even if the Fall had not taken place, even though the negative aspects of the temporal regiment would not have been necessary in that case, for if man had not sinned there would be no need for punishment. Tyndale's view that the temporal regiment stems from the creation places every man in a special relationship to God as his child – even though it is a relationship affected by the Fall. Passages such as, "God hath made them after the likeness of his own image, and they are his sons as well as we, and Christ hath bought them with his blood, and made them heirs of everlasting life as well as us:"[165] have added fuel to those scholars to accuse Tyndale of being a universalist.[166] However, Tyndale did not teach that every human being would find salvation, and this passage needs placing into its context, which teaches the changes which have taken place since Adam sinned.

Other misunderstandings of Tyndale's teaching about the temporal and the spiritual regiment concern the place of the king. Tyndale does not teach the divine right of kings nor the royal supremacy as it developed in Tudor England,[167] but that kings are appointed by God to govern the temporal regiment only. However, Kenneth Carleton wrote,

> Certainly, by the end of 1530 the King was aware of the arguments in favour of the vesting of supreme authority and jurisdiction over matters temporal and spiritual in the secular prince. William Tyndale's *The Obedience of a Christian Man,* which was known to Henry, taught the supremacy in matters both secular and spiritual of the king in his realm.[168]

J.J. Scarisbrick is even stronger in his claims for Tyndale's teaching (although he does not claim that Tyndale taught the king had rule over the spiritual regiment), "Tyndale's sweeping assertion of the rights and duties of princes and their claim to the undivided allegiance, body and soul, of their subjects, may well have opened up a new world for Henry."[169] But these statements, although found in Tyndale, are only one side of the coin, for the king also had his responsibilities to his subjects that were equally far reaching. Whereas Tyndale taught, firstly, that every man, clergy or lay, was part of the temporal regiment and therefore subject to the king. "The spiritual officer . . . is under the king's or temporal correction, how high soever he be."[170] Secondly, that the king, in the spiritual regiment, was subservient to the spiritual officers. "The king is as deep under the spiritual officer, to hear out of God's word what he ought to believe, and how to live, and how to rule, as is the poorest beggar in the realm."[171]

This chapter seems to point to certain conclusions regarding the relationship between the temporal and the spiritual regiments (see *Appendix 2),* but further work is needed on Tyndale's doctrine of the two regiments to establish his theology regarding their relationship to one another.

Notes

1. Lau, Franz, "The Lutheran Doctrine of the Two Kingdoms", p. 355
2. McGrath, Alister E., *Reformation Thought,* p. 211f
3. Luther also believed, "The law of this temporal sword has existed from the beginning of the world;" but Luther was using it as a response to sin, e.g. Cain slaying Abel, Luther, *Works,* vol 45, p. 86, whereas Tyndale used the term as the governance of society in general.
4. Tyndale, William, *Exposition Matthew,* p. 2/60f
5. Cargill Thompson, "The Two Regiments: The Continental Setting of William

Tyndale's Political Thought. p. 20
6. ibid. p. 22
7. ibid. p. 27
8. ibid. p. 27
9. Trevisa, John, *Dialogus inter Militem et Clericum,* pp 7-11 (quotes pp 9, 10f) "*Th*is is nou*gh*t vnderstonden for *th*e first state but for *th*e secunde; for in *th*e first state Crist vsed no siche power, but put hit awey fro*m* hym & vsed onlich *th*at longe*th* to *th*e gouer*n*au*n*ce of oure sauaciou*n*." . . . "*th*at he may take of p*r*inces & of kynges p*r*incipates and kyngdoms at his owne wille, and *g*eue where hym like*th*. But take hede how wrongfullich *th*at were y-do. . . . *Th*anne it is so*the* *th*at he feng nou*gh*t so grete power as C*r*ist in temporalte, but onlich *th*at power *th*at C*r*ist vsed & tau*gh*t in his de*th*lich lyuy*n*g."
10. Tyndale, William, *Exposition Matthew,* p. 2/5f
11. Tyndale, William, *Exposition Matthew,* p. 2/8
12. Tyndale, William, *Exposition Matthew,* p. 2/15. Trevisa, *Dialogus,* p. 9
13. In the *Conclusion* to this chapter I list certain statements regarding the two regiments, space does not allow these to be worked out in the confines of a chapter, and further work needs to be done on this aspect of Tyndale's theology. My STh dissertation of Tyndale's theology of Church and State was written before I realised that one could not understand his separate doctrines until the whole of Tyndale's theology had been discovered.
14. More, Thomas, *Dialogue, CWM* vol 6, p. 286. "Nowe where he calleth the chyrche alway the congregacyon / what reason had he therin? For euery man well seeth that thoughe the chyrch be in dede a congregacyon / yet is not euery congregacyon the chyrche / but a congregacyon of crysten people / whiche congregacyon of crysten people hath ben in Englande alway called and knowen by the name of the chyrche."
15. Tyndale, William, *Answer,* p 3/12
16. Tyndale, William, *Answer,* p. 3/158
17. Tyndale, William, *Answer,* p. 3/107
18. Tyndale, William, *Answer,* p. 3/113f
19. Tyndale, William, *Obedience,* p. 1/165
20. see Tyndale, William, *Sacraments,* p. 1/363
21. Tyndale, William, *1525,* p. 7
22. Tyndale, William, *1525,* p. 10
23. Tyndale, William, *Answer,* p. 3/13
24. Stafford, 106. Stafford points out that the "change in the status of laypeople has many sides, a complexity amplified by the multivalence of Tyndale as a writer. His voice had many undertones and overtones." He points out that different scholars have taken one or another of these voices as the full statement of Tyndale's thought.
25. Tyndale, William, *Sacraments,* p. 1/350
26. Tyndale, William, *Answer,* pp. 3/54, 69.
27. Tyndale, William, *Exposition Matthew,* p. 2/13
28. Tyndale, William, *Mammon,* p. 1/97
29. Tyndale, William, *Exposition 1 John,* p. 2/212
30. see chapters, *The Covenant Envisaged,* and *The Means to Achieve the Covenant.*
31. Tyndale, William, *Prelates,* p. 2/281

32. Tyndale, William, *Answer,* p. 3/31
33. Tyndale, William, *Prelates,* p. 2/249
34. Tyndale, William, *Prelates,* p. 2/250
35. Tyndale, William, *Prelates,* p. 2/249
36. Tyndale, William, *Exposition 1 John,* p. 2/168
37. Tyndale, William, *Obedience,* p. 1/274f
38. Tyndale, William, *Exposition 1 John,* p. 2/187
39. Tyndale, William, *Obedience,* p.1/211
40. Tyndale, William, *Prelates,* p. 2/253
41. Mayotte, Judith M., "William Tyndale's Contribution to the Reformation in England" p. 128
42. Tyndale, William, *Obedience,* p.1/230
43. Tyndale, William, *Prologue 1 Peter,* p. 1/528
44. Tyndale, William, *Prologue 1 Timothy,* p. 1/517f
45. Tyndale, William, *Prelates,* p. 2/275
46. Tyndale, William, *Obedience,* p.1/230f
47. Tyndale, William, *Obedience,* p. 1/283
48. Tyndale, William, *Exposition Matthew,* p. 2/36
49. Tyndale, William, *Exposition Matthew,* p. 2/33
50. Tyndale, William, *Answer,* p. 3/108f
51. Arnold, Thomas, *Select English Works,* p. 1/170f; 3/144. "Crist ordeynede *th*ree *th*ingis to be fillid by hise apostlis, first *th*at *th*ei shulden go forth in to *th*e world and preche his gospel, and *th*at *th*is shulde be fruytous to *th*us converte so myche peple, and si*th* *th*at *th*is fruyt dwelle, bo*th*e in *th*is worlde and in *th*e to*th*er."52 Again, "And herfore Jesus Crist occupyed hys mooste in *th*o werke of prechyng, and laft o*th*er werkes; and *th*us diden his apostils, and herfore God loved hom."
52. Tyndale, William, *Obedience,* p. 1/2
53. Tyndale, William, *Exposition 1 John,* p. 2/183f
54. Tyndale, William, *Answer,* p, 3/11
55. Tyndale, William, *Obedience,* p. 1/219
56. Tyndale, William, *Exposition Matthew,* p. 2/79
57. Tyndale, William, *Answer,* p. 3/88
58. Tyndale, William, *Mammon,* p. 1/106
59. Tyndale, William, *Exposition 1 John,* p. 2/210
60. Tyndale, William, *Answer,* p. 3/126
61. Tyndale, William, *Mammon,* p. 1/118f
62. Tyndale, William, *Obedience,* p. 1/255f
63. Tyndale, William, *Exposition 1 John,* p. 2/152f
64. see "The Fatherhood of God", p. 56
65. Tyndale, William, *Exposition Matthew,* p. 2/82
66. Tyndale, William, *Obedience,* p. 1/258
67. Tyndale, William, *Answer,* p. 3/125
68. Tyndale, William, *Epistle, 1526,* p. 1/390
69. Tyndale, William, *Obedience,* p. 1/275
70. Tyndale, William, *Obedience,* p. 1/300
71. Tyndale, William, *Obedience,* p. 1/295
72. Walter, Henry, *Biographical Notice, Tyndale, Parker Society* p. 1/lix

73. Tyndale, *Exposition 1 John,* p. 2/211
74. Tyndale, William, *Answer,* p. 3/64
75. Tyndale, William, *Mammon,* p. 1/94
76. Tyndale, William, *Obedience,* p. 1/293
77. Tyndale, William, *Exposition Matthew,* p. 2/116
78. Tyndale, William, *Prologue Numbers,* p. 1/437
79. Tyndale, William, *Obedience,* p. 1/142
80. see Chapter 10, *The Covenant Broken,*
81. Tyndale, William, *Obedience,* p. 1/280
82. Tyndale, William, *Exposition Matthew,* p. 2/83
83. Tyndale, William, *Sacraments,* p. 1/357
84. Tyndale, William, *Obedience,* p. 1/165
85. Tyndale, William, *Exposition Matthew,* p. 2/84
86. Tyndale, William, *Exposition Matthew,* p. 2/23
87. Tyndale, William, *Mammon,* p. 1/93
88. Tyndale, William, *Prologue 1 Timothy,* p. 1/518. This is expanded in the next paragraph.
89. Tyndale, William, *Exposition Matthew,* p. 2/41f
90. Tyndale, William, *Obedience,* p. 1/280
91. Tyndale, William, *Exposition Matthew,* p. 2/23
92. Tyndale, William, *Exposition 1 John,* p. 2/154
93. Tyndale, William, *1525,* p. 6. "with the lawe he conde*m*neth hym sylfe and all his deds / and geveth all the prayse to god. he beleueth the promyses / and ascribeth all trouth to god / thus every where iustifieth he god / and prayseth god."
94. Tyndale, William, *1525,* p. 14. "He bought it of his father derely with his bloud / ye with his moost bitter death and gave his lyfe for hit. What soever good thynge is in vs / that is geven vs frely with oute oure deservyng or meretts for Christs blouds sake. That we desyre to folow the will of god / it is the gyfte of Christs bloud. That we nowe hate the devylls will (where vnto we were so fast locked / and coude nott but love hit) is also the gyfte of Christes bloud / vnto whom belongeth the preyse and honoure of oure good dedes / and nott vnto vs."
95. Tyndale, William, *Prologue Exodus,* p. 1/418
96. Tyndale, William, *Exposition Matthew,* p. 2/78
97. Tyndale, William, *Jonas,* p. 1/465
98. Tyndale, William, *Exposition 1 John,* p. 2/171
99. Tyndale, William, *Prologue 1. Peter,* p. 1/527f
100. Tyndale, William, *Exposition 1 John,,* p. 2/188
101. Tyndale, William, *Answer,* p. 3/126
102. Tyndale, William, *Answer,* p. 3/7
103. Tyndale, William, *Answer,* p. 3/57
104. Tyndale, William, *Prologue Exodus,* p. 1/420
105. Tyndale, William, *Answer,* p. 3/88
106. Tyndale, William, *Sacraments,* p. 1/373
107. There is circumstantial evidence in Tyndale's writings that the division between the temporal and spiritual is a result of the Fall, and this could do with fuller treatment.

108. Tyndale, William, *Exposition 1 John,* p. 2/212
109. Tyndale, William, *Obedience*, p. 1/273
110. Tyndale, William, *Exposition Matthew,* p. 2/60
111. Tyndale, William, *Exposition Matthew,* p. 2/71.
112. Cargill Thompson, "Two Regiments" p. 17
113. Bast, Robert J., "From Two Kingdoms to Two Tables", p. 79
114. Boehrer, Bruce, "Tyndale's *The Practyse of Prelates",* pp 262, 263.
115. Tyndale, William, *Exposition Matthew,* p. 2/82
116. Tyndale, William, *Exposition Matthew,* p. 2/86f: see Boehrer, p. 261
117. This places the *temporal regiment* before the Fall, whilst the *spiritual regiment,* with its emphasis that our entry into it is through the blood of Christ, is therefore post Fall.
118. Tyndale, William, *Obedience,* p. 1/174f
1190. Jepson, Alfred, "What can the Old Testament contribute to the Discussion of the Two Kingdoms", p. 326
120. Tyndale, William, *Exposition Matthew,* p. 2/8
121. Tyndale, William, *Obedience,* p. 1/175
122. Tyndale, William, *Exposition Matthew,* p. 2/15
123. John 18:36
124. Tyndale, William, *Prelates,* p. 2/282
125. Tyndale, William, *Exposition Matthew,* p. 2/58
126. Tyndale, William, *Exposition Matthew,* p. 2/86
127. Tyndale, William, *1525,* p. 25. "No man shuld avenge hyme silfe / or seke wreeke / no nott by the lawe: butt the ruler which hath the swearde shuld do such thyngs of hym silfe / or when the negbures off love warne hym / and requyre hym." (Marginal Note, Matthew v.)
128. Tyndale, William, *Prelates,* p. 2/280
129. Tyndale, William, *Obedience,* p. 1/178
130. Tyndale, William, *Prologue Romans,* p. 1/506
131. More, Thomas, "Dialogue", *CWM* vol 6, p. 106. "obedyence to our superyours & rulers."
132. Tyndale, William, *Answer,* p. 3/94
133. Tyndale, William, *Exposition Matthew,* p. 2/86f
134. Tyndale, William, *Prologue Genesis,* p. 1/404
135. Tyndale, William, *Obedience,* p. 1/270
136. Tyndale, William, *Obedience,* p. 1/188
137. Tyndale, William, *Exposition 1 John,* p. 2/178
138. Tyndale, William, *Answer,* p. 3/27f
139. Tyndale, William, *Obedience,* p. 1/250 etc.
140. Tyndale, William, *Exposition Matthew,* p. 2/63
141. Tyndale, William, *Prologue Genesis,* p. 1/410
142. Tyndale, William, *Exposition Matthew,* p. 2/104f
143. Tyndale, William, *Obedience,* p. 1/206
144. Tyndale, William, *Obedience,* p. 1/271
145. Tyndale, William, *Mammon,* p. 1/95f
146. Tyndale, William, *Exposition Matthew,* p. 2/55
147. Tyndale, William, *Obedience,* p. 1/195
148. Tyndale, William, *Answer,* p. 3/180

149. Tyndale, William, *Exposition 1 John,* p. 2/209
150. 1 Samuel 24:4ff; 26:7ff
151. Tyndale, William, *Obedience,* p. 1/176f
152. Tyndale, William, *Obedience,* p. 1/141
153. Foxe, John, *Acts and Monuments,* vol 5. p. 131
154. Tyndale, William, *Prologue 1 Peter,* p. 1/527
155. Tyndale, William, *Exposition Matthew,* p. 2/111
156. Tyndale, William, *Pathway,* p. 1/25
157. Tyndale, William, *Obedience,* p. 1/193
158. Tyndale, William, *Pathway,* p. 1/25
159. Tyndale, William, *Pathway,* p. 1/26
160. Tyndale, William, *Exposition Matthew,* p. 2/56
161. Tyndale, William, *Exposition Matthew,* p. 2/63
162. Tyndale, William, *Pathway,* p. 1/18
163. Tyndale, William, *Obedience,* p. 1/296f
164. Tyndale, William, *Exposition Matthew,* p. 2/71
165. Tyndale, William, *Pathway,* p. 1/18
166. Baker, J.W., *Bullinger and the Covenant,* p. 209
167. Cargill Thompson, "Two Regiments", p 18, see also p. 20. "This has resulted in the emergence of a stereotyped view of Tyndale as a political thinker, largely based on a few famous quotations and repetition of second-hand ideas. In so far as there is a popular view of Tyndale as a political thinker it is contained in the widespread belief that he was an exponent of royal absolutism, and also that he foreshadowed the royal supremacy."
168. Carelton, Kenneth, *Bishops and Reform in the English Church, 1520-1559,* p. 9
169. Scarisbrick, J.J., *Henry VIII,* p. 247
170. Tyndale, William, *Exposition Matthew,* p. 2/67
171. Tyndale, William, *Exposition Matthew,* p. 2/67; see Boehrer, p. 270

10

The Covenant Broken

Introduction

Tyndale's criticism of the medieval Church was that it had broken God's covenant, and had replaced it with man's own ideas. Under the pope, the spiritualty had usurped power and now ruled over both the temporal and the spiritual regiments instead of serving the Church. In order to consolidate their power they had altered the meaning of scripture with their own glosses. Through their false interpretation of the meaning of the sacraments of baptism and the Lord's Supper, plus the addition of the five other sacraments which they had invented, they had gained a hold over the lives of Christians. Through their additions and alterations to the Scriptures, they had changed the pure worship of God into idolatry. Through their way of life and their covetousness, they had corrupted the Biblical teaching of how God wanted his people to live. "And as damnable as it is for the poor to trust in the riches of the richest upon earth, so damnable is it also to leave the covenant made in Christ's blood, and to trust in the saints of heaven."[1] Such were the main charges Tyndale levelled against the Church of his day to prove that it had broken God's covenant for our salvation from sin and the power of the devil. "Tyndale believed the rationale for this corruption could only be the clergy's advantage – that they might gain more power and more money from the people."[2]

For Tyndale all these errors of the Church were in reality only one, as they all depended on each other to create antichrist's kingdom on Earth. The pope had created an empire for himself and had gained power not only over the spiritual regiment, but he had also taken the temporal power from kings and emperors. He had enriched himself and impoverished the people, having caught them in the web of his deceit.[3]

There are large areas where Tyndale was concerned about the state of the Church that will not be covered in this chapter. Although they add force to Tyndale's attack on the Roman Church, they are not relevant to the covenant. The title of this chapter highlights the main reasons why Tyndale was so critical of the Church of his day because the Christian faith depends on the covenant. This chapter also highlights the reason why Tyndale could never have been a follower of Luther. Although he was prepared to translate large sections of Luther's writings into his own works, he altered and modified them, thus changing Luther's doctrine into his own.

Tyndale's *The Practice of Prelates* deals with how the spiritualty broke God's covenant through turning from God's word and listening to the devil's temptations. As the spiritualty sought their own glory, they broke God's commandments; there was then no way for the covenant to remain intact.

The Covenant Broken

Tyndale claimed that the covenant was broken when the spiritualty turned away from the word of God. In its place, they turned to their own imaginations and to the philosophy of Aristotle and other pagan philosophers, creating in the place of the covenant their own heathen ideas about God and salvation. Tyndale quotes (rather loosely) from Thomas More's *Dialogue*[4] that

> "We believe the doctrine of the scripture without scripture, . . . because only that the church so teacheth, though no scripture confirmeth it." Why so? "Because," saith he, "the Holy Ghost by inspiration, if I do my endeavour, and captivate mine understanding, teacheth me to believe the church concerning God's word, taught by the church and graven in men's hearts without scripture, as well as he teacheth us to believe words written in the scripture."[5]

Earlier, Tyndale had written that without scripture the Church's "doctrine is but the opinion of faithless people, which to confirm the devil hath wrought much subtilty." However, Tyndale did not seek to contradict More's claim that miracles prove the Church's doctrine; he only raised the question that we have to be sure the miracles are of God and points out that witches do miracles as well. But he allowed that miracles had happened "until the scripture was authentically received."[6] Tyndale meant they were to be received not only by the clergy but by every Christian. Judith Mayotte wrote, "In no circumstance was Tyndale's rage more pronounced than against the clergy's withholding from the English the scripture in their mother tongue."[7]

In spite of the lip service the spiritualty paid to the scriptures, in reality they did not accept them, for, wrote Tyndale, "If God's word appeared any where, they agreed all against it. When they had brought that asleep, then strove they one with another about their own traditions."[8] Then, instead of the scriptures, they teach "dreams of their own making."[9] Tyndale uses the example of how Cuthbert Tunstall got hold of the New Testament as it came into England:

> He burnt the new Testament, calling it *Doctrinam peregrinam,* 'strange learning.' Yea, verily, look how strange his living, in whose blood that testament was made, was from the living of the pope; even so strange is that doctrine from the pope's law.[10]

It was indeed "strange learning" for the Church because

> our great pillars of holy church, which have nailed a veil of false glosses on Moses's face, to corrupt the true understanding of his law, cannot come in. And therefore they bark, and say the scripture maketh heretics, and it is not possible for them to understand it in the English, because they themselves do not in Latin.[11]

In fact the prelates had lost "the understanding of the plain text, and of the Greek, and Latin, and specially of the Hebrew."[12]

The vernacular Bible would uncover "their false expounding the scripture."[13] In fact, their corruption of the scripture meant "he shall never speed well that will seek in the scripture whether our prelates teach us a true faith,"[14] for then the laity would know as much as the clergy.[15] Therefore, Tyndale wrote, the problem the spiritualty had with his translation of the New Testament was "not that they find just causes in the translation, but because they have lost their juggling and feigned terms."[16] In fact, according to Tyndale, "the pope first hath no scripture that he dare abide by, in the light; neither careth, but blasphemeth that his word is truer than the scripture;"[17] therefore he seeks "to quench the word of God,"[18] and so, by his corruption, "the scripture is hid, and brought into ignorance, and the true sense corrupt."[19]

Against the Church saying that the scriptures should not be in the vernacular, Tyndale pointed out that God's word was given to the Israelites "in their mother tongue" for "there was Christ but figured, and described in ceremonies, . . ." The laity need the "old Testament, with the new also, which is the light of the old" in the vernacular. Tyndale continued, "I can imagine no cause verily, except it be that we should not see the work of antichrist and juggling of hypocrites."[20]

By denying the laity the scriptures in their mother tongue and by the corruption of the word of God by their glosses and traditions, the spiritualty had hidden God's covenant from the laity, and the truth had been buried under every kind of ceremony and superstition. This accusation was the springboard from which Tyndale revealed the failings of the spiritualty.

False Faith

The medieval Church had turned from the scriptures to follow doctrines of its own imagination and thus had deceived the laity. Tyndale wrote of many ways in which More multiplied these deceits. He complained of More's methods, and wrote, "How juggleth he, to prove that all that pertaineth unto the faith was not written; alleging John in the last [chapter], that the world could not contain the books, if all should be written. And John meaneth of the miracles which Jesus did, and not of the necessary points of the faith."[21] He then lists many of the errors More makes into articles of faith: "the perpetual virginity of Mary," "the coming of antichrist," "traditions," the various errors in the Mass, justification by works, "the Saboth" (*sic*), etc. Then Tyndale wrote, "And, finally, to rock us asleep withal, he saith, that he shall never speed well that will seek in the scripture whether our prelates teach us a true faith; though ten preach, each contrary to other, in one day."[22]

The pope has left the scriptures also, and has joined "the spiritual doctrine of Christ and the fleshly doctrine of philosophers together; things so contrary that they cannot agree, no more than the Spirit and the flesh do in a christian man."[23] So the pope according to Tyndale, fulfils Paul's prophecy (2 Thessalonians), "that Antichrist should set up himself in the same place as God, and deceive the unthankful world with false doctrine, and with false and lying miracles, wrought by the working of Satan."[24]

In many of his writings Tyndale shows how the pope has corrupted the true Christian doctrine and substituted his own. "O how sore differeth the doctrine of Christ and his apostles from the doctrine of the pope and his apostles!"[25] And this corruption, says Tyndale, has an effect on all who follow the pope's teaching.

> Now the sum of all that the apostles taught, and how they built us upon Christ, is the New Testament. But the bishop of Rome's doctrine is not there found, but improved. Confounded therefore shall he be, which, witting and willing, shutteth his eyes at the true light, and openeth them to believe his lies.[26]

So Tyndale concluded that when we weigh up the pope's doctrines there "are tokens good enough that he is the right antichrist, and his doctrine sprung of the devil."[27]

The Destruction of the Covenant

For Tyndale all God-given, true doctrine, "buildeth thee upon Christ to put thy trust and confidence in his blood." He continues, "Examine the Romish bishop by this rule, and thou shalt find that all he doth is to the destruction of this article."[28] For, under the pope, the prelates "resist his Holy Spirit, enforcing with all craft and subtlety to quench the light of the everlasting testament, promises, and appointment made between God and us."[29] Because the pope has destroyed the true faith, the covenant has gone and forms no part of the preaching of the spiritualty. The result is that

> we Christians have been very seldom, or never, called again to the covenant of the Lord, the law of God, and faith of Christ; but to the covenant of the pope often: as he now clucketh apace for his chickens, and will both prove all his old policies, and seek and imagine new practices.[30]

In destroying the covenant the papists have, as far as Tyndale is concerned, destroyed every doctrine which we find in the Bible. For their doctrine is based on the heathen philosophy of Aristotle whose

> doctrine is, that the world was without beginning, and shall be without end; and that the first man never was, and the last shall never be, and that God doth all of necessity, neither careth what we do, neither will ask any accounts of that we do.[31]

God, Christ and Antichrist

Tyndale believed that the pope was Antichrist and that he had usurped God's power. He had dethroned Christ and sat on Christ's throne. Although we can trace a possible link between Tyndale and Luther, we also find Tyndale's arguments are found in Wycliffite writings, which often bridge the gaps between Tyndale's and Luther's theologies. There are many similarities in both Wyclif and Tyndale, for instance, between Peter following Christ's doctrine and the pope following Satan's doctrine.[32]

The pope has been given great power, and he has been placed above every man and on the same level as God. This false elevation happened through the Church's teaching. "Then came Thomas de Aquino, and he made the pope a god with his sophistry; and the pope made him a saint for his labour, and called him doctor Sanctus."[33] This was a doctrine the pope took up, and as we look at the doctrine and life of the Church "there also seest thou how the pope exalteth himself above God, and commandeth him to obey his tyranny."[34] Wyclif wrote, "Here I think that Antichrist presumes above Christ and all the Holy Trinity, as St. Paul says."[35] Therefore, replying to Sir Thomas More, Tyndale wrote, that "the pope, through falsehood and corrupting such poets as ye are, . . . leadeth in the darkness of death."[36]

Christ said there would be those claiming

> that they themselves are Christ. That do verily the pope and our holy orders of religion. For they, under the name of Christ, preach themselves, their own word and their own traditions, and teach the people to believe in them. The pope giveth pardons of his full power, of the treasure of the church, and of the merits of saints.[37]

The pope takes Christ's words about himself and claims they refer to the pope as well as to Christ. "Lo, saith the pope, Christ hath all power in heaven and earth without exception, and I am Christ's vicar; wherefore all power is mine." Then, turning to Hebrews 7, "Now, saith the pope, 'The priesthood is translated unto me; wherefore it pertaineth unto me to make laws, and to bind every man.' "[38]

In these ways the pope takes God's power, and instead of reverencing God's word "the pope putteth it under his feet, and treadeth on it; in token that he is lord over it, that it should serve him, and he not it."[39] The pope had made the word of God subservient to the Church. It was only because the Church had decided which books are scripture that they had authority. This meant that the Church had power to add to the scriptures the unwritten traditions that were part of the faith.

> Judge, therefore, reader, whether the pope with his be the church; whether their authority be above the scripture; whether all they teach without scripture be equal with the scripture; whether they have erred, and not only whether they can.[40]

The power which the pope claims stems from the idea that there is a continuous succession from Christ, through Peter and through all the Bishops of Rome, so that the pope sits on Peter's seat. Tyndale took up this idea and wrote,

> Peter's seat now is Christ's seat, Christ's gospel, on which all the apostles sat, and on which this day sit all they only that preach Christ truly. Wherefore, as antichrist preacheth not Peter's doctrine (which is Christ's gospel), so he sitteth not on Peter's seat, but on the seat of Satan, whose vicar he is, and on the seat of his own laws and ceremonies, and false doctrine, whereunto he compelleth all men with violence of sword.[41]

How contrary is the pope's practice to God's. "God is merciful and long-suffering, even so were all his true prophets and preachers; bearing the infirmities of their weak brethren, . . . until they sinned against the

Holy Ghost." But the pope is opposed to that, "which in sinning against God, and to quench the truth of his Holy Spirit, is ever chief captain and trumpet-blower to set other at work, . . . and in his own cause is so fervent, so stiff and cruel."[42] And this, Tyndale believes, leads to "the bishop of Rome and his defenders" saying, "'Then the devil hath God in him, and is also in God:' for other faith, than such as the devil hath, felt they never any."[43]

Christ's Kingdom and the Pope's Kingdom

We find that the pope has usurped God's power over both the spiritual and the temporal regiments; for since he has taken God's place in the world, these kingdoms must belong to him.

> Lo, saith he, in that he saith, whatsoever thou bindest in earth, he excepteth nothing; therefore I may make laws, and bind both king and emperor:" when Christ, as he had no worldly kingdom, even so he spake of no worldly binding, but the binding of sinners.[44]

Wyclif wrote that this ascendancy of spiritual over temporal authority was the work of the devil: "the fiend deceives the church in one way as by well known lying, that Christ was their worldly lord, most high of all other, and so should his vicar be that is called the pope of Rome."[45]

Tyndale said that every Christian, be he pope, clergy or lay, is part of the temporal kingdom, and therefore is under the authority of the God-appointed rulers. For, "Christ saith, Matt. iii. 'Thus becometh it us to fulfil all righteousness,' that is to say, all ordinances of God. If the head be then under the temporal sword, how can the members be excepted?"[46] Tyndale also refers to *Romans* 13, "'Let every soul obey the higher powers,' that are ordained to punish sin. The pope will not, nor let any of his."[47]

The pope had overturned the teaching of God's word and, in its place, set up his own. "The pope, contrary unto all conscience and against all the doctrine of Christ, which saith, 'My kingdom is not of this world,' (John xviii.) hath usurped the right of the emperor."[48] In *Prelates* Tyndale shows how the pope fell to the devil's temptation of worldly power, and the ways used by the pope to usurp the temporal sword. These temptations that

> Christ refused, (Matt. iv.) did the devil proffer unto the pope; and he immediately fell from Christ, and worshipped the devil, and received them. . . . The pope, after he had received the kingdom of the world of the devil, and was become the devil's

> vicar, took up in like manner all Christendom on high, and brought them from the meekness of Christ unto the high hill of the pride of Lucifer, and shewed them all the kingdoms of the earth, saying: 'Fall down and worship me, and I will give you these.'"[49]

The pope took over the governance of the countries, "deceiving the king of the country, and then with his sword compelled the rest."[50]

The pope prevented laymen from having temporal rule in the country "because that antichrist with the mist of his juggling hath beguiled our eyes, and hath cast a superstitious fear upon the world of christian men."[51] Tyndale showed how kings and emperor had become puppets in the hands of the spiritualty; all the political manipulations which went on at that time, were "not without our cardinal's and bishops' counsel, thou mayest well wit."[52]

The spiritualty needed freedom to live as they wanted, freed from the restraints of the spiritual regiment, and the punishment of the temporal regiment, and so they claimed that the church had liberties to sin without restraint. Therefore, "the kings, by the falsehood of the bishops and abbots, be sworn to defend such liberties."[53] The pope, to reward the king for his obedience, would confer on him a title: "So now, above seven hundred years, to be a christian king is to fight for the pope; and most christian, that most fighteth, and slayeth most men for his pleasure."[54]

Tyndale's clearest statement about the pope's workings in the temporal regiment are expressed in the "Prologue" to *The Obedience*:

> This seest thou, that it is the bloody doctrine of the pope which causeth disobedience, rebellion and insurrection: for he teacheth to fight and to defend his traditions, and whatsoever he dreameth, with fire, water, and sword; and to disobey father, mother, master, lord, king, and emperor; yea, and to invade whatsoever land or nation, that will not receive and admit his godhead.[55]

Christ's Ministers and the Pope's Ministers

The pope reigned supreme in the spiritual kingdom as well as in the temporal one. Here, also, he reigned as a tyrant and not as a servant of Christ, and all the spiritualty followed his lead.

> As soon as Nemroth, that mighty hunter, had caught this prey, that he had compelled all bishops to be under him, and to swear obedience unto him, then he began to be great in the earth; and called himself Papa, with the interpretation, Father of fathers."[56]

In answer to his question, "Judge, therefore, reader, whether the pope with his be the church?"[57] Tyndale answered very clearly

> That the pope and his spirits be not the church, may this wise be proved. He that hath no faith to be saved through Christ, is not of Christ's church. The pope believeth not to be saved through Christ: for he teacheth to trust in holy works for the remission of sins and salvation."

He then listed the main holy works people were expected to do before continuing,

> And a thousand such superstitiousnesses setteth he before us, instead of Christ to believe in; neither Christ nor God's word, neither honourable to God nor serviceable unto our neighbour, nor profitable unto ourselves for the taming of the flesh; which all are the denying of Christ's blood.[58]

The spiritualty have followed the pope's lead and exalted themselves in the Church. They set themselves up to capture more men than another to their "fashions," "yet to resist Christ are they all agreed, lest they should be all compelled to deliver up their prisoners to him." They hide behind all kinds of symbols, "mitres, crosiers, and hats," etc., and claim all kinds of titles, "My lord prior, my lord abbot, my lord bishop," etc., and their captives have to come to them in all humility, "if it please your fatherhood, if it please your lordship," etc. The result is we submit to them, "For both they, and whatsoever they make of their own heads, is more feared and dread than God and his commandments."[59] Although More feels that the spiritualty are good, Tyndale feels that their faith is no true faith. In fact he wrote,

> Our defenders do right well to foam out their own shame, and to utter the secret thoughts of their hearts. For as they write, so they believe. Other feeling of the laws of God and faith of Christ have they none, than that their God the pope so saith. And therefore as the pope preacheth with his mouth only, even so believe they with their mouth only whatsoever he preacheth, without more ado, be it never so abominable.[60]

The result of this teaching of the pope and the prelates is that the times Peter wrote about have come. "He warneth them of false teachers that should come, and through preaching confidence in false works, to satisfy their covetousness withal, should deny Christ."[61] The tragedy of all this is those "which are believed to minister the true word do slay the souls with false doctrine for covetousness' sake."[62]

Salvation: by Works or by Blood?

Man's salvation, as we have seen, depends on repentance and faith in the blood of Christ. But for the pope's church these were not important. Tyndale wrote, "Wycliffe preached repentance unto our fathers not long since. They repented not, for their hearts were indurate, and their eyes blinded with their own pope-holy righteousness." Now with the coming of the Reformation,

> Christ, to preach repentance, is risen yet once again out of his sepulchre, in which the pope had buried him, and kept him down with his pillars and poleaxes, and all disguisings of hypocrisy, with guile, wiles and falsehood, and with the sword of all princes, which he had blinded with his false merchandise.[63]

But still, the pope's church made a man believe that he "will be justified and saved through his own works."[64] For

> they had set up a righteousness of holy works to cleanse their souls withal; as the pope sanctifieth us with holy oil, holy bread, holy salt, holy candles, holy dumb ceremonies, and holy dumb blessings, and with whatsoever holiness thou wilt, save with the holiness of God's word.[65]

For the pope's doctrine leads us away from the salvation which is ours in Christ's blood; for

> with Pelagius, he preacheth the justifying of works; which is the denying of Christ. He preacheth a false binding and loosing with ear confession, which is not in the trust and confidence of Christ's blood-shedding. He preacheth the false penance of deeds; not to tame the flesh that we sin no more, but to make satisfaction, and to redeem the sin that is past: which what other can it be, save the denying of Christ, which is the only redemption of sin?[66]

We will be looking at what Tyndale considered the errors of the papists regarding salvation in more detail in the next two sections.

The Sacraments: True and False

Before we consider the individual sacraments there are, according to Tyndale, certain errors which relate to all the seven "sacraments" of the unreformed Church, as the spiritualty turn scripture from its literal sense into an allegory: "As when the pope saith, Ye be justified by the works of the ceremonies and sacraments, and so forth."[67]

The unreformed Church had taken away the true meaning of the sacraments and made them meaningless.

> Dumb ceremonies are no sacraments, but superstitiousness. Christ's sacraments preach the faith of Christ, as his apostles did, and thereby justify. Antichrist's dumb ceremonies preach not the faith that is in Christ; as his apostles, our bishops and cardinals do not. . . . And hereby mayest thou know the difference between Christ's signs or sacraments, and antichrist's signs or ceremonies; that Christ's signs speak, and antichrist's be dumb.[68]

Tyndale enlarged on these dumb ceremonies and called for his readers to decide their value.

> Judge whether it be possible that any good should come out of their dumb ceremonies and sacraments into thy soul. Judge their penance, pilgrimages, pardons, purgatory, praying to posts, dumb blessings, dumb absolutions, their dumb pattering, and howling, their dumb strange holy gestures, with all their dumb disguisings, their satisfactions and justifyings.[69]

With a catalogue of errors like that to contend with, it is no wonder that More accused Tyndale of being more extreme than Luther.[70]

To show the people's ignorance of the true meaning of baptism, Tyndale wrote that is was often called *volowing*, "because the priest saith, *Volo,* [I wish it] say ye. 'The child was well *volowed'* (say they); 'yea, and our vicar is as fair a *volower* as ever a priest within this twenty miles.'" The reason lying behind this attitude to baptism is that "they make us believe that the work itself, without the promise, saveth us; which doctrine they learned of Aristotle."[71] And this ignorance of the people was due to the spiritualty not teaching the people the truth. Tyndale wrote, "And therefore, because we be never taught the profession of our baptism, we remain always unlearned, as well the spiritualty, for all their great clergy and high schools (as we say), as the lay people."[72]

There were many ways the Church had destroyed the meaning of the Lord's Supper, and Tyndale believed that both transubstantiation and consubstantiation were erroneous. Although Tyndale could not see how the covenant could agree with either the Lutheran or the Roman doctrines of Christ's bodily presence with the elements of bread and wine, this was the one error he was prepared to overlook for the sake of Church unity. For Tyndale the covenant in the blood of Christ is all important, and he wrote of

> the damnable idolatry which the papists have committed with the sacrament, yet, whether they affirm the body and blood to be present with the bread and wine, or the bread and wine to be turned and transubstantiated into the body and blood, I am therewith content (for unity's sake) if they will there cease, and

> let him be there only to testify and confirm the testament or covenant made in Christ's blood and body.[73]

Tyndale found many opportunities to criticise the Roman Church for the doctrinal errors in the Mass. He drew attention to its teaching which appears to contradict its own belief in transubstantiation for

> the priest toucheth not Christ's natural body with his hands, by your own doctrine; nor seeth it with his eyes, nor breaketh it with his fingers, nor eateth it with his mouth, nor chammeth it with his teeth, nor drinketh his blood with his lips; for Christ is impassible.[74]

For the Mass to be called a sacrifice was also untrue, in Tyndale's view, so he attacked the spiritualty for teaching that it was. "I answer, that a sacrifice is the slaying of the body of a beast, or a man: wherefore, if it be a sacrifice, then is Christ's body there slain, and his blood there shed; but that is not so. And therefore it is properly no sacrifice, but a sacrament."[75]

The actions of the priest in the Mass also came under Tyndale's criticism. He picked up some words from More's *Dialogue,* "holy, strange gestures used in consecration or ministration of the blessed sacraments."[76] Tyndale wrote,

> And when he saith, "Holy strange gestures;" I answer, for the holiness I will not swear, but the strangeness I dare well avow: for every priest maketh them of a sundry manner, and many more madly than the gestures of jack-an-apes.[77]

Concerning the ceremonies used he wrote,

> And of the ceremonies of the mass we have none other imagination than that they be an holy service unto God; which he receiveth of our hands, and hath great delectation in them, and that we purchase great favour of God with them, as we do of great men here in the world with gifts and presents: insomuch that if a priest said mass without those vestments, or left the other ceremonies undone, we should all quake for fear; and think that there were a sin committed, enough to sink us all, and that the priest for his labour were worthy to be put in the bishop of Rome's purgatory.[78]

In fact those who believe "that all the ceremonies of the mass are a service to God by reason of the bodily works, to obtain forgiveness of sins thereby, and to deserve and merit therewith," are wrong, for they "be idolatry and image-service, and make God an idol or bodily image."[79]

The Five Non-Magisterial Sacraments

Tyndale passes onto the five sacraments of the medieval Church which he rejected as sacraments, that is, *Matrimony, Orders, Confirmation, Confession/Penance* and *Unction*.[80] He challenged More, "Now, sir, in your penance, describe us which is the sign and the outward sacrament, and what is the thing that I must do or believe; and then we will ensearch whether it may be a sacrament or no."[81] Of course, Tyndale has "ensearched" it and found that it is not a sacrament, but more than that he has found it to be evil.

> The sacrament of penance they thus describe: contrition, confession, and satisfaction: contrition; sorrow for thy sins: confession; not to God and them whom thou hast offended, but tell thy sins in the priest's ear: satisfaction, to do certain deeds enjoined of them, to buy out thy sins. And in their description they have clean excluded the faith in the satisfaction of Christ's blood.[82]

Tyndale expanded these remarks and then continued,

> And hereof ye may see how out of this open penance came the ear-confession, satisfaction of works, purgatory and pardons. For when they had put the satisfaction of Christ's blood out of the way, then as they compelled men to confess open sins, and to take open penance, even so they compelled them to confess secret sins, and to take secret penance.[83]

Tyndale's "ensearching" of the evils of penance and auricular confession led him to conclude, "Shrift in the ear is verily a work of Satan; and that the falsest that ever was wrought, and that most hath devoured the faith."[84]

Because the covenant in Christ's blood is denied, penance brings salvation through our holy works. "Holy-work men think that God rejoiceth in the deed self, without any farther respect. They think also that God, as a cruel tyrant, rejoiceth and hath delectation in our pain-taking, without any farther respect."[85] It is through these holy works that we must look for our salvation because "the pope believeth not to be saved through Christ: for he teacheth to trust in holy works for the remission of sins and salvation; as in the works of penance, enjoined in vows." Tyndale lists many other errors "which all are the denying of Christ's blood."[86]

Confession is also a source of wealth for the spiritualty.

> To believe they teach not in Christ, but in them and their disguised hypocrisy. And of them compel they all men to buy redemption

> and forgiveness of sins. The people's sin they eat, and thereof wax fat. The more wicked the people are, the more prosperous is their commonwealth.[87]

And the greed of the spiritualty can also be seen in the inventions they have conceived,

> And as for their feigned words, where findest thou in all the scripture purgatory, shrift, penance, pardon, *pœna, culpa, hyperdoulia,* and a thousand feigned terms more? And as for their merchandise, look whether they sell not all God's laws, and also their own, and all sin, and all Christ's merits, and all that a man can think. To one he selleth the fault only; and to another the fault and the pain too; and purgeth his purse of his money, and his brains of his wits, and maketh him so beastly that he can understand no godly thing.[88]

Marriage also was not to be counted as a sacrament, for,

> It was ordained for a remedy, and to increase the world; and for the man to help the woman, and the woman the man, with all love and kindness; and not to signify any promise, that ever I heard or read of in the scripture. Therefore ought it not to be called a sacrament.[89]

Tyndale is rather more sceptical of Orders,

> Subdeacon, deacon, priest, bishop, cardinal, patriarch, and pope, be names of offices and service, or should be, and not sacraments. There is no promise coupled therewith. If they minister their offices truly, it is a sign that Christ's Spirit is in them; if not, that the devil is in them.

Tyndale goes on to ask what is the sacramental sign, and what promise does it signify?[90] The conclusion Tyndale makes is that "Antichrist hath deceived us with unknown and strange terms, to bring us into confusion and superstitious blindness."[91] He then in many ways proves that those who follow the pope's teaching are indeed far from the teaching of Christ.[92]

Confirmation also is not a sacrament;[93] as it was practiced in the medieval Church it was an invention of the devil. Instead of preaching Christ's word,

> antichrist's bishops preach not; and their sacraments speak not; but as the disguised bishop's mum, so are their superstitious sacraments dumb. After that the bishops had left preaching, then feigned they this dumb ceremony of confirmation, to have somewhat at the leastway, whereby they might reign over their dioceses.[94]

It is the same with Extreme Unction, which Tyndale calls Anoiling, and says that it is "without promise, and therefore without the Spirit, and without profit; but altogether unfruitful and superstitious."[95]

All the sacraments of the unreformed Church were valueless; the ones Christ had ordained, "them minister they in the Latin tongue. So are they also become as unfruitful as the other. Yea, they make us believe that the work itself, without the promise, saveth us; which doctrine they learned of Aristotle."[96] From all the "sacraments" the spiritualty had taken the word of God so that they did not proclaim God's promises and made them into dumb ceremonies; and, "Dumb ceremonies are no sacraments, but superstitiousness."[97] They are valueless because "the keeping of men's traditions and dumb ceremonies make us not bold before God, nor certify our conscience that our faith is unfeigned."[98] It was then that Christians

> became servants unto the ceremonies; ascribing their justifying and salvation unto them, supposing that it was nothing else to be a christian man than to serve ceremonies, and him most christian that most served them; and contrariwise, him that was not popish and ceremonial, no christian man at all.[99]

Therefore, Tyndale wrote that they must be thrown out and trodden under foot for "What true christian man can give honour to that that taketh all honour from Christ? Who can give honour to that that slayeth the soul of his brother, and robbeth his heart of that trust and confidence, which he should give to his Lord that hath bought him with his blood?"[100]

Purgatory

Purgatory was, for Tyndale, perhaps the worst of the pope's inventions with no basis of fact found in God's word. Tyndale wrote that purgatory "is plainly impossible, and repugnant to the scripture."[101] The true Christians are "delivered from fear of everlasting death and hell." For it is through faith in Christ that we come to God and "are as familiar and bold with him as young innocent children, which have no conscience of sin, are with their fathers and mothers, or them that nourish them." What a difference faces those who listen to the pope's doctrine, who says that God commits us to "seven years' punishment, as sharp as the pains of hell, for every trespass we do; which trespasses for the number of them were like to make our purgatory almost as long as hell, seeing we have no God's word that we shall be delivered thence, until we have paid the last farthing."[102]

But even if God is not merciful, the pope is. For, according to the pope's doctrine, he will use the good deeds of those who have done more than God requires in this life to help those who are in purgatory. The

> *opera supererogationis* (howbeit *superarrogantia* were a meeter term), that is to say, deeds which are more than the law requireth; deeds of perfection and of liberality, which a man is not bound to do, but of his free will, and for them he shall have an higher place in heaven, and may give to other of his merits, or of which the pope, after his death, may give pardons from the pains of purgatory.[103]

However, when the pope released a soul from purgatory, or reduced the number of years to be spent there, it was not an act of mercy freely given, there was a cost placed on it. "Whatsoever any tyrant had robbed all his life, that, or the most part thereof, must he deal among them [the spiritualty] at his death, for fear of purgatory."[104] And then "the pope's letters do certify the believers of the pope's pardons."[105] But it is not just the wealthy who have to pay dear for the pope's pardons.

> Look at the pope's false doctrine: what is the end thereof, and what seek they thereby? Wherefore serveth purgatory, but to purge thy purse, and to poll thee, and rob both thee and thy heirs of house and lands, and of all thou hast, that they may be in honour? Serve not pardons for the same purpose?[106]

Tyndale exposes the folly of this doctrine in his *Answer to More,*

> M. More feeleth in his heart by inspiration, and with his endeavouring himself and captivating his understanding to believe it, that there is a purgatory as hot as hell; wherein if a silly soul were appointed by God to lie a thousand years, to purge him withal, the pope, for the value of a groat, shall command him thence full purged in the twinkling of an eye; and by as good reason, if he were going thence, keep him there still. He feeleth by inspiration, and in captivating his wits, that the pope can work wonders with a calf's skin.[107]

False Actions

The spiritualty had built a works righteousness unrelated to God's word and commandments; rather, like the Pharisees Christ condemned, they turned the truth of God upside down. We should help our parents,

> but to withdraw help from them at their need, for blind zeal of offering, unto the profit of the holy Pharisees, was then as meritorious, as it is now to let all thy kin choose whether they will sink or swim, while thou buildest and makest goodly foundations for holy people, which thou hast chosen to be thy

> Christ, for to supple thy soul with the oil of their sweet blessings; and to be thy Jesus, for to save thy soul from the purgatory of the blood that only purgeth sin, with their watching, fasting, woolward-going, and rising at midnight, &c., wherewith yet they purge not themselves from their covetousness, pride, lechery, or any vice that thou seest among the lay-people.[108]

Tyndale accuses John Fisher, Bishop of Rochester, of being "both abominable and shameless, yea, and stark mad with pure malice, and so adased in the brains with spite," that he cannot see or care for the truth. Tyndale continues, "In the end of his first destruction, I would say *instruction,* as he calleth it, intending to prove that we are justified through holy works, allegeth half a text of Paul." Moreover, Fisher did not even translate the half verse accurately.

> Which text he thiswise Englisheth: 'Faith which is wrought by love;' and maketh a verb passive of a verb deponent. Rochester will have love to go before, and faith to spring out of love. Thus antichrist turneth the roots of the tree upward.[109]

The spiritualty believed that God had set a certain amount of work for each one of us to do. It was not necessary for us to do anything extra in order to be saved. It was, therefore, possible for the friars to say, "They do more than their duty when they preach, and more than they are bound to."[110] The spiritualty were only bound to take the Church services, for as Kenneth Carleton wrote, "the constant teaching of the Middle Ages, that priests were ordained primarily to offer the sacrifice of the Mass, not for preaching or teaching the Word of God."[111]

Tyndale wrote of those who became martyrs because they resisted (as far as possible) being sexually abused. It was claimed that the value of their martyrdom was "partly for ensamples; partly, God through sin healeth sin. Pride can neither be healed, nor yet appear, but through such horrible deeds." Tyndale continued,

> Peradventure they were of the pope's sect, and rejoiced fleshly; thinking that heaven came by deeds, and not by Christ, and that the outward deed justified them and made them holy, and not the inward spirit received by faith, and the consent of the heart unto the laws of God.[112]

The "work" the martyrs did could not save them. Although there are some deeds which are wrong in themselves and must be resisted, yet even good deeds are powerless to save us and bring forgiveness to us. Christ warned against putting one's trust in works. Tyndale's comment on the first verses of *Matthew* 6 are,

> As he rebuked their doctrine above, even so here he rebuketh their works; for out of devilish doctrine can spring no godly works. But what works rebuketh he? Verily such as God in the scripture commandeth, and without which no man can be a christian man, even prayer; even fasting, and alms-deed."[113]

Baptism is seen as a holy work by the papists who believe "that the Holy Ghost be present in the water, and therefore the very deed or work doth put away sin." It is similar with the Lord's Supper, and the spiritualty believe "that it is a sacrifice as well for the dead as for the quick, and therefore the very deed itself justfieth and putteth away sin." Tyndale continues,

> But under the pretence of their soul-health, it is a servant unto our spirituality's holy covetousness; and an extortioner; and a builder of abbeys, colleges, chauntries and cathedral churches; . . . a pickpurse, a poller, and a bottomless bag.[114]

There were many other works that the spiritualty taught were a help towards man's salvation. "When the people believe therefore, if they do so much work, or suffer so much pain, or go so much a pilgrimage, that they are safe, [it] is a false faith."[115] Tyndale condemned this trust in good works, "For he that will be justified and saved through his own works, the same doth as much as he that denied Christ to be come in the flesh."[116]

False Worship

In his exposition of the *Sermon on the Mount,* Tyndale criticised the false prayers of the spiritualty, "their false intent in praying, that they sought praise and profit of that work." That they trusted

> in the multitude of words, and in the pain and tediousness of the length of the prayer, . . . and have turned it into a bodily labour, to vex the tongue, lips, eyes, and throat with roaring, and to weary all the members; so that they say . . . that there is no greater labour in the world than prayer."[117]

The spiritualty claim that they are the ones who have access to God, and so they exclude the laity from Christ. "They compel us to hire friars, monks, nuns, canons, and priests, and to buy their abominable merits, and to hire the saints that are dead to pray for us."[118] Because the Jews thought that they could worship God better in the temple, "And therefore they could not pray but there, as ours can nowhere but at church, and before an image."[119] Against that, "The temple wherein God will be worshipped is the heart of man."[120]

Tyndale constantly criticised the spiritualty for linking churches and images with the worship of God.

> But to believe that God will be sought more in one place than in another, or that God will hear thee more in one place than in another, or more where the image is than where it is not, is a false faith, and idolatry, or image-service.[121]

In spite of all the protestations of the spiritualty, the hallmark of the unreformed church was "image service". For the people are not taught what true worship is, and they spend their substance on images, therefore Tyndale asks how the sight of images adorned with "gold and silver and of precious stones should move a man's heart to despise such things, after the doctrine of Christ;" or how can seeing it clothed in a "rich coat help to move thy mind to follow the ensample of the saint." At the same time as they give all this wealth to the images "the poor are despised and uncared for."[122] Tyndale continues his attack on the worship of images by saying that if

> such things with all other service, as sticking up candles, move not thy mind to follow the ensample of the saint, nor teach thy soul any godly learning, then the image serveth thee not, but thou the image; and so art thou an idolater.[123]

If the person represented by the image could speak, "he would answer that he were a spirit, and delighted in no candle-light; but would bid thee give a candle to thy neighbour that lacketh, if thou hadst too many."[124]

Tyndale also called people to remember the words of Moses and God's commandments, "and to beware either of making imagery, or of bowing themselves unto images, saying, 'Ye saw no image when God spake unto you, but heard a voice only.'"[125] In reply to More when he said "that men know the image from the saint," Tyndale showed not only that people acted as if the image were the saint but also that "God is a spirit, and will be worshipped in his word only, which is spiritual; and will have no bodily service."[126]

Idolatry was found in the Church with the worship of images, but there was also "the damnable idolatry which the papists have committed with the sacrament."[127] "Let us take the mass, which after the Romish bishop's abuse of it, is the most damnable image-service that ever was since it began."[128] For those who believe in the bodily presence of Christ in the sacrament, and that the priest makes the bread and wine turn into Christ's body and blood are "serving God with bodily service, (which is idolatry, and to make God an idol or image,) in that they trust in the goodness of their works."[129]

The idolatry of the spiritualty was not only in the outward acts of worship before the images of the saints and the Host, they also prayed to the saints. In *A Dialogue,* More wrote, "The author proveth that if the worship of images were idolatry then the church, believing it to be lawful and pleasant to God, were in a misbelief and in a deadly error."[130] Tyndale answered him,

> In the nineteenth he proveth that praying to saints is good; . . . or else the church, saith he, doth err. It followeth indeed, or that the pope's church erreth. . . . And when he saith God is honoured by praying to saints, because it is done for his sake; I answer, if it sprang not out of a false faith, but of the love we have to God, then should we love God more. . . . And then if our faith in God were greater than our fervent devotion to saints, we should pray to no saints at all, seeing we have promises of all things in our Saviour Jesus, and in the saints none at all."[131]

If they follow the teaching of the pope's church about saints and images, then, Tyndale asks, "How can they believe that Christ died for their sins, and that he is their only and sufficient Saviour, seeing that they seek other saviours of their own imagination."[132]

In these and other ways the spiritualty taught the people to worship God, and led them astray from the truth and the true faith in Christ's blood.

> And yet in these works they have so great confidence, that they not only trust to be saved thereby, and to be higher in heaven than they that be saved through Christ, but also promise to all other forgiveness of their sins through the merits of the same; wherein they rest, and teach other to rest also, excluding the whole world from the rest of forgiveness of sins through faith in Christ's blood.[133]

The spiritualty teach the people that the saints, to whom they pray, are no more merciful than the pope himself. Tyndale condemns this,

> How wicked a thing then is it to think that the saints trouble and plague us, because we do them not such superstitious honour, which is their dishonour and our shame? It is verily a popish imagination, and even to describe the saints after the nature of our prelates, which be meek and lowly till they be where they would be; but when they be once aloft, they play the tormentors if we will not honour them, and do whatsoever they command more earnestly than that which God himself hath commanded, and fear them above God himself.[134]

Tyndale uses the example of St White[135] who "must have a cheese once in a year, and that of the greatest sort," and he asks, "What shall St

White do for thee again for that great cheese? For I wot well it is not given for nought. Shall she give abundance of milk, to make butter or cheese?" Finally he asks,

> What other thing then is thy serving of St White, than lack of faith and trust to God-ward in Christ's name; and a false faith of thy own feigning, to St White-ward, for thine image-service or serving her with cheese, as though she were a bodily thing? And like disputation is it of all other saints.

For everything that every saint is supposed to do for us is false, "but God hath promised, if we will keep his laws, to do so much for us at our own request, for the blood of his Son Jesus."[136]

The Spiritualty and the Broken Covenant

From the foregoing it is obvious that the spiritualty have erred, and they have led the laity astray. Although Tyndale was aware, from the New Testament, that the Church was never free from those who did not keep the true faith and sought to lead it into error, it is in *The Practice of Prelates* that Tyndale looks at the way the spiritualty turned away from the purity of the apostolic church. But until, approximately, the eighth century the worst excesses had been held at bay.

As the Church grew and persecutions ceased, the deacons who controlled the finances of the Church grew covetous. "And by the means of their practice and acquaintance in the world they were more subtle and worldly wise than the old bishops, and less learned in God's word."[137] They used their powers to their advantage and their wealth, and the Church turned away from Christ and the truth.

> Then, while they that had the plough by the tail looked back, the plough went awry; faith waxed feeble and fainty; love waxed cold; the scriptures waxed dark; Christ was no more seen. He was in the mount with Moses; and therefore the bishops would have a god upon the earth whom they might see, and thereupon they began to dispute who should be greatest.[138]

In the whole of that passage Tyndale traced the way by which the pope climbed to power and the papal church came into being. It was a time when covetousness and a lust for power gripped the spiritualty rather than a concern to serve God and build up his people.

Much of Tyndale's concern was with the pope's usurpation of the temporal regiment. Rainer Pineas in his article, "William Tyndale's use of History as a Weapon of Religious Controversy," is only concerned with this aspect. Pineas points out that the only Chronicle Tyndale mentions by name is Higden's *Polychronicon,* which was translated by Trevisa into English, although he does list others that Tyndale probably used.[139] It was the worldliness of the spiritualty which lay behind their errors.

> And if pride, covetousness, and lechery be the world, as St John saith, then turn your eyes unto the spiritualty, unto the Roman bishop, cardinals, bishops, abbots, and all other prelates, and see whether such dignities be not the world, and whether the way to them be not also the world![140]

In fact we had been warned against this danger in 2 Timothy, where Paul

> sheweth before, and that notably, of the jeopardous time toward the end of the world, in which a false spiritual living should deceive the whole world with outward hypocrisy and appearance of holiness; under which all abominations should have their free passage and course, as we (alas!) have seen this prophecy of St Paul fulfilled in our spiritualty unto the uttermost jot.[141]

The General Councils, which once had helped to maintain the truth of the Gospel, are now ineffectual. Tyndale first lists the ways by which the pope had seized power over kings and the clergy; then he continues,

> Moreover, the general councils of the spiritualty are of no other manner, since the pope was a god, than the general parliaments of the temporalty; where no man dare say his mind freely and liberally, for fear of some one and of his flatterers.[142]

As Christ condemned the scribes and Pharisees for doing their works so that men could see them, their pomp and glory in taking the chief places in the synagogue, and being called "Rabbi", so Tyndale criticised the spiritualty of his day. Tyndale drew attention to all their pomp, the titles they were to be called, and the humiliating way people have to approach them. "Behold how they are esteemed, and how high they be crept up above all; not into worldly seats only, but into the seat of God, the hearts of men, where they sit above God himself."[143] Tyndale tells the laity to "look on the works of our spiritualty, which will not only be justified with works before the world, but also before God."[144] He also warns the spiritualty to "take heed and look well about them, and see whether they walk as they have promised God, and in the steps of his Son Christ, and of his apostles, whose offices they bear."[145]

This failure of the Church to keep the purity of the gospel is because

> the pope, the father of all hypocrites, [has] put down the kingdom

> of Christ, and set up the kingdom of the devil, whose vicar he is; and hath put down the ministers of Christ, and hath set up the ministers of Satan, disguised yet in names and garments like unto the angels of light and ministers of righteousness.[146]

The result of this is that the spiritualty cannot even justify their actions before men, let alone God. "The pope consenteth not that God's law is good, . . . he hath granted unlawful whoredom unto as many as bring money." So the clergy are given licences, not to marry but to have whores, "and when the parishens go to law with them, to put away their whores, the bishop's officers mock them, poll them, and make them spend their thrifts, and the priests keep their whores still."[147] Tyndale challenges the immorality of the spiritualty and asks,

> If ye profess chastity, why desire ye above all other men the company of women? What do ye with whores openly in many countries, and with secret dispensations to keep concubines? Why corrupt ye so much other men's wives? And why be there so many sodomites among you?[148]

In fact, if a priest "keep a whore, then is he a good chaste child of their holy father the pope."[149]

At that point in the *Exposition of Matthew, v, vi, vii,* Tyndale lists many of the errors of the spiritualty. "Here Christ warneth thee, and describeth unto thee those captains that should so blind the great multitude that they should not find the strait gate, and lead them the broad way to perdition." They are the ones Christ warned against when he said, "There shall come many in my name, and deceive many." They preach and do miracles in Christ's name "to confirm the false doctrine which they preach in his name." "They preach to other, 'Steal not;' yet they themselves rob God of his honour, and take from him the praise and profit of all their doctrine and of all their works." "They have robbed the soul of man of the bread of her life, the faith and trust in Christ's blood; and fed her with the shales and cods of hope in their merits and confidence in their good works." Their obedience is to disobey those God has given authority over us. Their poverty causes Tyndale to ask, "Should a beggar ride with three or four score horses waiting upon him?" Their charity "is merciless to the rest of the world" and is "as is the charity of thieves." Their fasting makes them "as full and as fat as your hides can hold." Their prayer "is but the pattering without all affection"

In all, "Where they have fruit that seemeth to be good, go to and prove it, and thou shalt find it rotten, or the kernel eaten out, and that it is but a hollow nut."[150]

Conclusion

As one reads Tyndale's writings, one notices a uniformity and a clarity of thought. We realise that before we can attempt to study any individual doctrine we need to have grasped the overall view of Tyndale's theology. Careful reading of his works show the theological unity between Tyndale's first and last writings. This is confirmed in great depth by Paul Lauchlin in his doctoral dissertation "The Brightness of Moses' Face," and his findings were supported by Judith Mayotte's dissertation "William Tyndale's Contribution to the Reformation in England." The arguments which had been put forward that Tyndale's earlier use of the word "testament" and later use of "covenant" in his writings revealed a change in his theology are shown to be false and valueless. Tyndale pointed to this unity in his thought when he wrote, "testament, that is covenant."[1] Even Clebsch admitted that one of Tyndale's alterations in his revised translation of Genesis showed that these different words had the same meaning for he translated, in 1534, the Hebrew "*berith* as 'covenant,' discarding the 1530 alternatives 'appointment,' 'bond,' and 'testament.'"[2] It is incredible that Clebsch could build up a theory that "from 1532 . . . his theology, newly organised around the idea of covenant . . . shouts itself from every writing attributable to the period."[3] Many have accepted Clebsch's theory of the changes to Tyndale's theology,[4] and they have blindly followed him "and fallen into the ditch."[5] Even Clebsch himself expressed the problem his thesis created for his "Tyndale was a Lutheran" theory when he wrote, "Extant data display abundantly the theological breach and the literary debt, but they are mute as to Tyndale's motives."[6]

The problem facing William Clebsch, and those who followed him, is Tyndale's originality. They tried to make his theology fit into certain established patterns of theological thought and, like the feet of the ugly sisters, they had to mutilate Tyndale's theology in order to make it fit into what they thought was Cinderella's slipper. In fact, as I was told by two highly acclaimed Reformation historians, Tyndale's theology (as I have expounded it) is theologically impossible![7] Their criticism was also voiced by Paul Laughlin at the beginning of his dissertation,

> For on various occasions in his writings he offered two very different hermeneutical devices: . . . What makes this discrepancy more than merely intriguing, however, is that the two hermeneutical devices suggest two fundamentally contradictory and inimical underlying theological systems.[8]

However, his first thoughts changed, and in his "Conclusion" Laughlin could write,

> But it is now clear that he by no means employed two different theological frameworks, either simultaneously or successively, but rather maintained consistently throughout his writings an essentially covenantal framework for theological reflection and discourse.[9]

In the world of the sixteenth century Tyndale dared to think the unthinkable – simply because he restricted his theology to the scriptures and to what he understood God to be saying through them. He dared to reject man's reason, which had been tainted by the pagan philosophies of Aristotle, Plato and other Greek philosophers. This reliance on scripture alone led Tyndale to certain theological conclusions.

Firstly, the covenant is between the Persons of the Trinity. The doctrines that follow from Tyndale's understanding of the covenant shattered man's conceit in his own importance. There was a *feel* which seems to point to something larger and grander than the salvation of sinners. Even man's salvation, important as it is, seems to be relatively unimportant as we realise the place of God as Father and the elect as his children in Tyndale's theology. When the doctrine of the fatherhood of God is put alongside the statements in the Bible relating to the salvation of creation we seem to be entering into a different world to that normally occupied by the Christian community.[10]

Secondly, the stress Tyndale puts on creation – not as an event at the beginning of the universe, but that every man is a child of God through creation. Every man is therefore a brother or sister through creation. In loving them as we love ourselves, we may not make any difference between any human being – for whoever we are in race, colour, religion or gender we are all created by God. Taken out of context some of Tyndale's remarks sound as if he is bordering on universalism.[11] However, Tyndale wrote that

> two manner of people are sore deceived. . . . The first, that is to say, he which justifieth himself with his outward deeds, consenteth not to the law inward, neither hath delectation therein, yea, he would rather that no such law were. So justifieth he not God, but hateth him as a tyrant. . . . The second, that is to say, the sensual person, as a voluptuous swine, neither feareth God in the law, neither is thankful to him for his promises and mercy, which is set forth in Christ to all of them that believe.[12]

Tyndale's clearest denial of universalism comes from his teaching about the "little flock", "The kingdom of heaven is the preaching of the gospel, unto which come both good and bad. But the good are few, Christ calleth them therefore a 'little flock,' Luke xii."[13] But the multitude

> roar they out by and by, "what an heretic is this! . . . Thou art a strong heretic, and worthy to be burnt." . . . If little flock fear not that bug, then they go straight to the king: "And if it like your grace, perilous people, and seditious and even enough to destroy your realm, if ye see not to them betimes."[14]

Against that we have Tyndale's evangelical statement that we do good to those who are God's children through faith in order to strengthen their faith; and to those who have not been born again in order to win them for Christ. But there is also another reason behind loving our neighbour as we love ourselves which has a relevance towards proving this point. " 'Thou shalt not avenge thyself, nor bear hate in thy mind against the children of thy people; but shalt love thy fellow as thyself. I am the Lord.' As who should say, For my sake thou shalt do it." Tyndale continues,

> "The Lord your God is the God of gods and Lord of lords, a great God, mighty and terrible, which regardeth no man's person . . . but doth right to the fatherless and the widow, and loveth the stranger. . . . Love therefore the stranger. . . . But let the stranger, that dwelleth among you, be as one of yourselves, and love him as thyself: . . . I am the Lord." As who should say, Love him, for my sake.[15]

Thirdly, God's covenant is for the restoration of creation; therefore, Tyndale says, God wants us to care for the whole of his creation, and this care is especially seen in the compassion we must have towards animals.

> As that a man is forbid to seeth a kid in his mother's milk, moveth us unto compassion, and to be pitiful. As doth also that a man should not offer the sire, or dam, and the young both in one day. (Lev. xxii.) For it might seem a cruel thing, inasmuch as his mothers milk is, as it were, his blood: wherefore God will not have him sod therein; but will have a man shew courtesy upon the very beasts.[16]

The stress of Tyndale's theology is on God. It is God the Father who is our Father in a very real sense because one of the keys of Tyndale's covenant theology is the family, God's family. It is by one's entrance into that family, through the new birth, that one becomes a child of God. As a child one has access to our loving Father at any time and for whatever reason, and as loving children we seek always to please our Father in what we do.

It was God the Son who made the new birth and the new life possible. He shed his blood to satisfy God's justice so that the way for man's salvation could be opened and those who had been born again presented faultless to the Father as his children.

God the Holy Spirit applies the blood of Christ to those being saved, so that through the blood of Christ we are born again. Christ's blood is sprinkled on every aspect of our Christian life by the Holy Spirit as he gives faith and repentance and makes us righteous. "To believe in Christ's blood with a repenting heart is to make righteous, and the only making of peace and satisfaction to God-ward."[17] Through the blood of Christ, the Holy Spirit gives us love for God and his laws, love for our neighbour and all good works; the power to understand God's word and to worship God; and finally to bring us into God's eternal presence.

Luther, and most of the Reformers, had a doctrine of "the two regiments" or "kingdoms". Following the doctrine of the two swords of the medieval Church, the Reformers generally considered that the "spiritual regiment" was more important than the "temporal regiment" and that the temporal regiment was established post-Fall. However, Tyndale believed the temporal regiment is a creation ordinance and is fundamental for a proper functioning of society. For the basic unit of the temporal regiment is the family and "our fathers and mothers are to us in God's stead. Exod. xx."[18] With the growth of society the unit of society is no longer the family but the nation. "God therefore hath given laws unto all nations, and in all lands hath put kings, governors, and rulers in his own stead, to rule the world through them."[19] Although, since the Fall, they have the sword to maintain law and justice, this is not the main function of rulers. In the temporal regiment every man is a brother or sister to every one else. All are under God's laws, whether they are born again or not. Therefore, Tyndale wrote,

> God created the world of nought, and God worketh all things of his free will, and for a secret purpose; and that we shall all rise again, and that God will have accounts of all that we have done in this life.[20]

After the Fall the spiritual regiment became necessary for those born again by the Holy Spirit. But being members of the spiritual regiment did not separate them from those in the temporal regiment; the two regiments run side by side. The Christian king is under the rule of the bishop in the spiritual regiment, and the bishop is under the king in the temporal regiment (irrespective of whether the king were a Christian or a pagan).

As far as Tyndale was concerned, the problem of the medieval Church was that the clergy had broken the covenant. They had hidden the word of God from God's children and had forbidden the true Christians from having the scriptures and reading them in their own language. The clergy had made the spiritual regiment greater than the temporal regiment, and they had usurped the power and position of the rulers God had appointed over society. They believed that the spiritualty had been given an importance and power so that they alone could speak for God and interpret the scriptures and add to them the "traditions". But Tyndale accused them of following the Pharisees, who were condemned by Christ for hiding God's word from the people, and, by false interpretation, destroying the true meaning of the scriptures.

It was only by the laity having the scriptures in their own language that it was possible for them to see the truth and discern the errors of the spiritualty. It was Tyndale's desire for the laity to know the truth, and that lay behind Tyndale's life's work of translation. The laity would then be able to see how the spiritualty had followed in the steps of the Pharisees and broken the covenant. Through reading the authentic scriptures the laity would be able to discern the true doctrine from the false and become true followers of God and become his true children.

It is because a true Christian loves God's laws and commandments that he does good works that are pleasing to God. But these works are not done for any merit or reward; they come naturally to one who is a child of God for they reflect our likeness to our Father. And, as God shows his mercy, so must we;

> But lift up thine eyes unto thy heavenly Father, and as thy Father doth, so do thou love all thy Father's children. He ministereth sun and rain to good and bad; by which two understand all his benefits: . . . Even so provoke thou and draw thine evil brethren to goodness, with patience, with love in word and deed; and pray for them to him that is able to make them better and to convert them. And so thou shalt be thy Father's natural son, and perfect, as he is perfect.[21]

Once we have grasped Tyndale's doctrine of the covenant, we see the clarity of his thought and his total reliance on the scriptures. There is a simplicity and depth in his theology that make the Bible come alive in a way in which the ploughboy can rejoice as he finds he has become, through faith, a child of God the Father. There is much more research to be done that, I believe, will show that Tyndale was one of the greatest theologians of the Christian Church.

Notes

1. Tyndale, William, *Obedience,* p. 1/291f: *Sacraments,* p. 1/363, 381: *Prologue Matthew,* p. 1/468, "the new Testament, or covenant made with us in Christ's blood." and, *Prologue Matthew,* p. 1/476
2. Clebsch, *England's Earliest Protestants,* p. 182f
3. Clebsch, *England's Earliest Protestants,* p. 181
4. For example, Michael McGiffert, "Covenant flowered late in Tyndale's writings." "William Tyndale's Conception of Covenant", p. 169. Carl Trueman, *Luther's*

Legacy, although he acknowledged the idea of covenant going back to 1525, "It is in *I John* that Tyndale makes his first reference to an arrangement between God and man which approximates to that which he later describes with the term covenant." p. 111.

5. see Matthew 15:14.
6. Clebsch, *England's Earliest Protestants,* p. 183
7. I refrain from naming these persons, both of whom are historians and not theologians.
8. Laughlin, "The Brightness of Moses' Face:" p. 3f.
9. Laughlin, "The Brightness of Moses' Face:" p. 268
10. Romans 8:18-25; Acts 3:21
11. e.g. Tyndale, William, *Pathway,* p. 1/18: *Prelates,* p. 2/325: *Answer,* p. 3/6
12. Tyndale, William, *Pathway,* p. 12f.
13. Tyndale, William, *Obedience,* p. 165
14. Tyndale, William, *Answer,* p. 3/110
15. Tyndale, William, *Exposition Matthew,* p. 2/47
16. Tyndale, William, *Prologue Exodus,* p. 1/414: see also, *Sacraments,* p. 1/348, see also my paper given at the 4th International Tyndale Conference, Antwerp, 2002. "Divine Mercy and Human Compassion in the Prologues to Exodus and Deuteronomy".
17. Tyndale, William, *Answer,* p. 3/206
18. Tyndale, William, *Obedience,* p. 1/168 (Marginal Note)
19. Tyndale, William, *Obedience,* p. 1/174
20. Tyndale, William, *Obedience,* p. 1/155
21. Tyndale, William, *Exposition Matthew,* p. 2/71

11

Conclusion

As one reads Tyndale's writings, one notices a uniformity and a clarity of thought. We realise that before we can attempt to study any individual doctrine we need to have grasped the overall view of Tyndale's theology. Careful reading of his works show the theological unity between Tyndale's first and last writings. This is confirmed in great depth by Paul Lauchlin in his doctoral dissertation "The Brightness of Moses' Face," and his findings were supported by Judith Mayotte's dissertation "William Tyndale's Contribution to the Reformation in England." The arguments which had been put forward that Tyndale's earlier use of the word "testament" and later use of "covenant" in his writings revealed a change in his theology are shown to be false and valueless. Tyndale pointed to this unity in his thought when he wrote, "testament, that is covenant."[1] Even Clebsch admitted that one of Tyndale's alterations in his revised translation of Genesis showed that these different words had the same meaning for he translated, in 1534, the Hebrew "*berith* as 'covenant,' discarding the 1530 alternatives 'appointment,' 'bond,' and 'testament.'"[2] It is incredible that Clebsch could build up a theory that "from 1532 . . . his theology, newly organised around the idea of covenant . . . shouts itself from every writing attributable to the period."[3] Many have accepted Clebsch's theory of the changes to Tyndale's theology,[4] and they have blindly followed him "and fallen into the ditch."[5] Even Clebsch himself expressed the problem his thesis created for his "Tyndale was a Lutheran" theory when he wrote, "Extant data display abundantly the theological breach and the literary debt, but they are mute as to Tyndale's motives."[6]

The problem facing William Clebsch, and those who followed him, is Tyndale's originality. They tried to make his theology fit into certain established patterns of theological thought and, like the feet of the ugly sisters, they had to mutilate Tyndale's theology in order to make it fit into what they thought was Cinderella's slipper. In fact, as I was told by two highly acclaimed Reformation historians, Tyndale's theology (as I have expounded it) is theologically impossible![7] Their criticism was also voiced by Paul Laughlin at the beginning of his dissertation,

> For on various occasions in his writings he offered two very different hermeneutical devices: . . . What makes this discrepancy more than merely intriguing, however, is that the two hermeneutical devices suggest two fundamentally contradictory and inimical underlying theological systems.[8]

However, his first thoughts changed, and in his "Conclusion" Laughlin could write,

> But it is now clear that he by no means employed two different theological frameworks, either simultaneously or successively, but rather maintained consistently throughout his writings an essentially covenantal framework for theological reflection and discourse.[9]

In the world of the sixteenth century Tyndale dared to think the unthinkable – simply because he restricted his theology to the scriptures and to what he understood God to be saying through them. He dared to reject man's reason, which had been tainted by the pagan philosophies of Aristotle, Plato and other Greek philosophers. This reliance on scripture alone led Tyndale to certain theological conclusions.

Firstly, the covenant is between the Persons of the Trinity. The doctrines that follow from Tyndale's understanding of the covenant shattered man's conceit in his own importance. There was a *feel* which seems to point to something larger and grander than the salvation of sinners. Even man's salvation, important as it is, seems to be relatively unimportant as we realise the place of God as Father and the elect as his children in Tyndale's theology. When the doctrine of the fatherhood of God is put alongside the statements in the Bible relating to the salvation of creation we seem to be entering into a different world to that normally occupied by the Christian community.[10]

Secondly, the stress Tyndale puts on creation – not as an event at the beginning of the universe, but that every man is a child of God through creation. Every man is therefore a brother or sister through creation. In loving them as we love ourselves, we may not make any difference between any human being – for whoever we are in race, colour, religion or gender we are all created by God. Taken out of context some of Tyndale's remarks sound as if he is bordering on universalism.[11] However, Tyndale wrote that

> two manner of people are sore deceived. . . . The first, that is to say, he which justifieth himself with his outward deeds, consenteth not to the law inward, neither hath delectation therein, yea, he would rather that no such law were. So justifieth he not God, but hateth him as a tyrant. . . . The second, that is to say, the

> sensual person, as a voluptuous swine, neither feareth God in the law, neither is thankful to him for his promises and mercy, which is set forth in Christ to all of them that believe.[12]

Tyndale's clearest denial of universalism comes from his teaching about the "little flock", "The kingdom of heaven is the preaching of the gospel, unto which come both good and bad. But the good are few, Christ calleth them therefore a 'little flock,' Luke xii."[13] But the multitude

> roar they out by and by, "what an heretic is this! . . . Thou art a strong heretic, and worthy to be burnt." . . . If little flock fear not that bug, then they go straight to the king: "And if it like your grace, perilous people, and seditious and even enough to destroy your realm, if ye see not to them betimes."[14]

Against that we have Tyndale's evangelical statement that we do good to those who are God's children through faith in order to strengthen their faith; and to those who have not been born again in order to win them for Christ. But there is also another reason behind loving our neighbour as we love ourselves which has a relevance towards proving this point. " 'Thou shalt not avenge thyself, nor bear hate in thy mind against the children of thy people; but shalt love thy fellow as thyself. I am the Lord.' As who should say, For my sake thou shalt do it." Tyndale continues,

> "The Lord your God is the God of gods and Lord of lords, a great God, mighty and terrible, which regardeth no man's person . . . but doth right to the fatherless and the widow, and loveth the stranger. . . . Love therefore the stranger. . . . But let the stranger, that dwelleth among you, be as one of yourselves, and love him as thyself: . . . I am the Lord." As who should say, Love him, for my sake.[15]

Thirdly, God's covenant is for the restoration of creation; therefore, Tyndale says, God wants us to care for the whole of his creation, and this care is especially seen in the compassion we must have towards animals.

> As that a man is forbid to seeth a kid in his mother's milk, moveth us unto compassion, and to be pitiful. As doth also that a man should not offer the sire, or dam, and the young both in one day. (Lev. xxii.) For it might seem a cruel thing, inasmuch as his mothers milk is, as it were, his blood: wherefore God will not have him sod therein; but will have a man shew courtesy upon the very beasts.[16]

The stress of Tyndale's theology is on God. It is God the Father who is our Father in a very real sense because one of the keys of Tyndale's covenant theology is the family, God's family. It is by one's entrance into that family, through the new birth, that one becomes a child of God. As a child one has access to our loving Father at any time and for whatever reason, and as loving children we seek always to please our Father in what we do.

It was God the Son who made the new birth and the new life possible. He shed his blood to satisfy God's justice so that the way for man's salvation could be opened and those who had been born again presented faultless to the Father as his children.

God the Holy Spirit applies the blood of Christ to those being saved, so that through the blood of Christ we are born again. Christ's blood is sprinkled on every aspect of our Christian life by the Holy Spirit as he gives faith and repentance and makes us righteous. "To believe in Christ's blood with a repenting heart is to make righteous, and the only making of peace and satisfaction to God-ward."[17] Through the blood of Christ, the Holy Spirit gives us love for God and his laws, love for our neighbour and all good works; the power to understand God's word and to worship God; and finally to bring us into God's eternal presence.

Luther, and most of the Reformers, had a doctrine of "the two regiments" or "kingdoms". Following the doctrine of the two swords of the medieval Church, the Reformers generally considered that the "spiritual regiment" was more important than the "temporal regiment" and that the temporal regiment was established post-Fall. However, Tyndale believed the temporal regiment is a creation ordinance and is fundamental for a proper functioning of society. For the basic unit of the temporal regiment is the family and "our fathers and mothers are to us in God's stead. Exod. xx."[18] With the growth of society the unit of society is no longer the family but the nation. "God therefore hath given laws unto all nations, and in all lands hath put kings, governors, and rulers in his own stead, to rule the world through them."[19] Although, since the Fall, they have the sword to maintain law and justice, this is not the main function of rulers. In the temporal regiment every man is a brother or sister to every one else. All are under God's laws, whether they are born again or not. Therefore, Tyndale wrote,

> God created the world of nought, and God worketh all things of his free will, and for a secret purpose; and that we shall all rise again, and that God will have accounts of all that we have done in this life.[20]

After the Fall the spiritual regiment became necessary for those born again by the Holy Spirit. But being members of the spiritual regiment did not separate them from those in the temporal regiment; the two regiments run side by side. The Christian king is under the rule of the bishop in the spiritual regiment, and the bishop is under the king in the temporal regiment (irrespective of whether the king were a Christian or a pagan).

As far as Tyndale was concerned, the problem of the medieval Church was that the clergy had broken the covenant. They had hidden the word of God from God's children and had forbidden the true Christians from having the scriptures and reading them in their own language. The clergy had made the spiritual regiment greater than the temporal regiment, and they had usurped the power and position of the rulers God had appointed over society. They believed that the spiritualty had been given an importance and power so that they alone could speak for God and interpret the scriptures and add to them the "traditions". But Tyndale accused them of following the Pharisees, who were condemned by Christ for hiding God's word from the people, and, by false interpretation, destroying the true meaning of the scriptures.

It was only by the laity having the scriptures in their own language that it was possible for them to see the truth and discern the errors of the spiritualty. It was Tyndale's desire for the laity to know the truth, and that lay behind Tyndale's life's work of translation. The laity would then be able to see how the spiritualty had followed in the steps of the Pharisees and broken the covenant. Through reading the authentic scriptures the laity would be able to discern the true doctrine from the false and become true followers of God and become his true children.

It is because a true Christian loves God's laws and commandments that he does good works that are pleasing to God. But these works are not done for any merit or reward; they come naturally to one who is a child of God for they reflect our likeness to our Father. And, as God shows his mercy, so must we;

> But lift up thine eyes unto thy heavenly Father, and as thy Father doth, so do thou love all thy Father's children. He ministereth sun and rain to good and bad; by which two understand all his benefits: . . . Even so provoke thou and draw thine evil brethren to goodness, with patience, with love in word and deed; and pray for them to him that is able to make them better and to convert them. And so thou shalt be thy Father's natural son, and perfect, as he is perfect.[21]

Once we have grasped Tyndale's doctrine of the covenant, we see the clarity of his thought and his total reliance on the scriptures. There is a simplicity and depth in his theology that make the Bible come alive in a way in which the ploughboy can rejoice as he finds he has become, through faith, a child of God the Father. There is much more research to be done that, I believe, will show that Tyndale was one of the greatest theologians of the Christian Church.

Notes

1. Tyndale, William, *Obedience,* p. 1/291f: *Sacraments,* p. 1/363, 381: *Prologue Matthew,* p. 1/468, "the new Testament, or covenant made with us in Christ's blood." and, *Prologue Matthew,* p. 1/476
2. Clebsch, *England's Earliest Protestants,* p. 182f
3. Clebsch, *England's Earliest Protestants,* p. 181
4. For example, Michael McGiffert, "Covenant flowered late in Tyndale's writings." "William Tyndale's Conception of Covenant", p. 169. Carl Trueman, *Luther's Legacy,* although he acknowledged the idea of covenant going back to 1525, "It is in *I John* that Tyndale makes his first reference to an arrangement between God and man which approximates to that which he later describes with the term covenant." p. 111.
5. see Matthew 15:14.
6. Clebsch, *England's Earliest Protestants,* p. 183
7. I refrain from naming these persons, both of whom are historians and not theologians.
8. Laughlin, "The Brightness of Moses' Face:" p. 3f.
9. Laughlin, "The Brightness of Moses' Face:" p. 268
10. Romans 8:18-25; Acts 3:21
11. e.g. Tyndale, William, *Pathway,* p. 1/18: *Prelates,* p. 2/325: *Answer,* p. 3/6
12. Tyndale, William, *Pathway,* p. 12f.
13. Tyndale, William, *Obedience,* p. 165
14. Tyndale, William, *Answer,* p. 3/110
15. Tyndale, William, *Exposition Matthew,* p. 2/47
16. Tyndale, William, *Prologue Exodus,* p. 1/414: see also, *Sacraments,* p. 1/348, see also my paper given at the 4th International Tyndale Conference, Antwerp, 2002. "Divine Mercy and Human Compassion in the Prologues to Exodus and Deuteronomy".
17. Tyndale, William, *Answer,* p. 3/206
18. Tyndale, William, *Obedience,* p. 1/168 (Marginal Note)
19. Tyndale, William, *Obedience,* p. 1/174
20. Tyndale, William, *Obedience,* p. 1/155
21. Tyndale, William, *Exposition Matthew,* p. 2/71

Appendix 1

The Supper of the Lord

Through reading and re-reading *The Supper of the Lord,* I am convinced that it is the only writing wrongly attributed to Tyndale in the Parker Society Edition. *The Supper* did not have the same theology as Tyndale's writings, and it contradicts what Tyndale had written elsewhere. Others have rightly demonstrated that *The Supper* is not Tyndale's work. Whether it is George Joye's work I cannot say; I can say that it is not the work of Tyndale.

For the following reasons I believe Tyndale did not write *The Supper*:

1. It lacks the theological emphasis on the blood of Christ found in Tyndale's writings.[1]

2. The author of *The Supper* based his sacramental teaching mainly on John 6. Tyndale's comment on this is that "This oration is nothing to the purpose. For Christ spake to the blind and unbelieving Jews; testifying to them, that they could have no life except they should first eat his flesh, and drink his blood: . . . And therefore must it be understood of faith only, and not of the sacrament."[2] Tyndale never referred to John 6 in dealing with his sacramental theology.

3. The authorship of *The Supper of the Lord* has a history attributing it to George Joye, arguing that the English is closer to Joye than Tyndale. I can only comment on this that stylistically *The Supper* does not feel as if Tyndale wrote it. Anderegg, Cargill Thompson, Clebsch, Mozley, and O'Sullivan have explored the evidence. Without looking closely at the theology of George Joye I cannot say whether it was likely that Joye wrote *The Supper of the Lord* or not.

On these three grounds I reject Tyndale's authorship and so I ignore *The Supper of the Lord* in assessing Tyndale's theology. The fact that in every other work Tyndale has a consistent theology which we do not find in *The Supper* reinforces this decision.

[1] References to 'the blood of Christ' where there is a Tyndalian theological meaning, in *Sacraments* (106) is 39.6%. In *The Supper* (66), only 4.5%, whilst 15.5% have a non Tyndalian theology. The other references in both works refer to the bread and wine in the Lord's Supper.

[2] *Sacraments,* 1/368f

Appendix 2

The Temporal and Spiritual Regiments

Although the temporal regiment stems from creation, it would seem that the spiritual regiment was established as a result of the Fall. The following points appear to be a reasonable summary of the evidence found in Tyndale's writings. However, a more detailed examination of Tyndale's writings is needed in order to establish their validity.

1. God is the King of the temporal regiment, and kings are appointed to rule in his stead.
2. Through creation all men are brothers and sisters, and neighbours to each other, irrespective of race or creed.
3. Through creation all men are part of the temporal kingdom and belong to God and are his people.
4. The Fall meant that man was in rebellion against God – his King – and his kingdom, and was in the service of the devil.
5. Christ's blood was shed as a remedy for man's disobedience and sinful rebellion, so that all who turned back to God could be restored to their place in God's kingdom.
6. After the Fall some were elected to be brought back to obedience to their King, and be made his children and became the spiritual regiment.
7. Those who are in the spiritual regiment are doubly God's, first through creation, secondly through redemption.

Abbreviations

A&M	Foxe, John, *Acts and Monuments*
ARG	*Archiv für Reformationsgeschichte*
BIHR	*The Bulletin of the Institute of Historical Research*
BJRL	*The Bulletin of the John Rylands Library*
BL	The British Library
CWM	*Collected Works of St Thomas More*
Dialogue	More, Thomas, *A Dialogue Concerning Heresies*, CWM vol 6.
E.E.T.S.	Early English Text Society
EQ	*Evangelical Quarterly*
ET	*Expository Times*
HThR	*Harvard Theological Review*
ISBE	*International Standard Bible Encyclopaedia*
JBS	*Journal of British Studies*
JEH	*Journal of Ecclesiastical History*
JHI	*The Journal of the History of Ideas*
JMRS	*The Journal of Medieval and Renaissance Studies*
JRS	*Journal of Reformation Studies*
JThS	*Journal of Theological Studies*
LCC	Library of Christian Classics
LW	*Luther's Works* (American Edition)
MAE	*Medium Aevum*
MED	*The Middle English Dictionary*
MPh	*Modern Philology*
NAKD	*Nederlands Archief voor Kerkgeschiendenis*
N&Q	*Notes and Queries*
RQ	*Renaissance Quarterly*
SCH	Studies in Church History
SCJ	*Sixteenth Century Journal*
SCE&S	Sixteenth Century Essays and Studies
SJTh	*Scottish Journal of Theology*
SPh	*Studies in Philology*
SR	*Studies in the Renaissance*
TBGAS	The Bristol and Gloucestershire Archaeological Society
TS	The Tyndale Society
TSJ	*The Tyndale Society Journal*
WThJ	*Westminster Theological Journal*

Tyndale's Works

PS, The Parker Society. *Works of the Fathers and Early Writers of the Reformed English Church,* 55 vols, 1841-1854

Quotations from the Parker Society volumes where an author has more than one volume will be referred as: 1/pn: 2/pn

Parker Society works of William Tyndale will be referred to as follows

1. *Doctrinal Treatises and Introductions to different portions of the Holy Scriptures,* Parker Society 1
   Introduction, Walter, Henry, *Life of William Tyndale*
   Pathway, A Pathway into the Holy Scripture
   Mammon, The Parable of the Wicked Mammon
   Obedience, The Obedience of a Christian Man
   Sacraments, A brief declaration of the Sacraments
   Preface, Preface that he made before the five books of Moses, 1530
   Epistle, Epistle to the Reader; subjoined to the 1526 New Testament
   Prologue (followed by the title of the Biblical Book) *Prologues to Tyndale's Translations of the Old and New Testaments*

2. *Expositions and Notes on Sundry Portions of the Holy Scriptures, together with The Practice of Prelates,* Parker Society vol 2
   Exposition Matthew, Prologue to Exposition and *Exposition of Chapters 5, 6, and 7, of Matthew's Gospel*

Exposition 1 John, Introductory Notice, and *Prologue,* and *Exposition of the first Epistle of St. John*

Marg. Notes, Marginal Notes on first 21 chapters of St, Matthew's Gospel, 1525

Prelates, The Practice of Prelates

3. *An Answer to Sir Thomas More's Dialogue; The Supper of the Lord; and Wm Tracy's Testament Expounded,* Parker Society 3
   Answer, An Answer to Sir Thomas More's Dialogue
   Supper, The Supper of the Lord. This is not accepted as Tyndale's writing
   Tracy, The Testament of W. Tracy Esq.

Tyndale's Writings not in *The Parker Society*

The Cologne Fragment, (Arber)
Pater Noster, Bodleian PP274 TH
NT New Testament 1534 in Modern English (Daniell)
OT Old Testament, 1530, 1537, in Modern English (Daniell)

Bibliography

Source Materials

Arnold, Thomas, *Select English Works of John Wyclif,* 3 volumes, Oxford, 1869-1871

Bale, J., *Select Works of John Bale.* Christmas, Henry (ed.), PS, Cambridge, 1849

Barnes, R., *The Fathers of the English Church,* vol 1. John Hatchard, London, 509-626, 1807

Baxter, Richard, *The Practical Works of. . . ,*1, George Virtue, London. 4 volumes, 1845, 1845, 1845, 1838

Barnum, P.H. (ed.), *Dives and Pauper,* EETS OS275; OS280, Oxford, 1976 and 1980

Baylor, M.G. (ed.), *The Radical Reformation,* Cambridge Texts in the History of Political Thought, Cambridge University Press, Cambridge, 1991

Bayne, R. (ed.), *The Life of Fisher.* EETS ES117, Kraus Reprint, Millwood, 1988

Becon, Thomas, *Prayers and Other Pieces.* Ayre, John, (ed.), PS, Cambridge, 1844

Bettenson, H., *Documents of the Christian Church,* Oxford University Press, Oxford, 1959

Bray, Gerald, *Documents of the English Reformation,* James Clarke, Cambridge, 1994, revised ed, 2004

Bromiley G.W. (ed.), *Zwingli and Bullinger,* LCC (Ichthus Edition). Westminster Press, Philadelphia, 1953

Browne, Robert, *The Writings of Robert Harrison and Robert Browne.* Peel, Albert, and Carlson, Leland H. (eds), George Allen and Unwin. London, 1953

Bucer, M., *Common Places of Martin Bucer.* in Wright, D.F., trans and ed., Sutton Courteney Press, Abingdon.

Bühler, Curt F., "A Lollard Tract: On Translating the Bible into English" in *MAE,* vol VII No. 3. October, 1938, 167-183

Bullinger, Heinrich, *Decades,* Harding, Thomas, (ed) PS, Cambridge, 4 vols, 1849-52

Bullinger, Heinrich, *De testamento seu foedere Dei unico et aeterno.* in McCoy, C.S. and Baker, J.W. *Fountainhead of Federalism.* Westminster/John Knox Press, Louisville, 1991. 101-137

Bullinger, Heinrich, *Decades,* (4 volumes) The Parker Society, London, 1849-52

Bullinger, Heinrich, "Of the Holy Catholic Church." in Bromiley, G.W. (ed.), LCC (Ichthus Edition), 288-325

Bullinger, John, *The Works of. . .vols 1-3,* Offor, George (ed.), Blackie and Son, Glasgow, 1853, 1852, 1853

Calvin, John, *Institutes of the Christian Religion,* Translation by Beveridge, Henry, James Clarke, London, 1949

Calvin, John, *Commentaries on The Epistles of Paul to the Galatians and Ephesians,* Pringle, William (trans.), Wm B. Eerdmans Publishing Co. Grand Rapids, 1957

Calvin, John, *Commentaries on the Epistle of Paul to the Hebrews,* Owen, John, (trans.), Wm B. Eerdmans Publishing Company, Grand Rapids, 1949

Calvin, John, *Tracts and Treatises,* (3 volumes) Wm. B Eerdmans, Grand Rapids, 1958

Canons Ratified in the National Synod of the Reformed Church, Held at Dordrecht, in the years 1618 and 1619, in *The Psalter,* Wm. B. Eerdmans Publishing Co. Grand Rapids, 1927

Cardwell, Edward, *Documentary Annals of the Reformed Church of England,* Oxford University Press, Oxford, 1839

Cartwright. T., *Cartwrightiana.* Peel, A., and Carlson, L.H. (eds), George Allen and Unwin, London, 1951

Cartwright, T., *A Commentary upon the Epistle of St. Paul Written to the Colossians,* James Nichol, Edinburgh, 1864. [No editor attributed to this publication.]

Cigman. G. (ed.), *Lollard Sermons,* EETS OS294, Oxford, 1989

Colet, John, "Colet's 'Cathechyson' with the Articles for Admission to St. Paul's School, and other extracts from his Accidence," 284-289; "The Sermon of Doctor Colete, made to the Conuocacion at Paulis," 293-304; "A ryght fruitfull monicion . . ." 304-310; in Lupton, J.H., *A Life of Dean Colet D.D. Appendix, B,* George Bell & Son, London, 1909.

Colet, John, *An Exposition of St. Paul's Epistle to the Romans.* Lupton, J.H. (ed.), Bell and Daldy, London, 1873

Colet, John, *Commentary on First Corinthians.* O'Kelly, Bernard, and Jarrott, Catherine A.L., eds, Medieval and Renaissance Texts and Studies, Binghamton, 1985

Erasmus, D., *Erasmus' Annotations on the New Testament, the Gospels.* Reeve, Anne (ed.), Duckworth, London, 1986

Erasmus, D., *De Libero Arbitrio.* LCC (Ichthus Edition). The Westminster Press, Philadelphia, 1969, 35-97

Erasmus, D., *Enchiridion Militis Christiani.* O'Donnell, Anne (ed.), EETS OS282, Oxford, 1981

Erasmus, D., *Familiar Colloquies,* vols 1-3, Bailey, N. (trans.), Johnson, E. (ed.), Gibbings & Company, London. 1900

Erasmus, D., *In Praise of Folly,*[1] Reeves and Turner, London, 1876

Eusebius, *The Ecclesiastical History of the Martyrs of Palestine,* Lawlor, Hugh Jackson, and Oulton, John Ernest Leonard, (ed.), S.P.C.K., London, 1927

Fish, Simon., *A Supplicacyon for the Beggars,* Furnivall, Frederick J. (ed.), Kraus Reprint, EETS ES13, 1981

Fisher, John, *English Works of John Fisher.* Mayor, John E.B. (ed.), EETS ES27, London, 1876

Fisher, John, *Exposition of the Seven Penitential Psalms,* (in modern English with an introduction by Gardiner, Anne Barbeau). Ignatius Press, San Franscisco, 1998.

Foxe, John., *The Acts and Monuments of the Christian Martyrs.* Townsend, George (ed.), revised and corrected by Pratt, Josiah, The Church Historians of England, George Seeley, London, 1853-1870

Frith, John, *The Fathers of the English Church,* vol 1,[1] John Hatchard, London, 1807, 343-474

Gee, Henry and Hardy, William John., *Documents Illustrative of English Church History,* Macmillan and Co., London, 1910

Goodwin, Thomas, *The Works of. . .*vol 5,[1] James Nichol, Edinburgh, 1863

Henry, Matthew, *Works of the English Puritan Divines: Matthew Henry,*[1] Thomas Nelson, London, 1847

Herrtage, S.J. ed., *England in the Reign of King Henry the Eighth,* EETS ES12 & ES32, Kraus Reprint, 1981

Higden, Ranulphi, *Polychronicon, translated by Trevisa, John,* Babington, Churchill (ed.), "The Rolls Series", Longman, Green, Longman, Roberts, and Green 1865-1886.

Hitchcockand Chamberseds, *Harpsfield's Life of More.* EETS OS186, Oxford, 1982

Howe, John, *Works of the English Puritan Divines: John Howe,*[1] Thomas Nelson, London, 1846

Hudson, A. (ed.), *Two Wycliffite Texts,* EETS OS301, Oxford, 1993

Hudson, Anne ed, *Selections from English Wycliffite Writings,* University of Toronto Press, Toronto, 1997

Luther, Martin, *The Bondage of the Will,* Packer, J.I., and Johnston, O.R. (trans. and eds.), James Clarke, London, 1957

Luther, Martin, 1969, *De Servo Arbitrio.* LCC (Ichthus Edition), The Westminster Press, Philadelphia, 1969, 101-334

Luther, Martin, *Lectures on Genesis Chapters 1-5. LW-1.* Pelikan, Jaroslav (ed.), Concordia Publishing House, St. Louis, 1958

Luther, Martin, *The Sermon on the Mount (Sermons) and The Magnificat. LW-21.* Pelikan, Jaroslav (ed.), Concordia Publishing House, St. Louis, 1956

Luther, Martin, *Sermons on the Gospel of St. John, Chapters 1-4. LW-22.* Pelikan, Jaroslav (ed.), Concordia Publishing House, St. Louis, 1957

Luther, Martin, *Sermons on the Gospel of St. John, Chapters 14-16, LW-24.* Pelikan, Jaroslav, ed., Poellot, Daniel E., asst ed, Concordia Publishing House, St. Louis, 1961

Luther, Martin, *Lectures on Galatians 1535, chapters 1-4. LW-26* Pelikan, Jaroslav, ed., Hanson, Walter A., assistant ed, Concordia Publishing House, St. Louis, 1963

Luther, Martin, *Lectures on Galatians . . . LW-27.* Pelikan, Jaroslav (ed.), Hanson, Walter A. (assistant ed.), Concordia Publishing House, Saint Louis, 1964

Luther, Martin, *Lectures on Titus, Philemon, and Hebrews. LW-29.* Pelikan, Jaroslav (ed.), Hanson, Walter A. (asst ed.), Concordia Publishing House, St. Louis, 1968

Luther, Martin, *Career of the Reformer: I. LW-31.* Grimm, Harold J. (ed.), Muhlenberg Press, Philadelphia, 1957

Luther, Martin, *Career of the Reformer II. LW-32* Forell, George W. (ed.), Muhlenberg Press, Philadelphia, 1958

Luther, Martin, *Career of the Reformer, IV, LW-34* Spitz, Lewis W. (ed.), Muhlenberg Press, Philadelphia, 1960

Luther, Martin, *The Book of Concord*, Kolb, R., and Wengert, T.J. (eds), Fortress Press, Minneapolis

Luther, Martin, *Word and Sacrament, I. LW-35.* Bachmann, E. Theodore (ed.), Muhlenberg Press, Philadelphia, 1960

Luther, Martin, *Word and Sacrament II. LW-36.* Wentz, Abdel Ross (ed.), Muhlenberg Press, Philadelphia, 1959

Luther, Martin, *Word and Sacrament III. LW-37.* Fischer, Robert H. (ed.), Muhlenberg Press, Philadelphia, 1961

Luther, Martin, *Church and Ministry II, LW-40.* Bergendoff, Conrad (ed.), Muhlenberg Press, Philadelphia, 1958

Luther, Martin, *The Christian in Society II. LW-45.* Brandt, Walther I. (ed.), Muhlenberg Press, Philadelphia, 1962

Luther, M., *Table Talk. LW-54.* Tappert, Theodore G. (ed.), Fortress Press, Philadelphia, 1967

Matthew, F.D., *The English Works of Wyclif.* EETS OS74, Boydell & Brewer, Woodbridge, 1998

More, Thomas, *The Apologye of Syr Thomas More, Knyght.* Taft, A.I. (ed.), EETS OS180 Oxford, 1930

More, Thomas, *Responsio ad Lutherum. CWM-5* Headley, John M. (ed.), Translated by Sister Scholastica Mandeville, Yale University Press, New Haven, 1969

More, Thomas, *A Dialogue Concerning Heresies. CWM-6.* Lawler, Thomas M.C.: Marc'Hadour, Germain, and Marius, Richard C. (eds), Yale University Press, New Haven, 1981

More, Thomas, *The Confutation of Tyndale's Answer. CWM-8.* Schuster, Louis A.: et al., Yale University Press, New Haven, 1973

More, Thomas, *The Apology, The CWM-9.* Trapp, J.B. (ed.), Yale University Press, New Haven, 1979

More, Thomas, *The Answer to a Poisoned Book. CWM-11.* Foley, Stephen Merriam and Miller, Clarence H., eds, Yale University Press, New Haven, 1985

More, Thomas, *Treatise on the Passion, Treatise on the Blessed Body, Instructions and Prayers. CWM-13.* Haupt, Garry E. (ed.), Yale University Press, New Haven, 1976

More, Thomas, *The Correspondence of Sir Thomas More,* Rogers, Elizabeth Frances (ed.), Princeton University Press, Princeton, 1947

Pantin, T.P. (ed.), *Wycliffes Wycket,* Oxford, 1828

Parker, Douglas H. (ed.), *The Praier and Complaynte of the Ploweman vnto Christe,* University of Toronto Press, Toronto, 1997

Pauck, W. ed, *Melanchthon & Bucer.* LCC (Ichthus Edition), Westminster Press, Philadelphia, 1959

Perkins, William, *The Works of. . . .* Breward, Ian (ed.), The Courteney Library of Reformation Classics, The Sutton Courteney Press, Abingdon, 1970

Pollard, A.W. ed, *Records of the English Bible.* Oxford University Press, Oxford, 1911

Ro: Ba:, *The Life of Syr Thomas More.* Hitchcock, E.V., and Hallett, P.E. (ed.), EETS OS222, Oxford, 1950

Scattergood, V.J., "'The Two Ways': An Unpublished Religious Treatise by Sir John Clanvowe" in *English Philological Studies,* vol 7. 1961, 33-56

Sibbes, Richard, *The Complete Works of . . . ,* vol 2. Grosart, A.B. (ed.), James Nichol, Edinburgh, 1862

Simmons, T.F. & Nolloth, H.E. (ed.), *The Lay Folk's Catechism.* EETS OS118, Kegan, Trench, Trubner, London, 1901

Skeat, W.W. ed., *Pierce the Ploughmans Crede.* EETS OS30, Greenwood Press, New York, 1969

Swanson, R.N., *Catholic England, Faith, Religion and Observance before the Reformation.* Manchester University Press, Manchester, 1995

Swinburn, L.M. (ed.), *The Lanterne of Light.* E.E.T.S, OS151 Kraus Reprint, 1988

Tanner, J.R., *Tudor Constitutional Documents A.D. 1485-1603 with an historical commentary.* Cambridge University Press, Cambridge, 1951

Trevisa, John, *On the Properties of Things, John Trevisa's translation of Bartholomaus Anglicus, De Proprietibus Rerum,* vol 1. Seymour, M.C., et al. (ed.), Clarendon Press, Oxford, 1975

Trevisa, John, *Polychronicon.* Wynken de Worde, Westminster, Lambeth Palace Library 1495.5, 1495

Trevisa, John, *Polychronicon Ranulphi Higden, English Translation of John Trevisa,* Babington, C., Churchill, Longman, Roberts and Green, London, 1865-1886.

Trevisa, John, *Dialogus inter Militem et Clericum; Richard Fitzralph's Sermon 'Defensio Curatorum.* Perry, A.J. (ed.), E.E.T.S. 167, Oxford University Press, Oxford, 1925

Tyndale, W., *A Compendious Introduccion, Prologe or Preface vn to the Pistle off Paul to the Romayns – A Treates of the Pater Noster.* Bodleian PP274 TH (dated) 1526.

Tyndale, W., *Doctrinal Treatises, etc.* Walter, Henry (ed.), PS, Cambridge, 1951

Tyndale, W., *Expositions of Scripture and Practice of Prelates.* Walter, Henry (ed.), PS, Cambridge, 1849

Tyndale W., *An Answer to Sir Thomas More's Dialogue, etc.* Walter, Henry (ed.), PS, Cambridge, 1850

Tyndale, W., *An Answere Vnto Sir Thomas Mores Dialoge.* O'Donnell, Anne M., and Wicks, Jared (ed.), The Catholic University of America Press, Washington, 2000

Tyndale, W., *The Fathers of the English Church,* vol 1.[1] John Hatchard, London, 1807 1-340

Tyndale, W., *The First Printed English New Testament, translated by William Tyndale, 1525,* Facsimile Texts, Arber, Edward (ed.), London, 1871

Tyndale, William, *The New Testament, Translated by William Tyndale, The Text of the Worms edition of 1526 in original spelling,* (ed.), Cooper, W.R., British library, London, 2000

Tyndale, William, *The Obedience Of a Christian Man, 1528.* Facsimile, Scholar Press, Menston, 1970

Tyndale, William, *The Obedience of a Christian Man,* Daniell, David, ed., Penguin Books, London, 2000

Tyndale, W., *Tyndale's Old Testament (Modern Spelling Edition)* Daniell, David, ed., Yale University Press, New Haven, 1992

Tyndale, W., *Tyndale's New Testament (Modern Spelling Edition)* Daniell, David, ed., Yale University Press, New Haven, 1989

Vermigli, Peter Martyr., *Early Writings, The Peter Martyr Library,* vol 1. SCE&S, Kirksville, 1994

Williams, G.H. and Mergal, A.M. (ed.), *Spiritual and Anabaptist Writers.* LCC (Ichthus Edition), Westminster Press, Philadelphia, 1957

Wilson, Janet ed., *Sermons very fruitful, godly and learned by Roger Edgeworth: Preaching in the Reformation c. 1535- c. 1553.* D.S. Brewer, Woodbridge, 1993

Wood, Anthony á, *Athenae Oxoniensis*. Thomas Bennett at the Half Moon in St. Paul's Churchyard, 1691, 1692
Zwingli, Huldrych, "Of the Clarity and Certainty of the Word of God". LCC (Ichthus Edition), 59-95
Zwingli, Huldrych, "Of the Education of Youth". LCC (Ichthus Edition), 102-118
Zwingli, Huldrych, "Of Baptism". LCC (Ichthus Edition), 129-175
Zwingli, Huldrych, "On the Lord's Supper". LCC (Ichthus Edition), 185-238
Zwingli, Huldrych, "An Exposition of the Faith". LCC (Ichthus Edition), 245-279

Secondary Material

Ackroyd, Peter, *The Life and Times of Thomas More,* Chatto and Windus, London, 1998
Aland, Kurt, "Luther as Exegete," in *ET.* November, 1957, 45-48 December, 1957, 68-70
Allister, Donald, "The English Reformers' Teaching on Salvation. *Churchman,* vol 105, 1991, 148-165
Almasy, Rudolph P., "Contesting Voices in Tyndale's 'The Practice of Prelates,' " in Dick, John A.R., and Richardson, Anne, eds. *William Tyndale and the Law, SCE&S,* vol XXV Sixteenth Century Journal Publishers, Kirksville, 1994, 1-10
Althaus, Paul, *The Theology of Martin Luther,* Fortress Press, Philadelphia, 1966
Anderegg, Michael, "The Probable Author of 'The Souper of the Lorde: George Joye," in *CWM-11.* Foley, Stephen Merriam, and Miller, Clarence H., eds. Yale University Press, New Haven, 1985. 343-374
Anderson, J.J., "Introduction," in *BJRL,* vol 77, no. 3, 1995, 3-8
Anderson, Marvin W., "William Tyndale (d. 1536): A Martyr for all Seasons," in *SCJ,* vol XVII no. 3, 331-351
Ashley, Kathleen M., "Divine Power in Chester Cycle and Late Medieval Thought, in *JHI,* vol 39, 1978, 387-404
Aston, M., *Fire and Faith,* Hambledon Press, London, 1993
Aston, M., *Lollards and Reformers,* Hambledon Press, London, 1984
Aston, M. and Richmond, C. eds., *Lollardy and the Gentry in the Later Middle Ages,* Sutton Publishing, Stroud, 1997
Atkinson, James, "Huldreich Zwingli, Swiss Reformer." *Churchman,* vol 75. no. 1, 1961, 40-48.
Atkinson, James, "Confirmation: The Teaching of the Anglican Divines." *Churchman,* vol 77, 1963, 92-99
Atkinson, James, "Martin Bucer (1491-1551): Ecumenical Pioneer," *Churchman,* vol 79. no. 1, 1965, 19-28.
Augustijn, C., *Erasmus, His Life, Works, and Influence,* University of Toronto Press, Toronto, 1995
Auksi, Peter, *Reason and Feeling as Evidence: The Question of 'Proof' in Tyndale's Thought,* A Paper for presentation to the Leuven Tyndale Conference, "Tyndale and the First Revolution in European Communication" at K.U. Leuven, Sept 5-8, 1996, Printed in *Reformation Four,* TS, 1999, 1-20
Auksi, Peter, "Tyndale as Rhetorician: The Next Generation of Research," *TSJ. No. 6,* 1997, 17-25

Auksi, Peter, " 'So Rude and Simple Style' William Tyndale's Polemical Prose," *JMRS, 8,* 1978, 235-256

Auksi, Peter, "Tyndale on the Law of Reason and the Reason of Law," in Dick, John A.R., and Richardson, Anne, eds., *William Tyndale and the Law. SCE&S,* vol XXV, Sixteenth Century Journal Publishers, Kirksville, 1994, 41-49

Auksi, Peter, "Wyclif's Sermons and the Plain Style," in *A.R.G.*, vol 66, 1975, 5-23

Avis, P.D.L., *The Church in the Theology of the Reformers,* Marshall Morgan and Scott, London, 1981

Avis, P.D.L., "Luther's Theology of the Church," *Churchman*, vol 97, no 2, 1983, pp. 104-111

Ayris, Paul and Selwyn, David, eds. *Thomas Cranmer, Churchman and Scholar,* Boydell Press, Woodbridge, 1999

Bachtold, Hans Ulrich, "History, ideology and Propaganda in the Reformation: the Early Writing 'Anklag und ernstliches ermanen Gottes' (1525) of Heinrich Bullinger," in Gordon, Bruce, ed. *Protestant History and Identity in Sixteenth Century Europe,* Scolar Press, Aldershot, 1996, 46-59

Backus, Irena, "Bucer's Commentary on the Gospel of John," in Wright, D.F., *Martin Bucer: Reforming Church and Community,* Cambridge University Press, Cambridge. 1994, 61-71

Bagghi, David, "Diversity or Disunity? A Reformation Controversy over Communion in Both Kinds," in Swanson, R.N., *Unity and Diversity in the Church, SCH*, vol 32, Blackwell, Oxford, 1996, 207-219

Bagghi, D.V.N., "Tyndale, More, and the Anatomy of Heresy," in *Reformation,* vol 2, The TS, Oxford, 1997, 262-281

Bainton, R., *Here I Stand,* Mentor Books, New York, 1955

Bainton, R.H., *Studies on the Reformation,* Hodder and Stoughton, London, 1964

Bainton, R., *The Reformation of the Sixteenth Century,* Hodder and Stoughton, London, 1963.

Baker, J. Wayne, "Church, State, and Dissent: The Crisis of the Swiss Reformation, 1531-1536," in *CH*, vol 57, no 2, 1988, 135-152

Baker, J. Wayne, *Heinrich Bullinger and the Covenant: the other Reformed Tradition,* Ohio University Press, Athens, 1980

Baker, J. Wayne, "Heinrich Bullinger, the Covenant and the Reformed Tradition in Retrospect," in *SCJ*, XXIX no 2, 1998, 359-376

Bammel, C.P., "Justification by Faith in Augustine and Origen," in *JEH*, vol 47. no 2, 1996, 223-235

Barnard, R.K., "Bible Translation Today – Following in Tyndale's Amazing Footsteps," in *Christian History*, vol VI, no. 4, Worcester Pa., 29-31

Barr, J., *The Semantics of Biblical Language,* Xpress Reprints, London, 1996

Bast, Robert J., "From Two Kingdoms to Two Tables: The Ten Commandments and the Christian Magistrate," in *ARG* 89, 1998, 79-95

Bettey, J.H., "Early Reformers and Reformation Controversy in Bristol and South Gloucestershire," *TBGAS*, vol cxv, 1997, 9-18

Bierma, Lyle D., "Federal Theology in the Sixteenth Century: Two Traditions?" in *WThJ*, vol 45, 1983, 304-321

Bierma, Lyle D., "The Role of Covenant Theology in Early Reformed Orthodoxy," in *SCJ*, vol XXI no 3, 1990, 453-462

Biller, Peter, & Hudson, Anne., *Heresy and Literacy, 1000-1530,* Cambridge University Press, Cambridge, 1996

Bindoff, S.T., *Tudor England,* Penguin Books, London, 1950

Blickle, Peter, "The Popular Reformation," in Brady, Thomas A., Oberman, Heiko A., and Tracy, James D., eds., *Handbook of European History, 1400-1600,* vol 2, Eerdmans, Grand Rapids, 1996, 161-192

Boehrer, Bruce, "Tyndale's *The Practyse of Prelates:* Reformation Doctrine and the Royal Supremacy," in *Renaissance and Reformation,* vol 10, 1986, 257-276

Bone, G.D., "Tindale and the English Language," in Greenslade, S.L., *The Work of William Tyndale,* Blackie & Son, London and Glasgow, 1938, 50–68.

Bonini, C.R., "Lutheran Influences in the Early English Reformation: Richard Morrison Re-examined," *ARG,* vol 64, 1973, 206-224

Booty, J.E., *John Jewel, Apologist of the Church of England,* S.P.C.K. London, 1963.

Bostick, Curtis V., *The Antichrist and the Lollards, Apocalypticism in Late Medieval and Reformation England,* Brill, Leiden, 1998

Bornkamm. Heinrich., *Luther in Mid-Career, 1521-1530,* Fortress Press, Philadelphia, 1983

Bowman, Glen, "William Tyndale's Eucharistic Theology: Lollard and Zwinglian Influences," in *Anglican and Episcopal History,* vol LXIV no 4, 1997, 422-434

Boyle, Marjorie O'Rourke, "Erasmus and the 'Modern' Question: Was He Semi-Pelagian?" in *ARG,* vol 75, 1984 59-77

Bradshaw, Brendan, "Bishop John Fisher, 1469-1535: the man and his work," in Bradshaw, Brendan, & Duffy, Eamon (eds), *Humanism, Reform and the Reformation: the Career of Bishop John Fisher,* Cambridge University Press, Cambridge, 1989 1-24

Bradshaw, Brendan, "The Christian Humanism of Erasmus," in *JThS,* NS 33, 1982, 411-447

Brauer, Jerald C., "Reflections on the nature of English Puritanism," in *CH,* vol 23, no. 2, 1954, 99-108

Brecht, Martin, "Luther's Reformation," in Brady, Thomas A.; Oberman, Heiko A.; and Tracy, James D., eds. *Handbook of European History, 1400-1600,* vol 2 , Eerdmans, Grand Rapids, 1996, 129-159

Brecht, Martin, *Martin Luther: His Road to Reformation 1483-1521,* Fortress Press, Minneapolis, 1993

Bromily, G.W., *Baptism and the Anglican Reformers,* Lutterworth Press, London, 1953

Bromily, G.W., *Thomas Cranmer Theologian,* Lutterworth Press, London, 1956

Brown, Andrew J., *William Tyndale on Priests and Preachers,* Inscriptor Imprints, London, 1996

Bruce, F.F., "John Wycliffe and the English Bible," *Churchman,* vol 98, 1984, 294-306

Burnet, G., *The History of the Reformation of the Church of England,* 4 vols, Scott, Webster & Geary, London, 1837

Butterworth, Charles C., & Chester, Alan G., *George Joye 1495?-1553: A Chapter in the History of the English Bible and the English Reformation,* University of Pennsylvania Press, Philadelphia, 1962

Byington, E.H., *The Puritans in England and New England,* Sampson Low, Marston, London, 1896

Cameron, Euan, *The European Reformation,* Clarendon Press, Oxford, 1991

Campbell, W.E., *Erasmus, Tyndale and More,* Eyre and Spottiswoode, London, 1949

Campbell, W.E., "The Spirit and Doctrine of the Dialogue," in Campbell, W.E. (ed.), *The English Works of Sir Thomas More*, volume 2, Eyre and Spottiswoode, London, 1931

Caplan, Harry, "The Four Sense of Scriptural Interpretation and the Theory of Preaching," in *Speculum*, vol IV, 1929, 282-290

Carew-Hunt, R.N., "Zwingli's Theory of Church and State," in *CQR*, vol CXII, 1931, 20-36

Carey, G., "William Tyndale: Reformer and Rebel," in The *TSJ*, No. 2, 1995, 10-19

Carlson, Edgar M., "The Two Realms and the Modern World," in *Lutheran World*, vol xii, No. 4, 373-383

Carlson, Eric Josef, "Cassandra Banished? New Research on Religion in Tudor and Early Stuart England," in Carlson, Eric Josef, *Religion and the English People, 1500-1640: New Voices New Perspectives*, SCE&S, vol 45, Kirksville, 1998, 3-22

Carleton, Kenneth, *Bishops and Reform in the English Church, 1520-1559,* The Boydell Press, Woodbridge, 2001

Carrington, Laurel, "The Boundaries Between Text and Reader: Erasmus's Approach to Reading Scripture," in *ARG,* vol 88, 1997, 5-22

Carter, C.S., *The English Church and the Reformation,* Longmans Green & Co. London, 1925

Carter, C Sidney and Weeks, G.A. Alison (eds), *The Protestant Dictionary,* The Harrison Trust. London, 1933

Catto, J.I., "John Wyclif and the Cult of the Eucharist," in Walsh, Katherine, and Wood, Diana, eds. *The Bible in the Medieval World, SCH*, Subsidia 4, Blackwell, Oxford, 1985. 269-286

Chadwick, Henry, "Royal Ecclesiastical Supremacy," in Bradshaw, Brendan, & Duffy, Eamon (eds), *Humanism, Reform and the Reformation: the Career of Bishop John Fisher,* Cambridge University Press, Cambridge, 1989. 169-203

Chadwick, Owen, *The Reformation* in *The Penguin History of the Church.* Penguin Books, London, 1972

Christie-Murray, D., *A History of Heresy,* Oxford University Press, Oxford, 1989

Clark, Francis, *Eucharistic Sacrifice and the Reformation,* Darton, Longman & Todd, London, 1960

Clark, James Andrew, "Norm and License in Tyndale's New Testament Translation," in Dick, John A.R., and Richardson, Anne, eds. *William Tyndale and the Law, SCE&S,* vol XXV, Sixteenth Century Journal Publishers, Kirksville, 1994, 59-67

Clebsch, William, *England's Earliest Protestants,* Yale, New Haven, 1964

Clebsch, William, "More Evidence that George Joye Wrote the Souper of the Lorde." in *HThR,* vol lx, no. 1, January 1962, 63-66

Clebsch, William., "The Earliest Translations of Luther into English," in *HThR*, vol LVI, 1963, 75-86

Clement, C.J., *Religious Radicalism in England, 1535-1565,* Rutherford Studies in Historical Theology, Paternoster Press, Carlisle, 1996

Coggan, F.D., "The Bible in English: A Survey." in *Churchman*, vol lxxv, 1961, 78-87

Coggan, F.D., *The Life and Legacy of William Tyndale,* Gresham Special Lecture, 19 May, 1994.

Collinson, Patrick, "Biblical Rhetoric: the English Nation and National Sentiment in the Prophetic Mode," in McEarchen, Claire, and Shuger, Debora, (eds.) *Religion and Culture in Renaissance England,* Cambridge University Press, Cambridge, 1997, 15-45

Collinson, Patrick, *The Birthpangs of Protestant England,* Macmillan Press, Basingstoke, 1988

Collinson, Patrick, "England," in Scribner, Bob, Porter, Roy, and Teich, Mikulas (eds) *The Reformation in National Context,* Cambridge University Press, Cambridge, 1994, 80-94

Collinson, Patrick, *The Elizabethan Puritan Movement,* Clarendon Press, Oxford, 1998

Collinson, Patrick, "Protestant Culture and the Cultural Reformation," in TODD, Margo, *Reformation to Revolution: Politics and Religion in Early Modern England,* Routledge, New York, 1995, 33-50

Collinson, Patrick, "William Tyndale and the Course of the English Reformation," in *Reformation,* vol 1, TS, Oxford, 1996, 72-97

Cooper, Kenneth Schaaf., "The Revival of Lollardy in the English Reformation of the Sixteenth Century," unpublished PhD dissertation, University of Missouri, 1947

Cooper, W.R., "A Newly Identified Fragment in the Handwriting of William Tyndale," in *Reformation,* vol 3. TS, Oxford, 1998, 323-247

Coulton, G.G., *In Defence of the Reformation,* Simpkin Marshall, London, 1931

Coupe, L., "Tyndale, Interpretation and Revelation," in *TSJ,* no 2, June 1995, 29-36

Cowans, G., "Bible Translation since John Wycliffe," in *Christian History,* vol 2. no 2, 27-30, 35

Craig, John and Litzenberger, Caroline., "Wills as Religious Propaganda: The Testament of William Tracy," in *JEH,* vol 44 no. 3, July 1993, 415-431

Cranz, F. Edward, *An Essay on the development of Luther's Thought on Justice, Law, and Society,* Harvard Theological Studies XIX, Harvard University Press, Cambridge, 1959

Cressy, David and Ferrell, Lori Anne, *Religion and Society in Early Modern England,* Routledge, London, 1996

Cross, Claire, *Church and People, 1450-1660,* The Fontana History of England, William Collins, Glasgow, 1979

Culkin, Gerald., *The English Reformation,* Sands & Co., London, 1957

Cummings, B., "Justifying God in Tyndale's English," in *Reformation* vol 2, TS, Oxford, 1997, 143-171

Dahl, Nils A., "Is there a New Testament Basis for the Doctrine of the Two Kingdoms?" in *Lutheran World*, vol xii, no. 4, 1965, 337-354

Daniell, David ed., *Reformation,* vol 1, TS, Oxford, 1996

Daniell, David ed., *Reformation,* vol 2, TS, Oxford, 1996

Daniell, David, "Tyndale, Roye, Joye, and Copyright," in Dick, John A.R. and Richardson, Anne, eds., *William Tyndale and the Law, SCE&S,* vol XXV, Sixteenth Century Journal Publishers, Kirksville, 1994, 93-101

Daniell, David, *William Tyndale, a Biography,* Yale University Press, New Haven and London, 1994

Daniell, David, "William Tyndale, the English Bible, and the English Language," in O'Sullivan, Orlaith, ed., *The Bible as Book the Reformation,* BL, London. 2000, 39-50

D'Aubigne, J.H.M., *History of the Reformation,* Religious Tract Society, London, n.d.

D'Aubigne, J.H.M., *The Reformation in England,* Banner of Truth, London, 1962.

Davies, C.S.L., *Peace, Print and Protestantism 1450-1558,* Paladin, London, 1986.

Davies, Richard G., "Lollardy and Locality," in *Transactions of the Royal Historical Society*, Sixth Series, No. 1, London, 1991, 191-212

Davis, J.F., "Lollardy and the Reformation in England," in *ARG,* vol 73, 1982, 217-236

Davis, Thomas J., "The Truth of the Divine Words': Luther's Sermons on the Eucharist, 1521-28, and the Structure of Eucharistic Meaning," in *SCJ*, vol XXX/2 Summer 1999, 323-342

Dawley, P.M., *John Whitgift and the Reformation,* Adam and Charles Black London, 1955

Day, H., "Postwar Bible Translations," in *TSJ,* No 1, 37-43, No 2, 48-53. No 3, 53-57, No 4, 28-33, No 5, 31-37, No 6, 34-39, No 7, 30-35, No 8, 52-54

Day, John T., "William Tracy's Posthumous Legal Problems," in Dick, John A.R., and Richardson, Anne, eds., *William Tyndale and the Law, SCE&S*, vol XXV, Sixteenth Century Journal Publishers, Kirksville, 1994 103-113

Deansley, M., *A History of the Medieval Church,* Methuen & Co. London, 1954.

Deansley, Margaret, *The Lollard Bible and Other Medieval Biblical Versions,* Cambridge University Press, Cambridge, 1920

DeCoursey, Matthew, "Erasmus and Tyndale on Bible Reading." in *Reformation*, vol 1, TS, Oxford, 1996, 157-164

Dellar, Howard, "The Influence of Martin Bucer on the English Reformation," in *Churchman*, vol 106, 1992, 351-356

Demaus, Richard, *William Tyndale: a Biography,* Religious Tract Society, London, 1871

Dever, Mark E., "William Tyndale and Justification by Faith: 'Answer to Sir Thomas More'," in *Building on a Sure Foundation,* The Westminster Conference, 1994, 7-34

Devereux, E.J., "Tudor Uses of Erasmus on the Eucharist," in *ARG,* vol 62, 1971, 38-52

Dick, John A.R., "A Critical Edition of William Tyndale's The parable of the Wicked Mammon," unpublished PhD dissertation, Yale University, 1974.

Dick, John A.R., "Love within the Law: Tyndale's Examination of Marriage in 'The practice of Prelates,' " in Dick, John A.R., and Richardson, Anne, eds., *William Tyndale and the Law. SCE&S*, vol XXV, Sixteenth Century Journal Publishers, Kirksville, 1994, 81-92

Dick, J.A.R., "The Pen-and-Ink Wars, or Tyndale vs More," *Christian History*, vol VI, no. 4, Worcester, Pa., 24, 25

Dick, J.A.R., 'To trye his true frendes', Imagery as Argument in Tyndale's *The Parable of the Wicked Mammon*" in *Moreana* XXVIII, 106-107, July 1991, 69-82

Dickens, A.G., "The Early Expansion of Protestantism in England. 1520-1558," in *ARG,* vol 78, 187-221, 1995. Reprinted in Todd, Margo, *Reformation to Revolution: Politics and Religion in Early Modern England,* Routledge, New York, 1987, 157-174

Dickens, A.G., *The English Reformation,* Fontana Paperbacks, Glasgow, 1964

Dickens, A.G., *The English Reformation, second edition,* Batsford, London, 1999

Dickens, A.G., and Jones, Whitney R.D., *Erasmus the Reformer,* Methuen, London, 1994

Dowling, Maria, "John Fisher and the Preaching Ministry," in *ARG,* vol 82, 1991, 287-309

Duerdon, Richard, "Equivalence or Power? Authority and Reformation Bible Translation," in O'Sullivan, Orlaith, ed. *The Bible as Book the Reformation,* BL, London, 2000, 9-23

Duerdon, Richard Y., "Justice and Justification: King and God in Tyndale's 'The Obedience of a Christian Man,' " in Dick, John A.R. and Richardson, Anne eds. *William Tyndale and the Law,* SCE&S, vol XXV, Sixteenth Century Journal Publishers, Kirksville, 1994, 69-80

Duerdon, Richard, "The Temporal and Spiritual Kingdoms. Tyndale's Doctrine and Practice," in *Reformation,* vol 1, TS, Oxford, 1996, 118-128

Duffield, Gervase E., "William Tyndale and His New Testament," in *Churchman,* vol 90, 1976, 44-51

Duffy, Eamon, "The Spirituality of John Fisher," in Bradshaw, Brendan, & Duffy, Eamon (eds), *Humanism, Reform and the Reformation: the Career of Bishop John Fisher,* Cambridge University Press, Cambridge, 1989, 205-231

Duffy, Eamon, *The Stripping of the Altars,* Yale University Press, New Haven and London, 1992

Edwards, B.H., *God's Outlaw.* Evangelical Press, Welwyn, 1986

Elton, G.R., *Reformation Europe 1517-1559* Collins, Glasgow, 1963

Elton, G.R., *Reform and Reformation England 1509-1558,* Edward Arnold, London, 1993

Elton, G.R., "Persecution and Toleration in the English Reformation," in Sheils, W.J., ed., *Persecution and Toleration, SCH,* 21, Blackwell, Oxford, 1984, 163-187

Englander, David, et al. eds., *Culture and Belief in Europe, 1450-1600,* Blackwell, Oxford, 1990

Estes, James M., "The role of godly Magistrates in the church: Melanchthon as Luther's Interpreter and Collaborator," in *CH,* vol 67, no. 3, September 1998, 463-483

Evans, G.R., "Wyclif on Literal and Metaphorical," in Hudson, Anne, and Wilks, Michael, eds. *From Ockham to Wyclif. SCH,* Subsidia 5. Blackwell, Oxford, 1997, 259-266

Evans, Gillian R., "Wycliffe the Academic," *Churchman,* vol 98, 1984, 307-318

Evans, G.R., "Wyclif's Logic and Wyclif's Exegesis: the Context," in Walsh, Katherine, and Wood, Diana, eds., *The Bible in the Medieval World. SCH, Subsidia 4.* Blackwell, Oxford. 1985, 267-300

Fasolt, Constantin, "Visions of Order in the Canonists and Civilians," in Brady, Thomas A.; Oberman, Heiko A.; and Tracy, James D., eds., *Handbook of European History, 1400-1600*, vol 2, Eerdmans, Grand Rapids, 1996, 31-59

Fenlon, Dermot, "Thomas More and Tyranny," in *JEH*, vol 32, no 4, 1981, 453-476
Fines, J., "An Unnoticed Tract of the Tyndale-More Dispute," *BIHR*, xlii, 220-230
Fines, John, "Studies in the Lollard Heresy: Being and examination of the evidence from the Diocese of Norwich, Lincoln, Coventry and Lichfield, and Ely, during the period 1430-1530," unpublished PhD dissertation, Sheffield University, 1964
Fix, A.C. and Karant-Nunn, S.C. (eds), *Germania Illustrata, SCE&S*, XVIII, Sixteenth Century Journal Publishers, Kirksville, 1992
Flesseman-Van Leer, E., "The Controversy about Scripture and Tradition between Thomas More and William Tyndale," in *NAKD*, vol NS 43, 1959, 143-164
Flesseman-Van Leer, E., "The Controversy about Ecclesiology Between Thomas More and William Tyndale," in *NAKD*, vol NS 44, 1960, 65-86
Foley, Stephen Merriam, "Introduction, I. The Shape of the Eucharistic Controversy: II. The Argument of the Book," in *CWM-11*, Yale University Press, New Haven, 1985, xvii-lxixxvi
Fowler, David C., *John Trevisa, Medieval Scholar*, University of Washington Press, Seattle, 1995
Fowler, David C., "John Trevisa and the English Bible," in *MPh*, vol 58, 1960-61, 81-98
Friesen, Abraham, *Erasmus, the Anabaptists, and the Great Commission*, Eerdmans, Grand Rapids, 1998.
Gäbler, Ulrich, *Huldrych Zwingli, His Life and Work*, T. & T. Clark, Edinburgh, 1987
Gairdner, James, *Lollardy and the Reformation in England*, MacMillan, London, 1908
George, Timothy, *Theology of the Reformers*, Broadman Press, Nashville, 1994.
Gerrish, B.A., *The Old Protestantism and the New: Essays on the Reformation Heritage*, T. & T. Clark, Edinburgh, 1982.
Ginsberg, David, "Ploughboys versus Prelates: Tyndale and More and the Politics of Biblical Translation," in *SCJ*, XIX (1), 1988, 45-61
Gleason, Elizabeth A., "Catholic Reformation, counterreformation and Papal Reform in the sixteenth Century," in Brady, Thomas A. Oberman, Heiko A. and Tracy, James D. (eds), *Handbook of European History, 1400-1600*, vol 2, Eerdmans, Grand Rapids, 1996, 317-345
Gogan, Brian, *The Common Corps of Christendom: Ecclesiological Themes in the Writings of Sir Thomas More*, E.J. Brill, Leiden, 1982
Gogan, Brian, "Fisher's View of the Church" in Bradshaw, Brendan, & Duffy, Eamon (eds), *Humanism, Reform and the Reformation: the Career of Bishop John Fisher*, Cambridge University Press, Cambridge, 1989, 131-154
Golding, Peter, "Covenant Theology in Reformed Thought and Tradition: A Survey and an Evaluation," Unpublished PhD Dissertation, Greenwich University School of Theology, May 1993.
Gray, Lilian F., "William Tyndale: Translator, Scholar and Martyr," in *The Hibbert Journal*, vol xxxv, 1936, 101-107
Greaves, Richard L., "John Bunyan and Covenant Thought in the Seventeenth Century," in *CH*, 36, 1967, 151-169.
Green, Lowell C., "Luther's Understanding of the Freedom of God and the Salvation of Man: his Interpretation of I Timothy 2:4," in *ARG*, vol 87, 1996, 57-73

Greenblatt, Stephen, *Renaissance Self-fashioning from More to Shakespeare,* University of Chicago Press, Chicago, 1984

Greenhough, G.H., "The Reformers Attitude to the Law of God," in *WThJ*, vol 39, 1976, 81-99

Greengrass, Mark, *The European Reformation, c.1500-1618,* Longman, London, 1998

Greenslade, S.L., *The Work of William Tindale,* Blackie & Son, London and Glasgow, 1938

Greschat, Martin, "Church and Civil Community," in Wright, D.F., *Martin Bucer: Reforming Church and Community,* Cambridge University Press, Cambridge, 1994, 17-31

Gritsch, Eric W., "Lutheran Identity: What is this Augsburg Confession?" in *Sewanee Theological Review*, vol 40 no 2, 1997, 146-157

Guy, John, *Thomas More,* Arnold, London, 2000

Guy, John, *Tudor England,* Oxford University Press, Oxford, 1988.

Gwyn, Peter, *The King's Cardinal,* Pimlico, London, 1992.

Haas, Steven, "Simon Fish, William Tyndale and Sir Thomas More's Lutheran Conspiracy," in *JEH.* xxiii, 1972, 125-136

Hagen, Kenneth, "From Testament to Covenant in the Early Sixteenth Century," in *SCJ,* III no 1, 1972, 1-24

Haigh, Christopher, "Anticlericalism and the English Reformation," in *History*, vol 68, 1983, 391-407

Haigh, C., *The English Reformation Revised,* Cambridge University Press, Cambridge, 1992

Haigh, C., *English Reformations,* Clarendon Press, Oxford, 1993

Haigh, Christopher, "The Recent Historiography of the English Reformation," in Todd, Margo, *Reformation to Revolution: Politics and Religion in Early Modern England,* Routledge, New York, 1995, 13-29

Hall, Basil, *Humanists and Protestants, 1500-1900,* T & T Clark, Edinburgh, 1990

Hamm, Berndt, "The Urban Reformation in the Holy Roman Empire," in Brady, Thomas A.; Oberman, Heiko A.; and Tracy, James D., eds. *Handbook of European History, 1400-1600,* vol 2, Eerdmans, Grand Rapids, 1996. 193-227

Hammond, Gerald, "Law and Love in Deuteronomy" in Dick, John A.R., and Richardson, Anne, eds. *William Tyndale and the Law. SCE&S,* XXV, Sixteenth Century Journal Publishers, Kirksville, 1994, 51-58

Hammond, G., "What was the Influence of the Medieval English Bible upon the Renaissance Bible?" in *BJRL,* 77 no. 3, 1995, 87-95

Hammond, Gerald, "William Tyndale's Pentateuch: its Relation to Luther's German Bible and the Hebrew Original," in *RQ*, vol XXXIII, 1980, 351-385

Hanna III, Ralph, "Sir Thomas Berkeley and his Patronage," in *Speculum,* vol 64, 1989, 878-916

Hard, David C., "Doctrinal Adiaphora in the Debate Between Erasmus and Luther and its Impact on the Early English Reformation," Paper given at the Society for Reformation Studies Conference, Cambridge, April 15-17, 1998.

Harper-Bill, C., "Dean Colet's Convocation Sermon and the Pre-Reformation Church in England," in *History*, vol 73 no 238, 1988, 191-210

Harper-Bill, C., *The Pre-Reformation Church in England, 1400-1530,* Longman Group, London, 1989

Haslehurst, R.S.T., "Tyndale the Translator," in *CQR*, vol 123, 1936, 65-74

Hay, Denys, "The Church of England in the Later Middle Ages," in *History*, vol 53, 1968, 35-50

Hayden-Roy, Priscilla, "Hermeneutica gloriae vs hermeneutica crucis. Sebastian Franck and Martin Luther on the Clarity of Scripture," in *ARG*, 81, 1990, 50-67

Haynes, Roy, " 'Wilde Wittes and Wilfulness': John Swetstock's attack on those 'Poyswunmongeres' the Lollards," in Cuming, G.J., and Baker, Derek, eds. *Popular Beliefs and Practice*. SCH 8. Cambridge, 1972, 143-153

Hazlett, W. Ian P. , "Settlements: the British Isles," in Brady, Thomas A.; Oberman, Heiko A.; and Tracy, James D., eds. *Handbook of European History, 1400-1600*, vol 2, Eerdmans, Grand Rapids, 1996, 455-490

Headley, John M., "Introduction," in *CWM-5*, pt II, Yale University Press, New Haven and London, 1969, 732-774

Headley, John M., "Thomas More and Luther's Revolt," in *ARG*, vol 60, 1969, 145-160

Heath, P., *Church and Realm, 1272-1461*, Fontana Paperbacks, London, 1988.

Hecht, Jamey, "Limitations of Textuality in Thomas More's 'Confutation of Tyndale's Answer' ", in *SCJ*, XXVI no 4, 1995, 823-828

Hendrix, Scott H., *Luther and the Papacy*, Fortress Press, Philadelphia,1981

Hendrix, Scott, "Rerooting the Faith: The Reformation as Re-Christianization", in *CH*, vol 69 no. 3, September 2000, 558-577

Hendrix, Scott H., " 'We are all Hussites'? Hus and Luther revisited," in *ARG*, vol 65, 1981, 134-161

Herbert of Cherbury, *History of England under Henry VIII*, Alexander Murray, London, 1870

Hill, Christopher, *Society and Puritanism in Pre-Revolutionary England*, Secker and Warburg, London, 1964

Hill, Christopher, *The English Bible and the Seventeenth-Century Revolution*, Penguin Books, London, 1993

Hill, Christopher, "Tyndale and His Successors," in *Reformation*, vol.1, TS, Oxford, 1996, 98-112

Hillerbrand, Hans J., "The 'Other' in the Age of the Reformation", in Reinhart, Max (ed.) *Infinite Boundaries: Order, Disorder, and Reorder in Early Modern German Culture*, SCE&S, 40. Sixteenth Century Journal Publishers, Kirksville, 1998, 245-269

Hobbs, Gerald, "Martin Bucer and the Englishing of the Psalms: Pseudonimity in the service of early English Protestant Piety," in Wright, D.F., *Martin Bucer: Reforming Church and Community*, Cambridge University Press, Cambridge, 1994, 161-175

Hooker, M. D., "Tyndale as Translator," The Annual Hertford Lecture, Oxford, 19th October, 2000.

Hooker, M.D., "Tyndale's 'Heretical' Translation," in *Reformation*, 2, TS, Oxford, 1997, 127-142

Hope, Andrew (ed.), *Reformation*, 3, TS, Oxford, 1998.

Hudson, Anne, "A Wycliffite Scholar of the Early Fifteenth Century," in Walsh, Katherine, and Wood, Diana, eds. *The Bible in the Medieval World. SCH*, Subsidia 4, Blackwell, Oxford, 1985, 301-315

Hudson, Anne, " 'Laicus litteratus': the Paradox of Lollardy," in Biller, Peter & Hudson, Anne, *Heresy and Literacy, 1000-1530,* Cambridge University Press, Cambridge, 1996, 222-236.

Hudson, Anne, *Lollards and their Books,* Hambledon Press, London, 1985

Hudson, Anne, "The First Complete English Bible," in *TSJ, no 2* June 1995, 20-23

Hudson, Anne, *The Premature Reformation,* Clarendon Press, Oxford, 1988

Hughes, Philip, *The Reformation in England, I "The King's Proceedings,"* Hollis & Carter, London, 1952

Hughes, P. Edgecumbe, *The Theology of the English Reformers,* Horseradish, Abington, 1997

Hughes, P. Edgecumbe, "The Doctrine of Justification as Taught by the English Reformers," in *Churchman,* vol 76 no 3, 1962, 150-163

Hume, Anthea, "A Study of the Writings of the English Protestant Exiles 1525-35 (Excluding their Biblical Translations)," unpublished PhD Dissertation, University of London, 1961

Hunt, E.W., *Dean Colet and His Theology,* S.P.C.K., London, 1956

Hurley, Michael, " 'Scriptura Sola': Wyclif and his Critics," in *Traditio,* vol 16. 1960, 275-352

Hutchinson, F.E., *Cranmer and the English Reformation,* English Universities Press, London, 1951

Orr, James, et al. eds., *The International Standard Bible Encyclopaedia,* Eerdmans, Grand Rapids, 5 vols, 1957

Jacons, Henry Eyster, *The Lutheran Movement in England during the Reigns of Henry VIII and Edward VI,* G.W. Frederick, Philadelphia, 1890.

Jarrott, C.A.L., "Erasmus' Biblical Humanism," in *SR*, vol 17, 1970, 119-152

Jeanes, Gordon, "Cranmer and His Continental Colleagues: Identifying the Archbishop's Sacramental Theology", Paper given at The Society for Reformation Studies Conference, April 1988

Jedin, Hubert, *A History of the Council of Trent,* 1, Thomas Nelson & Sons, London, 1957

Jepsen, Alfred, "What can the Old Testament contribute to the discussion of the Two Kingdoms?" in *Lutheran World*, vol xii. no 4, 1965, 325-336

Johnson, Joan, *Tudor Gloucestershire,* Alan Sutton and Gloucestershire County Library, Gloucester, 1985

Johnston, James, *Pioneers of Protestantism,* Marshall Brothers, London, n.d.

Jones, R. Tudor, *The Great Reformation,* Inter-Varsity Press, Leicester, 1985

Kaminsky, Howard, "Wyclifism as Ideology or Revolution" in *CH*, vol 32, 1963, 57-74

Karlberg, Mark W., "Reformed Interpretation of the Mosaic Covenant," in *WThJ*, vol 43, 1980, 1-57

Karpman, Dahlia M., "William Tyndale's Response to the Hebraic Tradition," in *SR*, 14, 1967, 110-130

Kastan, David Scott, " 'The noyse of the new Bible': reform and reaction in Henrican England," in McEarchen, Claire, and Shuger, Debora, (eds.) *Religion and Culture in Renaissance England,* Cambridge University Press, Cambridge, 1997, 46-68

Kaufman, P.I., "John Colet and Erasmus' Enchiridion" in *CH*, vol 46, 1977, 296-312

Kaufman, P.I., "John Colet's *Opus de sacramentis* and Clerical Anticlericalism: the Limitations of 'Ordinary Wayes'," in *JBS,* vol 22, no. 1, 1982, 1-22

Keen, Maurice, *English Society in the Later Middle Ages,* Penguin Books, London, 1990

Kenny, A., *Wyclif,* Oxford University Press, Oxford, 1987

Kittleson, James M., *Luther the Reformer,* Augsburg Publishing House, Minneapolis, 1986

Kittleson, J.M., "Martin Bucer and the Sacramentarian Controversy: The Origins of his Policy of Concord," in *ARG,* vol 64, 1973, 166-183

Kleinhans, R.G., "Luther and Erasmus, Another Perspective," in *CH*, vol 39, 1970, 459-469

Klempa, William, "The Concept of Covenant in Sixteenth- and Seventeenth-Century Continental and British Reformed Theology," in McKim, D.K., ed. *Major Themes in the Reformed Tradition.* Eerdmans, Grand Rapids, 1992, 94-107

Knappen, M.M., *Tudor Puritanism,* University of Chicago Press, Chicago, 1939.

Knappen, M.M., "William Tyndale – First English Puritan" in *CH,* 5, 1936, pp 201-215

Knox, D.B., *The Doctrine of Faith in the Reignof Henry VIII,* James Clarke & Co. London, 1961.

Knox, D.B., *The Lord's Supper from Wycliffe to Cranmer,* Paternoster Press, Exeter, 1983

Koenigsberger, H.G., et al., *Europe in the Sixteenth Century,* Longman, London & New York, 1994

Kristeller, Paul Oskar and Wiener, Philip P. (eds), *Renaissance Essays,* vol 1, University of Rochester Press, Rochester, N.Y., 1992

Lahey, Stephen E., "Wyclif on Rights," in *JHI,* 58, 1997, 1-20

LaJoie, R.A., "What Tyndale owed Gutenberg," in *Christian History*, vol VI no. 4, Worcester Pa, 26-28

Lambert, Malcolm, *Medieval Heresy,* Blackwell Publishers, Oxford, 1994

Lane, Tony, "A Man for all People," in *Christian History*, vol VI, no 4, Worcester Pa, 6-9

Latré, Guido, "The 1535 Coverdale Bible and its Antwerp Origins", in O'Sullivan, Orlaith, ed. *The Bible as Book the Reformation,* BL, London, 2000, 89-102

Lau, Franz, "The Lutheran Doctrine of the Two Kingdoms," in *Lutheran World*, vol xii. No. 4, 1965, 355-372

Laughlin, Paul Alan, "The Brightness of Moses' Face: Law and Gospel, Covenant and Hermeneutics in the Theology of William Tyndale," Unpublished Ph.D. dissertation, Emory University, 1975

Lawton, David, *Faith, Text and History – the Bible in English,* University Press of Virginia, Charlottesville, 1990

Lechler, G.V., *John Wyclif and his English Precursors,* Religious Tract Society, London.

Leff, Gordon, *Heresy in the Later Middle Ages,* Manchester University Press, Manchester, 1967

Leff, Gordon, "John Wycliffe's Religious Doctrines" in *Churchman*, 98, 1984, 319-328

Leff, Gordon, "The Place of Metaphysics in Wyclif's Theology," in Hudson, Anne, and Wilks, Michael, eds. *From Ockham to Wyclif. SCH,* Subsidia 5, Blackwell, Oxford, 1987, 217-232

Lehmberg, Stanford E., "English Humanists, the Reformation, and the Problem of Counsel," in *ARG,* vol 52, 1961, 74-90

Lettinga, Neil, "Covenant Theology Turned Upside Down: Henry Hammond and Caroline Anglican Moralism: 1643-1660," in *SCJ,* vol XXIV no 3, 1993, 653-669

Levin, Carole, "A Good Prince: King John and Early Tudor Propaganda," in *SCJ,* vol XI no. 4, 1980, 23-32

Lewis, C.S., *English Literature in the Sixteenth Century, Excluding Drama,* Clarendon Press, Oxford,1954

Lindberg, Carter, *The European Reformations* Blackwell, Oxford, 1996

Lindberg, Carter, *The European Reformations Sourcebook,* Blackwell, Oxford, 2000.

Lindberg, C., "Literary Aspects of the Wyclif Bible," in *BJRL,* vol 77, no 3, Manchester, 1995, 79-85

Lindberg, C. ed, *Piety, Politics, and Ethics,* SCE&S, III, The Sixteenth Century Publishers, Kirksville, 1984

Litzenberger, Caroline, *The English Reformation and the Laity, Gloucestershire, 1540-1580,* Cambridge University Press, Cambridge, 1997.

Litzenberger, Caroline, "Local Responses to Religious Changes: Evidence from Gloucestershire Wills," in Carlson, Eric Josef, *Religion and the English People, 1500-1640: New Voices New Perspectives,* SCE&S, vol 45, Kirksville, 1998, 245-270

Loades, David, "England under the Tudors,", in Brady, Thomas A.; Oberman, Heiko A.; and Tracy, James D. (eds), *Handbook of European History, 1400-1600,* vol 1, Eerdmans, Grand Rapids, 1996, 403-43

Loades, David, *Politics, Censorship and the English Reformation,* Pinter Publishers, London, 1991

Loades, D.M., *The Oxford Martyrs,* Batsford, London, 1970

Loades, David, *Revolution in Religion, The English Reformation 1530-1570,* University of Wales Press, Cardiff, 1992.

Loane, Marcus L., *Masters of the English Reformation,* Church Book Room Press, London, 1956

Locher, Gottfried W., *Zwingli's Thought: New Perspectives,* E.J. Brill, Leiden, 1981

Lock, Julian, "Plantagenets against the Papacy: Protestant England 'Search for Royal Heroes' " in Gordon, Bruce, ed. *Protestant History and Identity in Sixteenth-Century Europe,* 1, Scolar Press, Aldershot, 1996, 153-173

Loeschen, John R., *The Divine Community Trinity, Church, and Ethics in Reformation Theologies,* The Sixteenth Century Journal, Publishers, Kirksville, 1981

Lohse, Bernhard, *Martin Luther, An Introduction to His Life and Work,* T.&T. Clark, Edinburgh, 1987

Lupton, J.H., *A Life of Dean Colet,* George Bell, London, 1904

Lytle, Guy Fitch, "John Wyclif, Martin Luther and Edward Powell: Heresy and the Oxford Theology Faculty at the Beginning of the Reformation," in Hudson, Anne, and Wilks, Michael, eds. *From Ockham to Wyclif. SCH,* Subsidia 5. Basil Blackwell, 1987, 465-479

McConica, James, *Erasmus,* Oxford University Press, Oxford, 1991

McCoy, Charles S. and Baker, J. Wayne, *Fountainhead of Federalism,* Westminster/ John Knox Press, Louisville, 1991

MacCulloch, D., "England," in Pettegree, A., ed. *The Early Reformation in Europe,* Cambridge University Press, Cambridge, 1992, 166-187

MacCulloch, Diarmaid, "The Myth of the English Reformation" in *JBS,* vol 30, Jan. 1991, 1-19

MacCulloch, Diarmaid, *Reformation,* Penguin Books, London, 2004

MacCulloch, D., *Thomas Cranmer,* Yale University Press, New Haven and London, 1996

McCutcheon, R.R., "Heresy and Dialogue: The Humanist Approaches of Erasmus and More," in *Viator,* vol 24, 1993, 357-384

McDiarmid, John F., "Humanism, Protestantism, and English Scripture, 1533-1540," in *JMRS,* 14:2, 1984, 121-138

McGiffert, M., "William Tyndale's Conception of Covenant," in *JEH,* 32 no. 2, April 1981, 167-184

McGrath, A.E., "Humanist Elements in the Early Reformed Doctrine of Justification," in *ARG,* vol 73, 1982, 5-19

McGrath, Alister, *The Intellectual Origins of the European Reformation,* Basil Blackwell, Oxford, 1987

McGrath, A., *Iustitia Dei*, 2 vols, Cambridge University Press, Cambridge. 1993-1994

McGrath, A.E., "Justification and the Reformation: The Significance of the Doctrine of Justification by Faith to Sixteenth Century Urban Communities," in *ARG,* vol 81, 1990, 5-18

McGrath, A.E., *Luther's Theology of the Cross,* Blackwell, Oxford, 1990

McGrath, A.E., *Reformation Thought,* Blackwell, Oxford, 1995

McHardy, A.K., "The Dissemination of Wyclif's Ideas," in Hudson, Anne and Wilks, Michael, eds. *From Ockham to Wyclif,* SCH, Subsidia 5, Basil Blackwell, 1987. 361-368

MacKie, J.D., *The Earliest Tudors, 1485-1558,* Oxford University Press, Oxford, 1994

McLelland, J.C., *The Visible Words of God,* Eerdmans, 1957.

Marc'Hadour, Germain, "Fisher and More: a note." in Bradshaw, Brendan, & Duffy, Eamon (eds), *Humanism, Reform and the Reformation: the Career of Bishop John Fisher,* Cambridge University Press, Cambridge, 1989, 103-108

Marc'Hadour, Germain, "Erasmus as Priest: Holy Orders in His Vision and Practice," in Pabel, Hilmar M. (ed.), *Erasmus' Vision of the Church,* SCE&S, XXXIII, Sixteenth Century Journal Publishers, Kirksville, 1995, 115-149

Marc'Hadour, Germain, "Tyndale and Fisher's 1521 Sermon Against Luther," in Day, John T., Lund, Eric, and O'Donnell, Anne M. (eds) *Word, Church, and State. Tyndale Quincentenary Essays,* The Catholic University of America Press, Washington D.C., 1998. 145-161

Marius, Richard, *Thomas More* Weidenfeld & Nicolson, London, 1993

Marius, R.C., "Thomas More and the Early Church Fathers," in *Traditio,* xxiv, 1968, 379-407

Marius, Richard, "Thomas More and the Heretics," unpublished PhD Dissertation, Yale University, 1961

Marius, Richard C., "Thomas More's View of the Church," in *CWM-8,* pt 3, Yale University Press, New Haven, 1973, 1271-1363

Marshall, Peter, "The Debate over 'Unwritten Verities' in Early Reformation England," in Gordon, Bruce, ed. *Protestant History and Identity in Sixteenth Century Europe,* 1, Scolar Press, Aldershot, 1996, 60-77

Marsh, Christopher, " 'Departing Well and Christianaly': Will-Making and Popular Religion in Early Modern England," in Carlson, Eric Josef *Religion and the English People, 1500-1640: New Voices New Perspectives,* SCE&S vol 45, Kirksville 1998, 201-244

Marsh, Christopher, *Popular Religion in Sixteenth-Century England,* MacMillan Press, Basingstoke, 1998.

Martin, Hugh, *Puritanism and Richard Baxter,* S.C.M. Press, London, 1954

Matteson, Peter, "Martin Bucer and the Old Church," in Wright, D.F., *Martin Bucer: Reforming Church and Community,* Cambridge University Press, Cambridge, 1994, 5-16

Maveety, Stanley R., "Doctrine in Tyndale's New Testament: Translation as a Tendentious Art," in *Studies in English Literature, 1500-1900,* 6, 1966, 151-158

Mayer, Thomas F., "If Martyrs are to be Exchanged with Martyrs: The Kidnapping of William Tyndale and Reginald Pole," in *ARG,* vol 81 1990, 286-307

Mayotte, Judith M., "William Tyndale's Contribution to the Reformation in England," unpub. PhD. Dissertation, Marquette University, 1976

Millius, Donald J., "The Tyndale Edition: Still Underground," in *Moreana,* vol XXIII, 91-92, Nov. 1986, 59-62

Møller, Jens G., "The Beginnings of Puritan Covenant Theology," in *JEH,* xiv. no. 1, April 1963, 46-67

Moltmann-Wendel, Elisabeth and Moltmann, Jurgen *Humanity in God,* The Pilgrim Press, New York, 1983

Mosheim, John Lawrence, *Ecclesiastical History, Ancient and Modern,* Blackie & Son, Glasgow, 1844

Mosse, George L., "Puritanism Reconsidered" in *ARG,* vol 55, 1964, 37-47

Moynihan, Brian, *If God Spare My Life*, Little, Brown, London, 2002

Mozley, J.F., "The English Enchiridion of Erasmus, 1533," in *The Review of English Studies*, vol XX No. 78, 1944, 97-107

Mozley, J.F., "Tyndale's 'Supper of the Lord,' " in *N&Q,* November 21st 1942, 305, 306

Mozley, J.F., *William Tyndale,* S.P.C.K., London, 1937

Mueller, Janet M., "Pain, persecution, and the construction of selfhood in Foxe's *Acts and Monuments*," in McEarchen, Claire, and Shuger, Debora (eds) *Religion and Culture in Renaissance England,* Cambridge University Press, Cambridge, 1997, 161-187

Myers, A.R., *England in the Late Middle Ages,* Pelican History of England. Penguin Books, London, 1988

Naphy, William G., *Documents on the Continental Reformation,* MacMillan Press, Basingstoke, 1996

Nauert, Charles G. Jr., *The Age of Renaissance and Reformation,* University Press of America, Lanham, 1981

Nauert, Charles G. Jr., "The Clash of Humanists and Scholastics: an Approach to Pre-Reformation Controversies," In *SCJ*, vol IV no 1, 1973, 1-18

Nauert, Charles G. Jr., *Humanism and the Culture of Renaissance Europe,* Cambridge University Press, Cambridge, 1998

Neill, Stephen, "The Bible in English History," in *The Churchman,* lxxv, 1961, 96-107

New, John F.H., *Anglican and Puritan: The Basis of their Opposition, 1558-1640,* Adam and Charles Black, London, 1964

Nicholls, Mark., *A History of the Modern British Isles, 1529-1603,* Blackwell, Oxford, 1999

Ni Chuilleanain, Eilean, "The Debate between Thomas More and William Tyndale, 1528-33: Ideas on Literature and Religion," in *JEH,* 39 no. 3, 1988. 382-411

Noll, Mark A., *Confessions and Catechisms of the Reformation,* Apollos, Leicester, 1992

Oberman, Heiko A., "The Shape of Late Medieval Thought: The Birthpangs of the Modern Era," in *ARG,* vol 64, 1973, 13-33

Oberman, H.A., *Forerunners of the Reformation,* Lutterworth Press, London, 1967

Oberman, Heiko A., "'Iustitia Christi' and 'Iustitia Dei'. Luther and the Scholastic Doctrines of Justification," in *HThR,* vol 59 no 1, January 1966 1-26

Oberman, Heiko A., *Luther: Man between God and the Devil,* Fontana Press, London, 1993

Oberman, Heiko A., *Masters of the Reformation,* Cambridge University Press, Cambridge, 1981

Oberman, Heiko A., "Some Notes on the Theology of Nominalism, with Attention to its Relations to the Renaissance" in *HThR,* vol 53. 1960, 47-76

Oberman, Heiko A., *The Dawn of the Reformation,* T. & T. Clark, Edinburgh, 1992

Oberman, Heiko A., *The Impact of the Reformation,* T. & T. Clark, Edinburgh, 1994

Oberman, Heiko A., *The Reformation: Roots and Ramifications,* T. & T. Clark, Edinburgh, 1994

Oberman, Heiko A., "*Via Antiqua* and *Via Moderna:* Late Medieval Prolegoma to Early Reformation Thought," in Hudson, Anne, and Wilks, Michael, eds. *From Ockham to Wyclif. SCH,* Subsidia 5, Basil Blackwell, 1987, 445-463

O'Day, R., *The Debate on the English Reformation,* Methuen, London, 1986

O'Day, Rosemary, *The Tudor Age,* Longman, London, 1995

O'Donnell, A.M., "Augustine in 'Unio Dissidentium' and Tyndale's 'Answer to More,' " in *Reformation,* vol 2, TS, Oxford, 1997, 241-260

O'Sullivan, O, "The Authorship of 'The Supper of the Lord,'" in *Reformation* vol 2, TS, Oxford, 1997, 207-232

O'Sullivan, Orlaith, "The Bible Translations of George Joye," in O'Sullivan, Orlaith (ed.) *The Bible as Book: the Reformation,* BL, London, 2000 25-38

O'Sullivan, Orlaith Aisling, "The Word and the Fire: A Critical Biography of George Joye" unpublished Ph.D dissertation, School of English, Trinity College, University of Dublin, 1997.

Ozment, Stephen, *Protestants: The Birth of a Revolution,* Fontana Press, London, 1993

Ozment, Stephen, *The Age of Reform: 1250-1550. An Intellectual and Religious History of Late Medieval and Reformation Europe,* Yale University Press, New Haven and London, 1980

Pabel, H.M. ed., *Erasmus' Vision of the Church. SCE&S,* XXXIII, Sixteenth Century Journal Publishers, Kirksville, 1995

Pabel, H.M., "Erasmus and Judaism" in *ARG,* vol 87, 1996, 9-37

Packer, J.I., *Among God's Giants,* Kingsway Publications, Eastbourne, 1997

Parish, Helen, "'Beastly is their Living and their Doctrine': Celibacy and Theological corruption in English Reformation Polemic," in Gordon, Bruce, ed. *Protestant History and Identity in Sixteenth Century Europe*, vol 1, Scolar Press, Aldershot, 1996, 138-152

Pelikan, Jaroslav, *Luther's Works: Companion volume, Luther the Expositor,* Concordia Publishing House, St. Louis, 1959. (Companion Volume to American Edition of *Luther's Works.)*

Penny, D. Andrew, *Freewill or Predestination – the Battle over Saving Grace in Mid-Tudor England,* Royal Historical Society, Studies in History 61, The Boydell Press, Woodbridge, 1980

Peters, R., "The Enigmatic 'Unio Dissidentium: Tyndale's Heretical Companion," in *Reformation,* vol 2, TS, Oxford, 1997, 233-240

Pettegree, Andrew, "Re-writing the English Reformation," in *NAKD*, vol 72, 1992, 37-58

Pineas, Rainer, "More Versus Tyndale: A Study of Controversial Technique," in *Modern Language Quarterly*, vol 24, 1963, 144-150

Pineas, Ranier, "Thomas More's Use of the Dialogue Form as a Weapon of Religious Controversy," in *SR*, vol 7, 1960, 193-206

Pineas, Rainer, "Thomas More's use of humor as a weapon of religious controversy," in *SPh*, vol LVIII, 1961, 97-114

Pineas, Rainer, "William Tyndale: Controversialist" in *SPh,* vol LX No 2, Pt. 1. 1963, 117-132

Pineas, Ranier, "William Tyndale's Influence on John Bale's Polemical Use of History," in *ARG,* 53, 1962, 79-96

Pineas, Ranier, "William Tyndale's Polemical Use of the Scriptures. in *NAKD,* vol NS45 1962, 65-78

Pineas, Ranier, "William Tyndale's Use of History as a Weapon of Religious Controversy" in *HThR*, lv, no 2, April 1962, 121-141

Pollard, Alfred, *Records of the English Bible,* Oxford, 1911

Porter, H.C., "Fisher and Erasmus" in Bradshaw, Brendan, & Duffy, Eamon (eds), *Humanism, Reform and the Reformation: the Career of Bishop John Fisher,* Cambridge University Press, Cambridge, 1989, 81-101

Post, Regnerus, "The Church on the Eve of the Reformation," in *Concilium,* vol 7. No 3, September 1967, 30-37

Powell, K.G., "The Social Background to the Reformation in Gloucestershire," in *TBGAS,* 92, 1973, 96-120

Powicke, Maurice, *The Reformation in England,* Oxford University Press, Oxford, 1961.

Prestige, G.L, *God in Patristic Thought,* S.P.C.K., London, 1981

Primus, J.H., "The Role of the Covenant Doctrine in the Puritanism of John Hooper," in *NAKD,* NS, 1967-8

Randell, Keith, *Henry VIII and the Reformation in England,* Hodder and Stoughton, London, 1997

Reardon, B.M.G., *Religious Thought in the Reformation,* Longman, London and New York, 1995

Renwick, A.M., *The Story of the Church,* I.V.F., London, 1958

Rex, Richard, *Henry VIII and the English Reformation,* MacMillan Press, Basingstoke, 1993

Rex, Richard, "The Polemical Theologian," in Bradshaw, Brendan, & Duffy, Eamon (eds), *Humanism, Reform and the Reformation: the Career of Bishop John Fisher,* Cambridge University Press, Cambridge, 1989, 109- 130

Rex, Richard, *The Theology of John Fisher,* Cambridge University Press, Cambridge, 1991

Reynolds, J.S., "The Reformation in Oxford: A Tentative Study," in *The Churchman,* 76, 1962, 216-226

Richardson, Anne, "Tyndale's Quarrel with Erasmus: A Chapter in the History of the English Reformation," in *Fides et Historia,* vol 25, 1993, 46-65

Richardson, Anne, "William Tyndale and the Bill of Rights," in Dick, John A.R., and Richardson, Anne, eds. *William Tyndale and the Law, CE&S,* vol XXV,Sixteenth Century Journal Publishers, Kirksville,1994,11-29

Rist, John M., "Augustine on Freewill and Predestination" in *JThS,* NS 20, 1969, 420-447

Roberts, D.L., "John Wycliffe and the Dawn of the Reformation," in *Christian History,* II no 21, Worcester Pa, 10-13, 30

Rollison, David, *The Local Origins of Modern Society, Gloucestershire 1500-1800,* Routledge, London. 1992

Rumble, A.R., "The Rylands, the Bible and Early English Literature: an illustrated note," in *BJRL,* 77, no 3, Manchester, 1995, 205-217

Rummel, Erika, *The Humanist-Scholastic Debate in the Renaissance and Reformation,* Harvard University Press, Cambridge, Mass, 1998

Rummel, Erika, "Voices of Reform from Hus to Erasmus," in Brady, Thomas A.; Oberman, Heiko A.; and Tracy, James D., eds. *Handbook of European History, 1400-1600,* vol 2, Eerdmans, Grand Rapids, 1996, 61-91

Rupp, Gordon, "Andrew Karlstadt and Reformation Puritanism," in *JRS,* NS vol X, 1959, 308-326

Rupp, Gordon, "Patterns of Salvation in the First Age of the Reformation," in *ARG,* vol 57, 1966, 52-66

Rupp, Gordon, "Protestant Spirituality in the first Age of the Reformation," in *SCH,* 8, Cambridge, 1972, 155-170

Rupp, Gordon, *Studies in the Making of the English Protestant Tradition,* Cambridge University Press, Cambridge, 1947

Russell, G.H., "Vernacular Instruction of the Laity in The Later Middle Ages in England: Some Texts and Notes" in *The Journal of Religious History,* vol 2, 1962-3, 98-119

Ryan, Barry T., "John Colet, Heretic? Tyndale's Assertion Reconsidered," in *TSJ,* No. 6, February 1997, 26-33

Ryrie, Alec, "The Problem of Legitimacy and Precedent in English Protestantism, 1539-47," in Gordon, Bruce, ed. *Protestant History and Identity in Sixteenth Century Europe,* Scolar Press, Aldershot, 1996, 78-92

Scarisbrick, J.J., *Henry VIII,* Eyre Methuen, London, 1981

Scarisbrick, J.J., "Fisher, Henry VIII and the Reformation Crisis," in Bradshaw, Brendan, & Duffy, Eamon (eds), *Humanism, Reform and the Reformation: the Career of Bishop John Fisher* Cambridge University Press, Cambridge, 1989, 155-168

Scarisbrick, J.J., *The Reformation and the English People.* Basil Blackwell, Oxford, 1997

Schaff, D.S. and P., *History of the Christian Church*, vols 5-8, Eerdmans, Grand Rapids, 1958-1960

Schaff, P., *History of the Christian Church*, vol 7, Eerdmans, Grand Rapids, n.d.

Schaff, P., *History of the Christian Church*, vol 8, Eerdmans Publishing, Grand Rapids, 1958

Scribner, Robert, W., "Elements of Popular Belief", in Brady, Thomas A.; Oberman, Heiko A.; and Tracy, James D. (eds), *Handbook of European History, 1400-1600*, vol 1, Eerdmans, Grand Rapids, 1996. 231-262

Scribner, Bob, Porter, Roy, and Teich, Mikulas, *The Reformation in National Context.* Cambridge University Press, Cambridge, 1994

Sergeant, L., *John Wyclif.* G.P. Putman's Sons. London. 1908

Shiels, W.J., *The English Reformation 1530-1570,* Longman, London, 1989

Shuger, Debora Kuller, *Habits of Thought in the English Renaissance, Religion, Politics. and the Dominant Culture,* University of Toronto Press, Toronto, 1997

Shuster, Louis A., "Thomas More's Polemical Career, 1523-1533," in CWM-8, pt 3, Yale University Press, New Haven, 1973, 1135-1268

Skeeters, Martha C., *Community and Clergy: Bristol and the Reformation c. 1530-1570,* Clarendon Press, Oxford, 1993.

Slavin, Arthur J., "Daniel Rogers in Copenhagen, 1588: Mission and Memory." in Thorp, Malcolm R, and Slavin, Arthur J., eds. *Politics, Religion and Diplomacy in Early Modern Europe,* SCE&S, vol XXVII, Sixteenth Century Journal Publishers, Kirksville, 1994, 245-266

Smart, Stefan J., "John Foxe and 'The Story of Richard Hun, Martyr,' " in *JEH*, vol 37, Jan. 1986, 1-14

Smeeton, D.D., "The Bible Translator who shook Henry VIII," in *Christian History*, 6 no, 4, Worcester Pa, 16-18

Smeeton, Donald Dean, *Lollard Themes in the Reformation Theology of William Tyndale,* SCE&S, vol VI, Sixteenth Century Journal Publishers, Kirksville, 1986

Smeeton, D.D., "Marriage, Motherhood and Ministry: women in the Dispute between Thomas More and William Tyndale," in *Churchman,* vol 108 no 3, 1994, 197-212

Smeeton, Donald Dean, "The Pneumatology of William Tyndale," in *Pneuma, The Journal of the Society for Pentecostal Studies,* vol 3, 1981, 22-30

Smeeton, Donald Dean, "The Wycliffite choice: Man's Law or God's," in Dick, John A.R., and Richardson, Anne, eds. *William Tyndale and the Law. SCE&S,* vol XXV Sixteenth Century Journal Publishers, Kirksville, 1994, 31-40

Smeeton, D.D., "Where did Tyndale get his Theology?" in *Christian History,* vol VI no 4, Worcester Pa, 19, 22, 23

Snyder, Susan, "The Left Hand of God: Despair in Medieval and Renaissance Tradition," in *SR*, vol 12, 1965, 18-59

Southern, R.W., *Scholastic Humanism and the Unification of Europe, 1. Foundations,* Blackwell, Oxford, 1997

Spitz, Lewis W., *The Protestant Reformation, 1517-1559,* Harper & Row, New York, 1985

Stackhouse, Ian, "The Native Roots of Early English Reformation Theology," in *EQ*, lxvi no 1, 1994, 19-35

Stafford, William S., "Tyndale's Voice to the Laity," in Day, John T., Lund, Eric, and O'Donnell, Anne M., eds. *Word, Church, and State. Tyndale Quincentenary Essays,* Catholic University of America Press, Washington D.C., 1998, 105-114

Stayer, James M., "The Radical Reformation," in Brady, Thomas A.; Oberman, Heiko A.; and Tracy, James D., eds. *Handbook of European History, 1400-1600,* vol 2, Eerdmans, Grand Rapids. 1996, 249-282

Steinmetz, David C. (ed), *The Bible in the Sixteenth Century,* Duke University Press, Durham, N.C., 1990

Stephens, Peter, "Bucer's Commentaries on Ephesians," in Wright, D.F., *Martin Bucer: Reforming Church and Community,* Cambridge University Press, Cambridge. 1994, 45-60

Stephens, Peter, *The Holy Spirit in the Theology of Martin Bucer,* Cambridge University Press, Cambridge, 1970

Stephens, Peter, *The Theology of Huldrych Zwingli,* Clarendon Press, Oxford, 1986

Stephens, W.P., *Zwingli: An Introduction to his Thought,* Clarendon Press, Oxford, 1994

Stowell, W.H., *The Puritans in England* Nelson, London, 1849

Strauss, Gerald, "Ideas of *Reformatio* and *Renovatio* from the Middle Ages to the Reformation," in Brady, Thomas A.; Oberman, Heiko A.; and Tracy, James D. (eds), *Handbook of European History, 1400-1600,* vol 2, Eerdmans, Grand Rapids, 1996, 1-30

Streater, David, "Renaissance and Reformation" in *Churchman,* vol 107, 1993, 294-306

Strickland, E., "The English Reformers' Teaching on Scripture," in *Churchman* vol 107, 1993, 38-53

Strype, J., *Annals of the Reformation,* (7 volumes) Clarendon Press, Oxford, 1824

Strype, J., *Ecclesiastical Memorials,* Clarendon Press, Oxford, 1822

Strype, J., *Memorials of Archbishop Cranmer,* Ecclesiastical History Society, Oxford, 1854

Strype, J., *Memorials of Thomas Cranmer,* George Routledge, London, 1853.

Stubbs, W., *The Constitutional History of England,* Clarendon Press, Oxford, 1875, 1875, 1878

Stupperich, R., *Melanchthon,* Lutterworth Press, London, 1966

Surtz, Edward., "John Fisher and the Scholastics," in *SPh,* vol 55, 1958, 136-153

Surtz, Edward L., " 'Oxford Reformers' and Scholasticism," in *SPh,* xlvii, 1950, 547-556

Swanson, R.N. (ed.), *Catholic England: Faith, Religion and Observance before the Reformation,* Manchester University Press, Manchester, 1995

Swanson, R.N., *Church and Society in Late Medieval England,* Blackwell, Oxford, 1993

Sykes, Norman, *The Crisis of the Reformation,* Geoffrey Bles, London, 1950

Talbert, Ernest William, "A Lollard Chronicle of the Papacy," in *Journal of English and Germanic Philology,* vol 41, 1942, 163-193

Tanner, N., *Kent Heresy Proceedings 1511-1512,* Kent Archaeological Society, 1997

Tavard, George H., *Holy Writ or Holy Church – The Crisis of the Protestant Reformation,* Burns & Oates, London, 1959

Taylor, J.B., "William Tyndale, Bible Translator," in *Anvil,* 1995, 35-43

Theide, C.P., "Tyndale and the European Reformation," in *Reformation,* 2, TS, Oxford, 1997, 283-300

Thiselton, A.C., "Authority and Hermeneutics: Some Proposals for a more Creative Agenda," in Satterthwaite, P.E., and Wright, D.F., eds. *A Pathway into the Holy Scripture,* Eerdmans, Grand Rapids, 1994, 107-141

Thompson, Stephen, "The Bishop in his Diocese" in Bradshaw, Brendan, & Duffy, Eamon (eds), *Humanism, Reform and the Reformation: the Career of Bishop John Fisher,* Cambridge University Press, Cambridge, 1989, 67-80

Thompson, W.D.J. Cargill, "The Two Regiments: The Continental Setting in William Tyndale's Political Thought," In Baker, Derek, ed. *Reform and Reformation: England and the Continent c1500-c1750. SCH, Subsidia 2,* Oxford, 1979, 17-33

Thompson, W.D.J. Cargill, "Who Wrote the Supper of the Lord?" in *HThR,* vol liii, no 1 January 1960, 78-91

Thomson, J.A.F., *The Early Tudor Church and Society,* Longman, London, 1993

Thomson, J.A.F., *The Transformation of Medieval England. 1370-1529,* Longman, London, 1983

Thorp, Malcolm R. & Slavin, Arthur J., *Politics, Religion and Diplomacy in Early Modern Europe. SCE&S,* XXVII, Sixteenth Century Journal Publishers, Kirksville, 1994

Tomlin, Graham S., "The Medieval Origins of Luther's Theology of the Cross," in *ARG,* vol 89, 1998, 22-39

Torrance, T.F., *Kingdom and Church: A Study in the Theology of the Reformation,* Oliver and Boyd, Edinburgh and London, 1956

Tracy, James D., 'Two Erasmuses, Two Luthers: Erasmus' Strategy in defense of *De Libero Arbitrio*' in *ARG,* vol 78, 1987, 37-59

Trapp, J..B., "An English Late Medieval Cleric and Italian Thought: the Case of John Colet, Dean of St Paul's (1467-1519)," in Krautzmann, Gregory, et al eds. *Medieval English Religious and Ethical Literature,* D.S. Brewer, Cambridge, 1986, 233-250

Trapp, J.B., *Erasmus, Colet and More: The Early Tudor Humanists and their Books,* BL, London, 1991

Trevelyan, G.M., *A Shortened History of England,* Penguin Books, Harmondsworth, 1959

Trevelyan, G.M., *English Social History,* Longman, Green, London, 1945

Trinterud, L.J., "A Reappraisal of William Tyndale's Debt to Martin Luther," in *CH,* vol 31, 1962, 24-43

Trinterud, Leonard J., "The Origins of Puritanism" in *CH,* vol XX, 1951. 37-57

Trotman, Anthony E.F., "Hutchyns/Tyndale/Trotman Links," in *TSJ,* No 2, June 1995, 6,7

Trueman, Carl R., *Luther's Legacy* Clarendon Press, Oxford, 1994

Trueman, Carl R., "Pathway to Reformation: William Tyndale and the Importance of the Scriptures" in Satterthwaite, Philip E. and Wright, David F. (eds), *A Pathway into the Holy Scripture.* Wm B. Eerdmans Publishing. Grand Rapids, 1994. 11-29

Trueman, Carl R., " 'The Saxons be sore on the Affirmative': Robert Barnes on the Lord's Supper," in Stephens, W.P. (ed.), *The Bible, the Reformation and the Church,* Journal for the Study of the New Testament, Supplement Series, 105, Sheffield, 1995, 290-307

Trueman, Carl R., and Clark, R.S. (eds), *Protestant Scholasticism*, Paternoster Press, Carlisle, 1999

Underwood, Malcolm, "John Fisher and the Promotion of Learning" in Bradshaw, Brendan, & Duffy, Eamon (eds), *Humanism, Reform and the Reformation: the Career of Bishop John Fisher.* Cambridge University Press, Cambridge, 1989, 25-46

Urban, Linwood, "Was Luther a Thoroughgoing Determinist?" in *JThS*, ns 22, 1971. 113-139

Van Den Brink, J.A.B., "Bible and Biblical Theology in the Early Reformation" in *Scottish Journal of Theology*, vol 14, 1961, 1962. 337-352: 50-65

Van Engen, John, "The Church in the Fifteenth Century", ", in Brady, Thomas A.; Oberman, Heiko A.; and Tracy, James D., eds., *Handbook of European History, 1400-1600*, vol 1. , Eerdmans, Grand Rapids, 1996, 305-330

Vaughan, Robert, *John De Wycliffe D.D.*, Seeleys, London, 1853

Wallace, Dewey D., "The Doctrine of Predestination in the Early English Reformation" in *CH*, vol 43, 1974, 201-215

Walsh, W., *England's Fight with the Papacy*, James Nisbet, London, 1912

Wand, J.W.C., *A History of the Modern Church*, Methuen, London, 1952

Watkin, E.I., *The Church in Council*, Darton, Longman and Todd, London, 1960

Weitzman, Michael, "On Translating the Old Testament: The Achievement of William Tyndale," in *Reformation*, vol 1, TS, Oxford, 1996, 165-180

Wengert, Timothy J., *Law and Gospel: Philip Melanchthon's Debate with John Agricola of Eisselben over* Poenitentia, Paternoster Press, Carlisle, 1997

Werrell, Ralph S., "The Authority of Scripture for the Anglican Reformers," in *EQ*, vol xxxv, 1963, 79-88

Werrell, Ralph S., "Church and State in Reformation England," in *EQ*, vol xxxviii, 1966, 219-232

Werrell, Ralph S., *The Doctrine of Church and State in the Writings of William Tyndale*, unpublished dissertation for the Lambeth Diploma, 1991

Werrell, Ralph S., "Tyndale and the Blood of Christ" in *TSJ*, No 2, June 1995. 42-47, Paper given at *The Oxford International Tyndale Conference*, September 1994.

Werrell, Ralph S., "Tyndale's Use of the Blood of Christ in the Meaning of Baptism" in *Churchman*, vol 108, no 3, 1994, 213-221

Whitehead, R., "Tyndale – The Pith and Marrow of the Thing" in *TSJ*, no 12 March 1999, 5-14, 20, Paper given at the *International Tyndale Conference*, Oxford, September 1988.

Whiting, Robert, *Local Responses to the English Reformation*, MacMillan Press, Basingstoke, 1998

Whitney, J.P., *The History of the Reformation*, S.P.C.K., London, 1958

Whitney, J.P., *Reformation Essays*, S.P.C.K., London, 1939

Wilkinson, B., *The Later Middle Ages in England, 1216-1485*, Longman Group, Harlow, 1969

Wilkinson, Robert J., "Reconstructing Tyndale in Latomus: William Tyndale's last, lost book" in *Reformation 1*. TS, Oxford, 1996, 252-285

Wilks, Michael, "Misleading Manuscripts: Wyclif and the Non-Wycliffite Bible" in *SCH*, 11, Blackwell, Oxford, 1975, 147-161

Wilks, Michael, "Predestination, Property, and Power: Wyclif's Theory of Dominion and Grace" in *SCH*, 2, Nelson, London, 1965. 220-236

Williams, C.H., *William Tyndale,* Nelson, London, 1969
Williams, E.N., *The Penguin Dictionary of English and European History 1485-1789,* Penguin Books, London, 1980
Williams, Glanmor, *Reformation Views of Church History.* Lutterworth Press, London, 1970
Williams, Glanmor, "Some Protestant Views of Early British Church History" in *History,* NS 38, 1958. 219-233
Williams, Rowan, *Anglican Identities,* Darton, Longman and Todd, London, 2004
Williams, R.R., *Religion and the English Vernacular,* S.P.C.K., London, 1940
Windsor, Graham, "The Spiritual Issues of the Reformation" in *Churchman,* vol lxxiv, 1960, 152-165
Witt, Ronald G., "The Humanist Movement". in Brady, Thomas A.; Oberman, Heiko A.; and Tracy, James D. (eds), *Handbook of European History, 1400-1600,* vol 2, Eerdmans, Grand Rapids, 1996, 93-125
Wood, A.S., "Luther's Concept of Revelation" in *EQ,* xxxv, 1963, 149-159
Wood, A.S., "Nicholas of Lyra" in *EQ,* vol xxxiii, 1961, 196-206

Index

This Index is not comprehensive but selective. It is also generic (e.g. 'Election' includes 'elect', 'chosen'). Many words, such as 'Christ', 'Tyndale', etc. are so frequent that they have not been shown their page numbers.

Printed in the United Kingdom
by Lightning Source UK Ltd.
110528UKS00001B/52-93

9 780227 679852